He took out his trachea, put a finger over
the hole in his throat, and thanked each
of us nurses. Then he died.
　　　　—A nurse, *Vietnam: The Women Who*
　　　　　　Served, Turner Broadcasting 1994

EMBRACING THEIR MEMORY

Loss and the Social Psychology of Storytelling

John H. Harvey
University of Iowa

Executive Editor: Sean Wakely
Editorial Assistant: Jennifer Normandin
Executive Marketing Manager: Joyce Nilsen
Editorial-Production Service: Susan McNally
Composition Buyer: Linda Cox
Manufacturing Buyer: Aloka Rathnam
Cover Administrator: Suzanne Harbison

Copyright © 1996 by Allyn & Bacon
A Simon & Schuster Company
Needham Heights, MA 02194

Library of Congress Cataloging-in-Publication Data

Harvey, John H., 1943–
    Embracing their memory : loss and the social psychology of story-
telling / John H. Harvey.
        p.   cm.
    Includes bibliographical references and index.
    ISBN 0-205-17478-7
    1. Loss (Psychology)   2. Bereavement—Psychological aspects.
3. Storytelling—Psychological aspects.   4. Discourse analysis,
Narrative—Psychological aspects.   I. Title.
   BF575.D35H37   ~~1995~~ 1996
   155.9'2—dc20   95-24025
                                                  CIP

Printed in the United States of America

10 9 8 7 6 5 4 3 2 1   00 99 98 97 96 95

Photo Credits:
All photos: AP/Wide World Photos.

CONTENTS

This book is dedicated to all those who show great courage and example in the face of major loss. May we all learn and grow in their midst. May we embrace the memory of those who are no longer with us, no matter who they are. This book also is dedicated to the loved ones, students, and colleagues I have known over the years who have taught me a portion of what I know about loss, grieving, and the human spirit to renew and be generative. I am grateful and hope that the ideas in these pages do justice to your contributions. Finally, the book is dedicated to my foremost writing colleagues and friends, Terri Orbuch and Ann Weber, who have shared with me much wisdom about the nature of loss and life.

PREFACE

> *For, although it is true that fear and despair can
> overwhelm us, hope cannot be purchased with the
> refusal to feel.*
> —Susan Griffith

Griffith's quote succinctly expresses a major point of this book. All of us in our lives will come face-to-face with many occasions of major loss (i.e., a loss that greatly diminishes us or our resources). The loss of loved ones, health, and even hope is the bane of all humans. The book clearly is about pain and the importance of recognizing, knowing, and not running away from pain. It is about all that can be learned that is invaluable to living and the contributions we make when sorrow and mourning have walked with us. I argue in this book that we can use our major losses to grow stronger and give back to others through learning from our own pain.

I have written the book in a style that I hope will make it accessible to a large group of readers who also wish to probe and grapple with the meanings of loss and adaptation to loss. While I have provided some coverage of the extensive literature on grief and recovery, in no way is the book a comprehensive treatment of the literature. It is, in fact, quite idiosyncratic to my own sense of what loss is and how it can be analyzed. I hope that both the professional in this area and the layperson, perhaps someone who has recently experienced a major loss and is seeking help by reading on the topic, will gain insights from these pages.

The book is about stories and their value. The assumptions behind the storytelling approach are discussed in Chapter 2, A Social–Psychological Perspective on Loss and Storytelling, and the Epilogue, New Directions in the Storytelling Approach to Loss. Also, in the Epilogue, I have discussed the possible merit of developing a formal field of work that integrates approaches to the study of personal and interpersonal loss. Stories about loss are pervasive in the book. In Chapter 6, Losses Resulting from War and Violence, I report narratives presented to my colleague Christina Davidson and myself during discussions with the veterans of World War II's Normandy Invasion returning to Normandy, France, in June 1994, to commemorate the fiftieth anniversary of the invasion. In Chapter 10, Shelley K. Stein, Nils Olsen, and I present an actual study of loss that emphasized the storytelling approach.

Other chapters in the book deal with loss in the more personal way. Chapters 1, We Grieve, 3, Meanings of Loss, 11, Experiencing Dying, and 12, Losses that Heal and Are Generative, illustrate this personal statement. These chapters are directed most clearly to any person who is struggling with major loss and the challenge of grieving and growing from the pain of such loss. This includes us all, at one time or another.

As I note in the dedication, this book owes a huge debt to my many loved ones, colleagues, and students who have taught me more than any book can about the nature of loss and grief. As a college teacher for over twenty years, I cannot count the number of times that students have come to talk to me about their losses, including relationship dissolutions, deaths, and lost relationships with parents and close others.

I wish to thank Terri Gullickson for superb work on the permissions for this book. I am very grateful for feedback from several persons who read drafts of the manuscript including Sheila Mulligan-Webb, Laura Pearson, and Elaine Pirrone and to the reviewers Stephanie M. Clancy Dollinger, Southern Illinois University, Carbondale; Phyllis Ladrigan, Nazareth College, Rochester; R. Kevin Rowell, University of Central Arkansas; Ann L. Weber, University of North Carolina at Asheville; Brian DeVries, University of British Columbia; and Terri Orbuch, University of Michigan at Ann Arbor.

As a social psychologist, my own study of this topic began in the 1970s in studies of the dynamics of failing close relationships, and continued until the present in studying a host of groups who have experienced different types of major losses. Each of these groups has contributed greatly to our understanding of this topic. In truth, though, my study of major loss has been most intense and devoted when I have experienced my own personal, major losses. I suspect that is true for many workers in this broad field of inquiry. I only hope that the plethora of stories found in these pages will give each of us a little bit more courage to face major loss and to recognize the value of telling our stories of loss and grief.

John H. Harvey
December, 1995

1

WE GRIEVE

Well, everyone can master grief
'cept he that has it.
                    —William Shakespeare

Who never mourned hath never known,
What treasures grief reveals,
The sympathies that humanize,
The tenderness that heals.
                    —Anonymous

On these pages I offer a set of speculations that undergirds much of the logic of this book of stories of loss. I believe that each of us begins a journey of grieving very soon in life. For each of us, there must be countless stories of loss and grief. *These particular stories form the whole of diminishment, and sometimes renewal, that is at the core of who we are, and they create the big picture of what has happened in our lives.*

We begin to grieve just as soon as we learn that we have lost something that mattered quite a bit to us; that probably is as young children. Then, throughout our lives, we grieve both in tiny, difficult-to-discern ways and in huge, tumultuous, but subtle ways. We grieve mostly in private but sometimes in public, too. We have different styles of grieving, some outwardly showing the power of our emotions and some outwardly showing little of the tempest within us.

Sometimes we are aware of our grieving; sometimes we are unaware. For some, the grieving often is quite visible and prolonged throughout their lives. For others, the realization comes later—maybe in the middle of the night— that they have lost someone or something that mattered a lot and that they have been grieving this loss for a long time. Some of us may try, and possibly succeed, in hiding our grief from others and even ourselves all of our lives. In Anne Tyler's novel *The Accidental Tourist* (1985), the character Macon Leary tries to hide his grief after his son's death in a freak shooting at a fast-food restaurant. As his wife tells him:

> *Everything that might touch or upset you or disrupt you, you've given up without a murmur. . . . And when Ethan died, . . . you emptied his closet and his bureau as if you couldn't be rid of him soon enough. You kept offering people his junk in the basement, stilts and sleds and skateboards, and you couldn't understand why they didn't accept them. . . . There's something so muffled about the way you experience things, I mean love or grief or anything; it's like you're trying to slip through life unchanged.* (p. 142)

To recognize that we need to grieve our losses is healthy. Active participation in one's own inevitable change as a human being is a vital step in living. In his wife's commentary, Macon Leary gets a critical wake-up call that can be the stimulant not only to the necessary grieving for his son's death but also to beginning a passage in which he produces in his own life, as well as in his memory of his son's life, greater meaning and accomplishment.

SUNNY DAY—TO DRIVE MY CARES AWAY?

> *What's the use of worrying?*
> *It never was worthwhile,*
> *So, pack up your troubles in your old kit-bag*
> *and smile, smile, smile.*
> —Popular Song from World War I

Even in the sunniest weather, outside and in our own lives, we often experience the nagging feeling that we are missing something. I have often encountered in myself and other people a sense of sadness on very beautiful days when nothing seemed to be terribly wrong in my life or theirs. Why? Is it the knowledge that, sooner or later, beautiful days will give way to dreary days? Is it the feeling that there is a huge gap between the beauty of nature and what our lives have achieved or can achieve? Is it the fact that we wish some absent loved one were there to share the day with us? At times it could be all of these.

Raymond Carver, whose penetrating writing about human relations will be discussed again later in this chapter, wrote a poem called "This Morning" (1986) that mentions his "usual musings"—the existential anxiety that permeates the thoughts of all humans.

This morning was something. A little snow lay on the ground.
The sun floated in a clear blue sky. The sea was blue, and
blue-green, as far as the eye could see.
Scarcely a ripple. Calm. I dressed and went for a walk—
determined not to return until I took in what Nature had to
offer. I passed close to some old, bent-over trees.
Crossed a field strewn with rocks
where snow had drifted. Kept going until I reached the bluff.
Where I gazed at the sea, and the sky, and
the gulls wheeling over the white beach far below.
But, as usual, my thoughts began to wander.
I had to will myself to see what I was seeing
and nothing else. I had to tell myself this
is what mattered, not the other. (And I did see it,
for a minute or two!) For a minute or two it
crowded out the usual musings on
what was right, and what was wrong—duty,
tender memories, thoughts of death, how I should treat
my former wife. All the things
I hoped would go away this morning.
The stuff I live with every day. What
I've trampled on in order to stay alive.
But for a minute or two I did forget
myself and everything else. I know I did.
For when I turned back I didn't know
where I was. Until some birds rose up
from the gnarled trees. And flew
in the direction I needed to be going. (pp. 3–4; emphasis added)

At the heart of Carver's usual musings are the problems of living he has experienced, whether in divorce, death, or decisions that affect himself and others in decisive ways. These are the types of issues many of us spend a lot of time worrying about and trying to address. The essence of this poem is that in nature there is solace from these worries, even if it is but for a brief time.

It is the "exits"—to borrow from Shakespeare's lines about the world as a stage on which each person makes entrances and exits—that engage our minds and emotions most definitively as humans. At some point relatively early in our experience as social beings, we learn to dread exits, both our own and those of others for whom we care. At the heart of loss is the experience of "missing." We have developed many points of reasoning, some of which are simply rationalizations, about our losses. In this way, we try to protect ourselves against recognition of the incessant nature of our grief. We say: "That's life." "Whatever will be, will be." "Easy come, easy go." "Into every life, a little rain must fall." "What does it matter?" We use these expressions to try to rid ourselves of the experience of missing what we have lost.

Whether or not we succeed in easing our minds with these clichés and attempts to avoid contemplation of our losses, there is great cogency in a William Faulkner quote: "The past is never dead. It is not even past." All that matters to us and has gone on still is a part of us. It may be a part of our deep memories. Our losses and experience of missing do not totally go away into some abyss of nothingness in our lifetimes. They often just lurk around, sometimes rising above the level of consciousness in our daily lives and shaking us powerfully. While occasionally they bubble up, usually they just sit in our psyches having some small, indelible impacts on what we consciously feel, think, and do. We would be fortunate if we could say as Rita Mae Brown (1991) said, "I still miss those I loved who are no longer with me but I find that I am grateful for having loved them. The gratitude has finally conquered the loss" (p. 100).

The development of gratitude after loss takes grace and perspective about the suffering and joy of one's life. Jacqueline Kennedy Onassis showed these qualities in how she lived her life—a life that included the loss of a child, the assassination of a husband and a brother-in-law, and her own battle with cancer at age sixty-four. She said, "I have been through a lot and I have suffered a great deal. But I have had lots of happy moments as well. I have come to the conclusion that we must not expect too much from life."

In many other ways we have sought to routinize and formalize our grieving. Holidays such as Martin Luther King Day have been designed not only to recognize people's contributions but also to grieve their passing. We have developed memorial days and memorial gardens. We have built the Vietnam Veterans Memorial, perhaps the most effective wailing wall of our time to signify our recognition of the deaths of over 50,000 U.S. troops, nurses, and Red Cross workers in that war. The memorial, a black granite monument dug into the earth, is actually composed of two walls of over 240 feet each that meet at an angle of 125 degrees.

The Wall, as it is called, was designed by Maya Ying Lin to reflect our own images in its blackness. It connotes that we could be among the dead, or that in a certain sense we are they and they are we, that we were all caught in a historical time and web of logic that led to the Vietnam War and to hundreds of thousands of deaths and disabling injuries. We are invited to recognize our own blessing in living while grieving for these young persons who had their lives cut short. Many people who have stood and stared at a name on the Wall have indicated that they felt they could see a reflection of that person in the Wall. This feeling is depicted by a famous picture of the Wall showing a man, head bowed, with his finger pointing to a name and the soldier's reflection shining forth in the granite of the Wall. Lin wanted the Wall to be honest and healing. She said:

I felt a memorial should be honest about the reality of war and be for the people who gave their lives. . . . I didn't want a static object that people would just look at, but something they could relate to as a journey, or passage, that would bring each to his own conclusions. . . . I had an impulse to cut open the earth . . . an initial violence that in time would heal. . . . It was as if the black-brown earth were polished and made into an interface between the sunny world and the quiet dark world beyond, that we can't enter. . . . The names would become the memorial. There was no need to embellish. (1987, p. 16)

Vietnam veteran Ken Smith described his first visit to the Wall:

I remembered certain guys, I remembered certain smells, I remembered certain times, I remembered the rain, I remembered Christmas eve, I remembered leaving. I'd been in a couple of nasty things there; I remembered those. I remembered faces. I remembered. . . . It's more like a religious experience. It's kind of this catharsis. It's a hard thing to explain to somebody: I'm part of that and I always will be. And because I was able to come to peace with that, I was able to draw the power from it to do what I do." (Herman, 1992, p. 71)

We have created the American Holocaust Museum to remember a loss that is so great and so terrible that it defies human imagination. The journey to this museum is becoming as common as the journey to the Wall. Many of us feel that it is absolutely imperative that we make this pilgrimage. We owe it to those who died and those whose grief for them knows no end. We owe it to our own grief that humanity could ever stoop to this level in its hatred and brutality. In this hallowed structure, we cannot deny the enormity of those human losses. We cannot readily assuage our grief by paying this homage. That grief is necessary and will always be so. What the pilgrimage may do, however, is give us greater courage and vigilance not to turn our backs on prejudice and genocide occurring anywhere in the world—even if we must risk our own lives in the process.

We often try to ease our grief by placing our losses within the context of our spiritual beliefs. We may believe that we will meet our loved ones again in heaven or that some day God, or the Universal Spirit, will make everything right and perfect, including us and our human frailties. We sometimes bury the remains of the wife beside the remains of the husband, as if that step is critical to the continued connection of their lives. We often engage in elaborate private and public acts to express such beliefs. These sentiments and acts may help ease the feeling of loss. But seldom are people—believers, nonbelievers, or agnostics—able to comprehend and accept totally their losses. The psychologist Harry Sullivan contended that we simply are "more human than anything else." To be human is to have fear. The greatest fear is losing what matters to us most, whether it is our own lives, the lives of those whom we dearly love, or the opportunity to use our lives to work for some cause in which we believe deeply.

We read books and articles about grief, and sometimes write them (this book, for example), as a way of dealing with our own grief. In her book *Necessary Losses* (1986), Judith Viorst argues that we "necessarily" lose something every step of the way in life. We may lose health or a friend or lover who goes away or dies. Viorst believes that through such losses, emotional growth can occur. I do too. But I do not believe we can begin to appreciate the toll that is taken of our mental and emotional strength in dealing with these losses— sometimes occurring in tidal-wave fashion in our lives. As Majorie Kinnan Rawlings said, "Sorrow was like the wind. It came in gusts."

ACCEPTING THE UNIVERSALS OF GRIEF AND LOSS

John Donne in Meditation from *Devotions Upon Emergent Occasions* XVII issued the famous dictum:

> *No man is an island entire of itself; every man is a piece of the continent . . . . Any man's death diminishes me, because I am involved in mankind and therefore never send to know for whom the bell tolls; it tolls for thee.*

As we contemplate death all around us, we grieve for ourselves as well as our losses. In this book I write of loss resulting from war, violence, and stigmatization, as when we grow very old or infirm. I also write of being haunted by losses, which occurs when our minds cannot control the intrusive images and memories of those losses. From this broad view of our involvement in "the continent of the whole," the bell tolls unendingly as we continue to love and remember others. A woman, age seventy-four, who survived the Holocaust was quoted in Judith Herman's *Trauma and Recovery* (1992) as saying: "Even if it takes one year to mourn each loss, and even if I live to be 107 [and mourn all members of my family], what do I do about the rest of the six million?" (p. 188).

To assume the explicit task of grieving the atrocities that regularly occur in the world would be exceedingly daunting. A 1994 example of staggering loss is the deaths of over 200,000 people in a two-year period in the Bosnian civil war and a like number in two weeks in the tribal warfare in Rwanda. As *Chicago Tribune* columnist Bob Greene asked in a May 4, 1994, article, how could the world have come to this shocking state of affairs only fifty years after a world war in which literally millions of people died to save the world from the hideous reality of Nazi domination? How could civilization not have progressed beyond such points of barbarism and cruelty?

Although grieving and loss are pervasive in human life and take an enormous toll on us emotionally, the grieving process can motivate us to use our lives effectively for what we believe in. Thus, in the end, the grieving process can give us hope that our lives and what we diligently strive to do matter. Consistent with this, one of the primary goals of this book is Dennis Ryan's recognition of the importance of educating people to appreciate and express grief:

> *We need to teach people how to be in touch with their feelings of grief and how to express these to others in words. Also, we need to teach them how they can express their grief by acting it out. This area is not only the most creative area but also the one most easily misunderstood. For the acts are often irrational, if not in their design then in the intensity with which they are executed. However, it is the nature of grief to be irrational. This fact needs to be repeated until everyone accepts it and allows it in themselves and others. . . . if we empower them to express grief and to help others to express theirs, then there may no longer be a need to deal with disenfranchised grief. (1992, p. 133)*

It is a powerful extension of self to proclaim, "I agree that I am my brother's keeper." I hope that the stories of loss reported in this book reinforce our collective belief in our interdependence with one another and our empathy for one another's sufferings. Let there be no illusion, though: Grief is grief and it hurts; grieving is a big part of what we must experience as humans. There is no alternative! William Faulkner perceptively spoke when he said, "Between grief and nothing I will take grief."

PEACE

Thus, I have argued that at some level we all grieve most of the time. Does this possibility also suggest that we must be hopeless and helpless in our ability to react in any positive way to our grief? No, we all have the capacity to use our grief as a motivator, to devote the precious moments of our lives to constructive action. I conclude this chapter with a perceptive passage by T. Earl Yarborough that deals with what all of us search for: peace. The message, I think, is that even though we experience loss and grieve, we still can find peace through our contributions to others:

> *Once there was a man lost in the woods. For days and nights he wandered around in the deep woods and found that there were no roads leading out.*

One long and lonely night as he walked through the dark, he came upon a monastery. He knocked at the door. A monk came, and before opening the door he called out and asked the man what he wanted. The lonely, lost man didn't answer the monk. Again the monk asked him, "What do you want?" Finally the man said, "All I want is peace."

Peace is what we all are searching for most of the time. Even the monk, who in this story was the helper, was looking for peace. The monk could never have found peace had he refused to open the door to this lonely, lost man. We are all, at some point in our lives, standing and knocking at the door of the monastery, crying out for peace. . . . Until all of us learn the true meaning of giving, we ourselves are helpless people, not helpers. . . . The lost, hurting stranger is still knocking at the door of our monasteries. All he wants is peace. . . . Will you open the door for him? (1988, pp. 179–181)

2

A SOCIAL–PSYCHOLOGICAL PERSPECTIVE ON LOSS AND STORYTELLING

You cannot tell people what to do. You can only tell them parables.

—W.H. Auden

DEFINITIONS

Auden's insight epitomizes the message of this chapter and most of the chapters in this book. We are all storytellers. We have in our memories a multitude of stories. As people share their stories with others, they name and shape the meanings of their unique life experiences. They also pass on their stories to their confidants. When confidants or listeners become new tellers, they reshape the original stories, incorporating their own particular issues and matters of moment. Thus, a story is never retold in exactly the same way. Stories and storytelling, therefore, permit both continuity and change.

Storytelling can be both an informative and powerfully persuasive act. It has consequences for the self because the act can influence both the teller and the listener in profound ways. For example, when I confide in a close friend about a difficult conflict I am experiencing in a close relationship, I may be trying to convince the friend that my view on the issues has merit (a point first articulated by Orvis, Kelley, and Butler, 1976). Further, I am probably venting some emotion about how I feel, or I may be trying to clarify my own thinking. The act of venting, or releasing, my emotions may be quite helpful to me in dealing with my problems, at least in the short run. Clearly, then, storytelling fulfills many functions.

In this chapter, I sketch out a theoretical perspective that undergirds the logic of this book's emphasis on storytelling. I make a case for the value of stories, storytelling, and story-listening in dealing with loss and argue that they are essential elements of effective grieving. Much of what I argue is a refinement of what Harvey, Weber, and Orbuch (1990) contend in *Interpersonal Accounts: A Social Psychological Perspective*. That book equates account-making with the more commonly used terms *storytelling* and *narration*. Weber, Orbuch, and I define account-making as "the act of explaining, describing, and emotionally reacting to the major events in our lives in story-like form." We suggest that account-making often begins in our private reflections and then is communicated to other people in whom we confide. As I elaborate later, we also argue for the great value of account-making in dealing with life's major stressors.

I define social psychology using pioneering social psychologist Gordon Allport's (1968) suggested definition, which is "the study of how the thought, feeling, and behavior of an individual are affected by the real, imagined, or implied presence of others." This definition covers a lot of territory, but it is centered around one person's mind, feelings, and behavior and the influence of one or more people on that person. A social–psychological perspective on loss and storytelling finds that the following steps are involved in the process of grieving: (1) the private construction of a story that fits people into roles and that contains a story line or theme and passages such as a beginning, middle, and end; (2) often, the person's imagining the act of telling the story to others and their reactions in turn; and (3) the actual act of confiding to close others parts of the story about events of loss and grief in one's life. Thus, the story is social both in its imagined mental construction and playing out and in its interactive nature. Even if the individual is alone on a desert isle, he or she will probably narrate his or her story as if others were present—the implied part of Allport's definition. As Judy Dunn's (1988) work on narrative in developmental psychology suggests, we learn about stories and storytelling early in our lives in our interactions with parents and other caretakers. Then, as we grow older, we develop our own stories and storytelling styles.

When major loss occurs, both persons in a confiding situation may comfort one another and tell stories of loss. I know that is often what happens when I am engaged in a confidence-sharing experience with a dear friend. We usually take turns discussing our perceptions of what is happening, sometimes asking for input, sometimes asking each other if we see things the same way, sometimes asking if we have had similar experiences. It is the reciprocal communicative act that makes this experience a powerfully social event that has implications both for the listener and the teller. Hence, the

ed in the form of quantifiable indices. The coding itself, however, is an
pretative act, and as Berscheid suggests, that act can distort the data and
needs to be carefully implemented and assessed. Alternatively, the in-
gator may leave the material as it is and report it, or excerpts of it, as I do
in this book, without imposing quantitative categories. This technique
nown as qualitative or descriptive research. But even the decision about
t to excerpt is an interpretative act. I personally believe that either ap-
ach to stories, accounts, and narratives is tenable, depending on the ob-
ive of the investigator. What is important is that the material is
resentative of the phenomenon and people being investigated. If it is rich
d evocative, either approach may pull out or present valuable insights
out how the people think, feel, and behave (see Harvey, Orbuch, and
eber, 1992, for a number of types of methodological approaches to studying
ose relationships, all of which embrace accounts and narratives as key con-
epts).

A MODEL OF REACTIONS TO MAJOR LOSS AND STEPS TOWARD RECOVERY

Figure 2-1 presents the model of theorized reactions to major loss and the
steps toward recovery formulated by Harvey, Weber, and Orbuch (1990).
This model, which initially was adapted from Horowitz's (1976) model of
coping with loss, is an idealized depiction. All people do not follow such a
course in dealing with stressful events such as the death of a loved one.
Also, people may jump around in the sequence. For example, a person may
show little outcrying early, but later, well after the traumatic event, may exhibit signs of crying out to others for help—perhaps in an indirect way
without knowing that the loss is still raw. I discuss the model and elaborate
on its possible merit in dealing with grief in Chapter 11, which focuses on
the healing process.

This model suggests that people experience states such as numbing,
panic, despair, and hopelessness early after learning of a personally traumatic event. In this early stage, it is common for a person to show denial, isolation, and avoidance as he or she tries to regroup. Over time, however, the
individual may begin to accept the reality of the event and may begin looking to others for emotional support. I would suggest that the type of support
that is most helpful is first simply being there for a person in shock from loss
and second being a confidant—someone who listens well and offers suggestions when asked. During the time that early confiding occurs, the individual
is doing private account-making about the loss. "Why did it happen?" "Why
did it have to happen to her?" "Why me?" "If only . . . ." These are the kinds
of questions that may not have answers but that lead to thinking and feeling

theoretical perspective I present here must deal with what happens when
people share, via some form of communication, their troubles and joys.

How important is it that the accounts or stories that people develop
about major events in their lives are sometimes distorted and untrue? It may
be very important. The issue of false memory, especially in regard to sexual
abuse and incest occurring early in a person's life, is prominent in the United
States now. Using the thesis of false memory, or implanted false memory, parents have sued children who had accused them of incest. In fact, highly emotional events may be quite subject to distortion in memory (Nigro and
Neisser, 1983).

We contend, however, that accounts and stories help those involved in
loss to recover—whether or not the stories are true. In some circumstances,
certainly, it may be very important for the researcher to try to establish the
truth of an account. Yet we also may study how the account is related to factors such as psychological and physical health and its impact on others, independent of its truth. In an account of the meaning of a loved one's recent
death to cancer, a survivor may not choose to emphasize the loved person's
smoking in the development of the cancer—even if the smoking was clearly
linked to the death by the person's physicians. Nevertheless, the development of the account may help the survivor heal and recover.

Our use of the concept of account follows Robert Weiss's (1975) persuasive use of this term. Weiss first used the term to help us understand how
people in the process of marital separation organize and manage their chaotic
thoughts and feelings about why their marriage is ending. Weiss argued that
work on the account or story often gives the survivor a greater sense of control over what are otherwise confusing and dismaying events. He suggested
that the account begins to settle the issue of who is responsible for what and
that it imposes on the events leading to separation a plot structure with a beginning, middle, and end, and so organizes the events into a conceptually
manageable unity. Once understood in this way, Weiss suggested, the events
can be dealt with, and detachment from emotionally searing stimuli can be
achieved.

The concept of account has another root in sociological theory. Based on
E. Goffman's (1959) influential writing about the presentation of self in everyday life, Scott and Lyman (1968) developed the concept of account to refer to
people's use of justifications and excuse-making in general in presenting actions that have been associated with negative outcomes. For example, a
driver may blame running a red light on a bee that was buzzing around the
interior of the car.

More generally, if we link the account to a story about why and how
events occurred (whether it represents a justification for action or a more general statement without reference to justification), there is a plethora of recent
writing in the social and behavioral sciences that emphasizes the value of sto-

rytelling. The psychiatrist Robert Coles (1989) has written about the value of storytelling as a humanizing and meaning-giving force for human betterment in a variety of life contexts, such as education and medicine. The eminent cognitive psychologist Jerome Bruner, in his book *Acts of Meaning* (1990), suggests that the lives and selves we construct are the outcomes of the process of meaning construction that is embedded within a culture of meaning. He contends that social scientists should give greater attention to how people construct and use meaning in different cultures.

In presenting what they term a *dramaturgical* approach (which views life as a theater) to emotion and understanding Cochran and Claspell (1987) write about how life is punctuated by overlapping and interweaving beginnings, middles, and ends of stories. They contend that we vacation, daydream, plot, love, meet challenges, do chores, pursue careers, seek redress, raise children, and play *in story*. We also grieve in story, which is the message that is at the heart of this book. Cochran and Claspell persuasively argue that to object to viewing the story as the very root of what it is to be alive requires enacting a counterargument in the form of yet another story!

The counseling psychologist George Howard had this to say about storytelling:

> *A life becomes meaningful when one sees himself or herself as an actor within the context of a story—be it a cultural tale, a religious narrative, a family saga, the march of science, a political movement, and so forth. Early in life we are free to choose what life story we will inhabit—and later we find we are lived by that story. (1991, p. 196)*

Still other important work on the storytelling metaphor is being done by scholars who emphasize the value of human narrative activity, including Gergen and Gergen (1987). Baumeister (1991) has provided interesting experimental explorations of people's narrative activity and has written influentially about human meaning-making. From his thinking and research about meaning-making, he has concluded:

> *Happiness is a state full of meaning. Happy people have meaningful lives that make sense. They have purpose, they feel their actions are right and good and justified, they have a sense of personal efficacy, and they have a firm sense of positive self-worth. (1991, p. 232)*

Finally, the cognitive psychologist Frank Smith has noted:

> *Most of the beliefs we have about the world and our place in it come in the form of stories. Most of the beliefs we have about other people, and the way we regard and treat them, are in the form of stories. Stories are the mortar*

> *that holds thoughts together, the grist of all our explanatio...* *and values.*
>
> *Thought is inseparable from a literally fabulous congl... personalized stories—religious, political, social, economic, p... and psychological. . . . Armies, terrorists, and bigots are moti... stories they believe—and so are peacemakers, philanthropists... tyrs. (1990, p. 144)*

STUDYING STORIES, NARRATIVES, AND ACCOUNTS

By what means can we systematically and reliably study accoun... and narratives? Ellen Berscheid (1994) wrote an important review... personal relations for the *Annual Review of Psychology* and addres... she called account–narrative approaches to studying close relati... Berscheid suggested that there were two main approaches in soc... chology: (1) the ethnographic tradition represented by Gergen and... (1988), and (2) the information processing represented by Harvey,... and Orbuch (1990). While she did not clearly differentiate these two... tions, one possible distinction is that the ethnographic tradition empha... the participant observation techniques commonly used in cultural an... pology, whereas the information-processing technique involves a mor... moved, noninvolved approach in which the investigator presumably... observes and listens to the respondent. My own view of this distinction,... is widely entertained, is that it is arbitrary. In our own work on accoun... my colleagues and I have been somewhat removed from our respondent... How else could it be? We cannot live their lives and truly understand the... circumstances without being in their shoes. Yet, we also are close to being... ethnographers in our seeking respondents and then listening at length to... their stories. Unless investigators evolve into the confidants of research par... ticipants, they will remain distanced from their respondents.

Another possible distinction is that ethnographic approaches involve the... assumption that causal relations are recursive. That is, everything may... causally affect everything else, and causal loops of reciprocal influences dom... inate in the real world. Yet, my colleagues and I have also made that as... sumption in our general work on accounts and in the model outlined in the... following section. For example, an account may be influenced by the type of... grief the person is experiencing (if it is high grief), and the account then may... affect the nature and extent of grief experienced.

Finally, with all social–psychological approaches to accounts, stories, and... narratives, respondents' written or spoken material may be coded and...

to find the best answers the individual can develop. Sharing confidences with a close other during this period may help the individual find an acceptable answer and start the process of resolving the inquiry and achieving a degree of tranquility.

Our model emphasizes the dual importance of private account-making and social interaction through confiding as essential components of healing from a major loss. Alone, either one may be insufficient; together, they may only advance the healing process to a certain point. All evidence indicates, however, that both are probably the best type of medicine the survivor can take. Each involves a process of thinking and feeling, but confiding also involves a process of reaching out to others for assistance in the further thinking and feeling that must occur for resolution. It is often said that "time will heal all wounds." I personally believe it is *what we do over time* that best heals the wounds. We may want to forget, but it may be better if we deal with, work on, and resolve a loss and then file it away in memory. Even with resolution, memory intrusions about the loss (see Chapter 9) are common and must be accepted. I believe that the available evidence, some of which I describe in the following discussion, strongly supports the efficacy of an active approach to healing, in contrast to denial, avoidance, or trying to go on without a significant struggle of the mind and heart in dealing with the loss. It is true that people sometimes begin the struggle well before the actual loss. For example, some people have noted that they started grieving an impending divorce or the death of an elderly parent well before the event occurred. Nonetheless, the act of grieving and a particular form of expressing that grief (through "worked on" story and social interaction with close others) seem essential to recovery or adaptation and to moving on with life.

The middle and final aspects of our model emphasize the importance of "working through," which involves account-making and confiding. It is to be hoped that the process of "working through" culminates in feeling of completion or understanding and greater acceptance of facts of the loss. Along with these feelings, we may believe that we have become more tenacious or hardened as a consequence of our grief. Such a belief probably represents a positive outcome because we think that we are stronger. We may even feel that we can better help others (see Chapter 11), based on our own experiences and learning. Thus, the challenge to the survivor is to work on his or her story until the account *feels complete* and along the way confide parts of the account to a close other. Completion, in fact, occurs only to the extent the survivor accepts what has happened and its meaning for him or her. Once completion occurs, the individual may see his or her losses in the broader spectrum of human loss and realize that a positive response is to be there for others suffering similar losses (Harvey and Martin, in press).

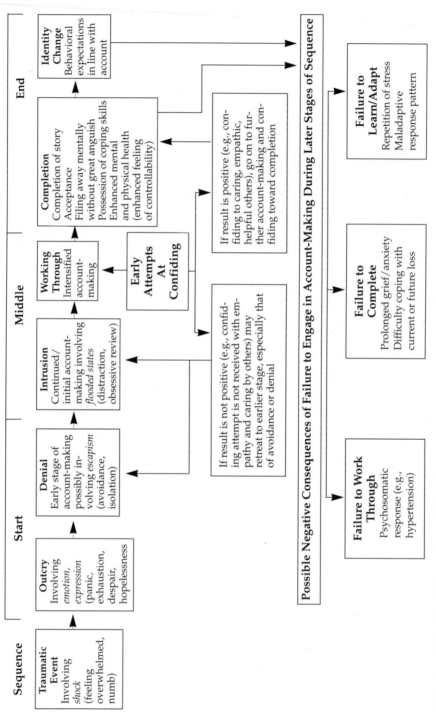

FIGURE 2-1 Revision of model in Harvey, Weber, and Orbuch (1990)

The model further suggests that failure to work through the grieving process may have various negative consequences, both physical (e.g., hypertension) and psychological (e.g., prolonged depression). In a sense, becoming stuck is the downside of completion, acceptance, and moving on. We may become stuck in an unending period of grieving, like the wife who, six years after her husband's death, keeps his room the way it was the day he died. That is, we perseverate in grieving, not acting to put our grief in a resting place after we have given it ample opportunity to affect us. Or, we may become stuck in the sense that we will not face up to the loss and what it means to us.

The last step in resolution is identity change. Harvey, Agostinelli, and Weber (1989) argue and have provided evidence that people change in significant ways when they incur major losses. This reality is especially true when we lose a loved one with whom we have had a close relationship, such as a spouse or primary partner. As discussed in Chapters 4 and 5, at the time of death or dissolution, we go from being a member of a couple to being alone, both in the eyes of others and in our own minds. C.S. Lewis's (1961) insightful notes about dealing with grief reveal his great sense of being adrift when his wife died. More generally, though, any truly major stressor changes who we are in some perceptible ways. Whether the stressor makes us less naive, less trusting, wiser, more confident, less apt to become seriously involved so quickly, or fed up with the system, it exacts some relatively permanent change in our identity.

Our work on the importance of confiding is similar to the influential work of James Pennebaker (1990) and his colleagues, who have provided impressive evidence that survivors of major loss experience improved psychological and physical health if they have confided their trauma to others. These researchers have shown that writing or talking about trauma may positively affect factors such as physiological skin conductance (less reactivity reflects nervousness) and number of visits to a physician (less frequent visits), as well as self-reported improvement in feelings about the event. Pennebaker and associates do not emphasize the particular content of stories or accounts to the extent that we do in our work. We believe that an account that is conducive to healing involves a relatively complete story that embodies acceptance of the event and, possibly, an understanding of how the survivor has learned from the event.

Our work also emphasizes the critical role of the confidant in cases of trauma that are embarrassing or anxiety-producing for the survivors. In studies of incest survivors, Harvey et al. (1991) found that middle-aged women who had experienced incest as young children and confided in family members or close others were better off only to the extent that the people in whom they confided showed empathy for them and believed their stories. If the confidant (usually a parent) indicated lack of empathy or disbelief, this experience led to the worst of outcomes: The women went into a shell with their hurt and did not come out until they reached midlife. Hence, a nonempathic confidant may be even worse than no confidant at all! As an example of the often elaborate account-making and confiding that we found among incest survivors who in their thirties and forties are working to deal with their wounds, consider this statement:

> *I stayed a virgin for many years . . . [but I began to recover in my early thirties] after going to counseling, taking an emotional healing course . . . writing letters and making phone calls to my family, parents, sisters and brothers, to my brother the abuser. I'm right now making a tape and letter to my ex-husband who was emotionally and physically abusive. (p. 525)*

In further work on account-making, confiding, and incest, Orbuch et al. (1994) found that males, too, need to experience empathy among their confidants if the confiding behavior is to be effective. This work also found that over an extended time period, male incest survivors seemed to have more difficulty dealing with serious acts of incest than did females. One man, age forty-seven, said:

> *The assaults [by his father and cousins] were violent and occurred over a six-year period . . . [and I've tried to recover by going to] . . . therapists, incest recovery groups and confiding by mail with my siblings and father and mother. . . . Dad says he doesn't remember anything about that period. (p. 260)*

Overall, work on the long-term effects of incest suggests how special and particular every type of loss may be for survivors. It may be much more difficult to confide about something so personal and painful as incest than it is to confide about the death of a close other. We do not yet have the type of research evidence about how people cope with different types of major losses that we need. What we do know, however, is that account-making and confiding usually help, as long as the incest survivor confides in an empathic other. In general, it appears that writing about troubling experiences, when a person cannot talk to others, is a positive way to begin to heal. As Hal Adams (1994), a writing instructor, has said, "Writing is magical. It gives people access to a level of their experience they usually don't touch."

I certainly believe that account-making through reflection, writing, and confiding in close others can help anyone dealing with stress in any situation, however hostile the outside world or barren a person's life in terms of helpful, caring others. Pain needs to be expressed in some way; pain that is unreleased is crippling. We know that based on research and reports of survivors. Pain unreleased is like a straitjacket; it keeps us from reaching out, from feeling, from being real.

EXAMPLES OF STORIES OF LOSS
AND GRIEF EVERYWHERE

Loss, grieving, and storytelling are omnipresent in the media and in our daily lives. A brief review of some of the major stories in the media attests to this point.

The British and world presses, in the summer and fall of 1994, printed many stories about Princess Diana and the gossip about how this thirty-three-year-old princess was beginning to crack under the strain of a number of midlife pressures. In a way, it seems strange that a woman so famous, wealthy, and generally beloved by her public could be facing a huge turning point in her life. But the British press implied as much. Why? There was her separation from Prince Charles in 1992, and the prince's own admission of adultery during their marriage. Most important, Prince Charles indicated in an authorized biography that he had never loved Di and had felt compelled by his family to marry her. He is said to have depicted Di as a neurotic, bulimic person who was essentially incapable of intimacy.

For a while, press accounts suggested that divorce was imminent and that Di would receive a multimillion dollar parting present, probably as an inducement not to take a crack at Charles in the media. In 1994, however, the press began to convey an image of Di as a young woman with few friends who was increasingly isolated and constantly hounded by snooping cameras and tabloid journalists, not to mention a public that seemed to have an unquenchable thirst for information about her private life. The stories about her behavior with other men were endless. One story had her making harassing phone calls to men in whom she presumably had an interest and then hanging up when they answered the phone. While these stories may be lies, they are illustrative of the press's regular speculation about the intimate details of her life. Some papers have suggested that Di should depart into a discreet exile to better preserve the propriety of the throne and facilitate her personal life. Thus, whether or not we believe all of the particular sub-stories in her life, we can view the life story of Princess Di in 1994 as one of major losses that may impact her future decisions and behavior.

Another famous person in the news in the summer 1994 was Marlon Brando, who published his autobiography, *Brando: Songs My Mother Taught Me*. Aside from reporting several romantic–sexual liaisons he had had with different people, this book is notable for describing the great losses Brando suffered as a youth and how he feels those experiences have affected him. For example, Brando has said he and his two sisters were always close "because we were all scorched by the experience of growing up in the furnace that was our family" (p. 97). Regarding his mother, he notes "She was an alcoholic whom I loved but who ignored me. . . . I was beside her hospital bed with her hand in mine when she died" (p. 98). Brando's relationship with his father was even more distant. We have a picture—this time, painted by the actor in the story—of how much of Brando's life was shaped by loss of parenting when he was young.

A final story from the summer of 1994 that probably will grow in scope over the years concerns the number of children who are being raised by foster parents and grandparents because of the economic difficulties or health problems faced by their single parents. The Census Bureau reported that in the United States in 1991, 4.7 million children under the age of eighteen were living with a grandparent and that 81 percent of those children also had a single parent living in the same home. Obviously, this situation, which has mushroomed in the last decade, is creating hardships for senior citizens, many of whom expected to spend these years traveling or on the golf course rather than raising young children. The number of children expected to be orphaned and, if lucky, placed in foster families because their mothers suffer from AIDS is expected to be on the order of 100,000 by the turn of the century.

Hardship and loss are not particular in their choice of the famous or the ordinary. Will this book be only about such depressing stories and statistics? Yes. But they are realistic, and that is what is most important. Not only must the stories be realistic, but also we must be willing to face and consider them and learn that in the midst of pain is hope. For each of the types of losses in this book, I tell stories of people displaying courage, surviving, and giving the gift of hope and willpower to others who suffer similar losses. In Chapter 1, I argued that we grieve implicitly on a regular basis because we observe so many losses in the world, including our own. But the transcending message of this book is that we can use our grief to make ourselves deeper, stronger, and more able to celebrate the good in life.

> *Mourning is the constant reawakening that things are different now.*
> —Wild, 1995

3

MEANINGS OF LOSS

Working through our endings allows us to redefine our relationships, to surrender what is dead and to accept what is alive, and to be in the world more fully to face the new situation.
—Stanley Keleman

You don't get to choose how you're going to die. Or when. You can only decide how you're going to live. Now.
—Joan Baez

The meaning of major loss can be described most powerfully not with words but with images and feelings that occur at the immediate point of learning of the loss, especially an unexpected loss. Turned into words, these images and feelings approximate the following expressions, reported by people reflecting on their first reactions to the sudden loss of a loved one:

Oh, my God! Oh no, please no! It can't be true.

She wasn't there anymore. I felt so empty.

This can't be real. We were happy and laughing only hours before. I couldn't believe the lifeless body I discovered.

I can't feel anything. It doesn't feel real.

I cried hysterically, and then I went numb; kind of like I was watching myself from the outside.

With death, the images and feelings often pertain to the physical entity being gone, perhaps swiftly and unexpectedly. With dissolution and divorce, the images and feelings often relate to the void left by the person who is missing, and even missed. Psychologically, a loss is best represented by the sense of missing, of being bewildered, of being without, and even, in some cases, of being hopeless. People have often reported that they felt numbed and overwhelmed upon learning about a great personal loss.

Photographs, especially those showing the expressions of children, poignantly tell the stories of loss. It may be true that children are not as likely as adults to mask their grief. In the picture below, a family grieves at the burial of their father/husband, who was killed in the 1991 Gulf War. The young boy's expression is that of humble, insuperable despair. In the picture on the next page, two children weep at the grave of their brothers, who were accidentally killed in 1994 while playing with an anti-personnel bomb planted during the Vietnam War. These young children look as if they are frantically trying to get to the bodies of their siblings—maybe to bring them back to life. These children were not a part of the war that led to their grief, and yet the battles of that war presaged this scene of despair

more than twenty years later. Both photographs dramatically pinpoint the immediate experience of loss as a feeling of little personal control over what has happened. Both plumb the depth of anguish to which great loss can drive individuals.

Images that convey the sense of missing a deceased loved one were described by C.S. Lewis in *A Grief Observed* (1961), after the death of his wife, Joy Davidman, from cancer. Lewis, an English writer, teacher, and theologian, had been a confirmed bachelor well into midlife when he met Davidman, an American poet. They fell deeply in love and married. Within a few years, however, her advanced stage of cancer was discovered. Perhaps her death was even more devastating to Lewis because of the whole set of unexpected events: he had been single for years but then had fallen in love overnight, gotten married quickly, and just as quickly lost that which had brought him his greatest happiness. Lewis was inconsolable. He soon began the notes about his grief that not only helped in his healing but also served as a beautiful memorial to his love for his wife. These notes are a magnificent contribution to anyone who has lost a loved one. These are Lewis's words about missing Joy:

Her absence is like the sky, spread over everything. (p. 11)

I have no photograph of her that's any good. I cannot even see her face distinctly in my imagination. Yet the odd face of some stranger seen in a crowd this morning may come before me in vivid perfection the moment I close my eyes tonight. No doubt, the explanation is simple enough. We have seen the faces of those we know best so variously, from so many angles, in so many lights, with so many expressions—waking, sleeping, laughing, crying, eating, talking, thinking—that all the impressions crowd into our memory together and cancel out into a mere blur. But her voice is still vivid. The remembered voice—that can turn me at any moment to a whimpering child. (pp. 16–17)

This chapter depicts the meaning of loss for people who have undergone this experience and felt it deeply. I refer to this type of loss as *major loss*. My colleagues and I (Harvey et al., 1992) have examined the reactions of a variety of people to events in their lives that have involved significant personal loss. These events have run the gamut from the loss of love and companionship through divorce and death, to the loss of self, safety, and trust on the part of incest survivors, to the loss of major possessions by people whose property was severely flooded in 1993 in the Midwest.

Each of these losses has involved somewhat different social–psychological dynamics, but all of these people *have lost valuable resources. All of them have been transformed in some critical way as a result of their loss.* Most major losses lead to fundamental changes in our identity—who we think we are and what we see as the basic reasons for our existence. For example, a widower who has lost his wife after a long marriage is no longer a married man; he is single. He no longer has a companion with whom to share most of the important events of his life. He no longer sleeps with someone with whom the sleep and dreaming experiences have been defined over a long period of time. He no longer can readily describe his life to friends as involving "us" or tell them that "we" did so and so. The transformation to singlehood may be daunting for the man, and he will have many starts and stops in his new life. But when the process of grieving has run its course, he will be fundamentally different. He will not necessarily be better or worse, just different. All through life, we change, yet major loss quickens the changing.

For each type of major loss, a scenario like the widower's can be traced. Certainly, each person who experiences major loss shows a distinctive pattern of responses, but at the same time, there is considerable commonality, such as the feelings when a spouse dies. This book is concerned with both the particular aspects of experiences of loss and the aspects that overlap across different types of losses.

AN EXTENSIVE LITERATURE

Loss and associated grief work have undergone extensive analysis and research by behavioral scientists and social commentators. The present discussion mentions only a fragment of that literature as a basis for later discussion of different types of losses and how people deal with them.

Judith Viorst's classic book on loss, *Necessary Losses* (1986), deals with many of the natural losses that people incur. Viorst points out that losses such as virginity, friends as we move from place to place, and physical health as we reach the later stages of our lives are natural and come in due course for every person. Some people, however, experience out-of-season losses. Loved ones die at an early age because of accidents, cancer, AIDS, and the like. Still, in Viorst's view, loss is

> [N]atural, unavoidable, inexorable. And these losses are necessary because we grow by losing and leaving and letting go. . . .
>
> For the road to human development is paved with renunciation. Throughout our life we grow by giving up. We give up some of our deepest attachments to others. We give up certain cherished parts of ourselves. We must confront, in the dreams we dream, as well as in our intimate relationships, all that we never will have and never will be. Passionate investment leaves us vulnerable to loss. And sometimes, no matter how clever we are, we must lose. (p. 16)

But does everyone who experiences these losses experience growth as a consequence? I doubt it. I argue in this book that the key to transforming losses into something positive lies in our efforts to give our losses meaning, to learn and gain insights from them, and to impart to others something positive based on the experience. Not all of us will be inclined to search for meaning in our losses. Not all of us will want to learn from them. Not all of us will use losses to motivate us toward helping others who also are struggling with their diminished hopes and resources. Some people who have experienced losses are too diminished to consider how they might help others. The power of Viorst's book, however, is in realizing that people experience *a plethora of types of losses in their lifetime.*

Therese Rando, in *Treatment of Complicated Mourning* (1993), provides a comprehensive discussion of the nature of loss as it pertains to psychological intervention. She suggests that there are primary losses and secondary losses. A primary loss is an event that leads to a major reduction in a person's resources, such as loss of a spouse. A secondary loss is a physical or psychosocial loss that coincides with or develops as a consequence of the initial loss. For example, with the death of a loved one, a survivor will experience the secondary loss of the loved one's presence, may have financial difficulties associated with the loss, and may have to relocate. I will return to Rando's interesting analysis in Chapter 12 when I discuss treatment for extended mourning.

I believe that these secondary losses may be seen as part of the primary loss package. They occur, however, at distant points from the initial loss. Rando's argument about secondary loss is important because it highlights the rippling, long-term effects associated with major loss. In some cases, it is unclear when the end of the chain of associated losses occurs—in fact, it may not end until the survivor dies.

As discussed in Chapter 9, some people are overwhelmed by a key loss at one point in their lives. They never fully deal with the loss and then are staggered even more by losses later in life. Psychoanalysts have long contended that unmastered losses—such as the unresolved death of a parent when a person was young—come back to interfere with mourning a current loss (Volkan and Zintl, 1993). Other types of particularly haunting losses are the loss of a child, a suicide, and any kind of loss that occurs unexpectedly and early in the life cycle.

George Levinger (1992) presents a useful set of distinctions about the nature of perceived loss. He notes that the extent to which a person *perceives loss* (or a deprivation in personal resources) after the death of a close other depends on several factors, including: How close (or involving or interdependent) was the relationship? Did the death occur unexpectedly, or did it occur only after a protracted period of illness? If the individual's death involved a long terminal phase, survivors probably were able to begin the process of mourning (which may have involved story development and confiding). Levinger posits that when a dying person expresses a clear desire to stop living, it helps his or her loved ones to accept the ultimate death. In fact, the survivors have a clearer answer to the question of why he or she died—the individual wanted to. Levinger also suggests that when there is a prolonged severe illness, survivors may begin to pull away emotionally from the dying person, which is a defense mechanism that helps survivors to accept the certainty of the impending death and to begin the mourning process.

Along the lines of Viorst, Robert Weiss has made the following valuable statement about the nature of healing from loss:

> *Loss is inescapable. Deaths, estrangements, and separations are part of life. Recoveries tend to be either more or less adequate; only rarely can they be said to be either complete or entirely absent. Most of us have character structures influenced by partial recovery from loss. . . . Loss and pain are inescapable, but permanent damage should not be. (1988, pp. 50–51)*

Emily Dickinson said as much when she wrote, "Heavenly Hurt, it gives us— / We can find no scar, / But internal difference, / Where the Meanings, are.—" It is to these meanings that I turn next.

AN EMPHASIS ON STORIES

They talked about their fears as if talking about it would make the images go away.

—News Reporter on the Survivors of Flight 232

All sorrows can be borne if you put them into a story or tell a story about them.

—Isak Dinesen

This book is mainly about stories of loss and the importance of these stories in our search for meaning in our lives and in the healing process. Our argument closely follows Dinesen's contention as well as Shakespeare's lines in *Macbeth*:

Give sorrow words; the grief that does not speak
Whispers the o'er-fraught heart and bids it break. (Act IV, iii)

Let's begin with a story. An advertisement in the *Chicago Tribune* on March 20, 1994, announced, *"The Night of the Iguana* by Tennessee Williams . . . America's laureate of loss." This advertisement was accompanied by a review of the production at Chicago's Goodman Theater. A quick survey of the play explains why Williams may be considered "America's laureate of loss." The play tells the story of two people who are at the end of their ropes and verging on madness. One is a disgraced minister with a taste for underage girls, who now conducts bus tours throughout backwater Mexico. In the play, the minister is holed up in a hotel on an island, experiencing a mental and spiritual breakdown. The hotel proprietor has shackled him to a hammock on a veranda to stop him from harming others. The other main character is a young woman who is a guest at the hotel and who counsels the minister in his time of torment. She has experienced a mental breakdown in the past and now fears that her elderly grandfather, who is her lifelong companion, is about to die. In their dialogue, the lead characters discuss carnality and spirituality—forces that energize much of Williams's writing.

The two characters dominate the stage and engage in dramatic colloquies about life and death. The essence of the debate pits the woman against evil, despair, insanity, and surrender. The woman tells the minister that as she dealt with her breakdown, she "began to see this faint, very faint gray light—the light outside me—and I kept climbing to it. I had to," which is the message of hope that undergirds the play. As *Chicago Tribune* art critic Sid Smith (1994) noted in his review, the play tackles the elusive, intangible, inarticulate human feelings and fears about death. The play reaches a climax when the woman cuts loose an iguana that the hotel staff had caught and tied to the veranda banister, and a horrendous storm begins. While the young woman helps the minister get through the night, the peace they create together is temporary. We are led to believe that the minister may never find permanent peace—a dilemma that Williams too faced for twenty-two years after writing this play, his last commercial success. The play ends with these lines from Emily Dickinson: "And so, as Kinsmen met a Night— / We talked between the Rooms— / Until the Moss had reached our lips— / And covered up—our names—" These lines sum up the play's main argument that, as Smith writes, "the temporary hope of spiritual communion is the most one can expect from a path to a resting place, where, no matter our triumphs or tormented struggles, the moss will inevitably cover our names and skulls at last" (1994, p. 34).

Night of the Iguana involves universal principles of struggle, uncertainty, and turmoil. Depending on the interpretation, it may also involve hope. Subtly woven into the fabric of this story is hope—a derivative of loss that may be just as likely to emerge from grief as despair and hopelessness.

In our discussion of the stories presented here, we probably will not come to any more profound conclusion than Emily Dickinson's lines. Yet, I believe that the human will to find a "very faint gray light" is epitomized in people's stories of loss and recovery. The act of telling these stories is a timeless antidote to the feeling that there is no hope in dealing with loss. Just as loss is continuous and inevitable in human experience, so is the capacity of humans to tell of their loss and thereby find light and the hope and will to live.

By creating an account, the widower in my earlier example may gain a more complete sense of the meanings of his wife's death for the present and future. He will probably search for an answer to why she died suddenly. He will begin to see himself as a single man who no longer has a clear plan for companionship and intimacy in the future. He will begin to formulate and work on images of himself involved with someone new and/or a new life course. In creating this account, the widower may eliminate his early feelings of overwhelming despair and hopelessness.

I believe that the sharing we do when we confide in others is most useful for our catharsis (or emotional release) and cognitive clarification about a loss when we can do it regularly and with someone whom we deeply trust. We all have acquaintances who do not want to hear about our problems. They may want us to hear about theirs, but not the reverse. A valuable confidant is someone to whom we can talk at almost any moment about our most troubling thoughts and feelings. And usually the process of confiding with such a person goes both ways. Irwin Altman and Dalmus Taylor (1973) have done some creative thinking about the process of self-disclosure that embodies the confiding act. They refer to the process of people getting to know others as *social penetration*. They suggest that we may never let anyone know our deepest qualities—we may even shy away from thinking about them ourselves.

Based on my belief that we need a valuable confidant, I suspect the widower's healing will be greatly facilitated if he can find someone who appreciates his sorrow and is willing to listen and offer support. This is one of the reasons why grief support groups are so important to people who are actively working on their grief. These groups represent people who know what it feels like to lose a close other and who are in the process of mourning and trying to adapt to the absence of their loved ones.

A towering question for most people is, Do I have a confidant in whom I can share my deepest sorrows, fears, and joys? For many, that confidant is a spouse. For others, that person may be someone other than a spouse—perhaps a parent or very close friend. Still others, however, are uncertain about whom to trust. These people may have learned as a consequence of perceived betrayals not to trust others. They may feel that no one truly cares. They are the ones who suffer most because their losses are compounded by their inability to work on them through storytelling to close others.

Colin Parkes (1988) notes that grief following bereavement is aggravated if the person lost is the one to whom the bereaved would turn in times of trouble. Faced with the biggest trouble ever experienced, the bereaved repeatedly turns to a confidant who is not there. Parkes suggests that such a situation, which often occurs when a spouse dies, is exceedingly difficult to resolve: "The familiar world suddenly seems to have become unfamiliar, habits of thought and behaviour let us down, and we lose confidence in our own internal world" (p. 55).

Every person has the capacity to create and tell his or her own stories and thus deal with losses. As Robert Coles (1989) eloquently argues, storytelling is each person's gift regardless of how educated or literate the person is. Indeed, Coles suggests that stories are the bedrock of every human being. Certainly, Tim O'Brien's *The Things They Carried* (1990) well illustrates the power of stories and storytelling in dealing with loss. In referring to his experience as a soldier in Vietnam, O'Brien argues for the timeless value of stories in giving connectedness to human experience:

> *Forty-three years old, and the war occurred half a lifetime ago, and yet the remembering makes it now. And sometimes remembering will lead to a story, which makes it forever. That's what stories are for. Stories are for joining the past to the future. Stories are for those late hours in the night when you can't remember how you got from where you were to where you are. Stories are for eternity, when memory is erased, when there is nothing to remember except the story. (p. 40)*

ILLUSTRATIVE STORIES OF LOSS

Death is not the enemy; living in constant fear of it is.
—Norman Cousins

The following stories are examples of the great diversity of loss that people experience. They were also chosen to reflect variations in how people deal with their losses.

The first illustration involves a story of a loss that left a thirty-two-year-old father alone to raise his daughter, Amie, age four. Amie's mother was killed in an automobile accident during a snowstorm. One year after her death, Amie's father, Barry, was interviewed by a local reporter. During the course of the interview, he said, "Everything is not like it was. . . . It can never be like it was again. . . . You can't predict tomorrow. If you could, January 5 [the date his wife died] would never have happened. You don't go through life thinking: 'Tomorrow my life is going to be turned around on me.' " He went on to say that every anniversary, birthday, and holiday evoked painful memories. He said,

> *We've gone through them all once now. . . . They say it's supposed to get easier. . . . I live day to day, just trying to get by. . . . I've just got too many things to keep my mind occupied. I don't sleep that well anymore. . . . You can't take for granted how much your spouse means to you. . . . You just think they'll always be there. And then, they aren't. (Rasdal, 1992)*

Although it had been a year since the accident, Barry still would not drive when it was snowing heavily, and he said that he believed the accident would never leave his mind. Amie, who was in the automobile with her mother, still suffered from motor control problems due to spinal injuries from the accident and could not walk. The future for this single-parent father and his young daughter will be full of challenges. The problems he alluded to in the article, such as sleeping difficulty, are normal. It may be a long time before he is in a position to try to address the incomplete business that exists because of his wife's sudden death. Amie, too, may encounter difficulties later. At the time of the article, she was too young to articulate what may need to be addressed to achieve peace of mind and body.

The second illustration is different in that the survivor has begun to reach a point of completion in her story and mourning. In this case, the survivor is a nurse, Edie, from the Vietnam War. Edie McCoy Meeks saw a lot of death and destruction during her tour in Vietnam in 1968. When her year there ended, she returned to the United States and said that she experienced no joy, just pain for the men she could not help because of the seriousness of their injuries. Within two years, she was married and raising a family. But like so many who served in Vietnam, she put off her grieving. She did not recognize that this step had to take place if she ever was to achieve any peace about what she had experienced in Vietnam. When she first went to the Vietnam Veterans Memorial in Washington, D.C., although obviously upset, she was unable to talk to her family about her feelings.

Then in 1983, fifteen years after her service in Vietnam, Meeks found herself often feeling edgy and afraid. In casual conversation, a friend mentioned that maybe she had not faced up to Vietnam yet. At the very same time, Edie received a call from a former colleague in Vietnam who was raising money for a memorial to the women who served there and wanted Meeks to help in the effort. Meeks said that she would not help:

> *Why commemorate what I was trying to forget? I thought that was the end of it until one night I turned on* 60 Minutes *and there on the screen was Diane [her nurse friend from Vietnam] and some other army nurses who'd served in Vietnam! I couldn't watch; I had to leave the room. At the time, I'd been having flashbacks. While driving I'd suddenly see and remember whole scenes of horror. . . . To keep my family from worrying, I made a joke of it. After all, I hadn't been hurt. (Meeks, 1994, pp. 50–59)*

Soon thereafter, Meeks began to see a psychologist who helped her to recognize that her Vietnam experience was coloring her whole life. She was withdrawing from her family because she feared that she would lose them—just as she lost many of her patients in Vietnam. But what really allowed her to express her feelings about her experience was a presentation that she made to her daughter's college class about what it was like to be a nurse in Vietnam.

> *I cleared my throat and said, "If you want facts, you'll need someone else. I'm going to tell you what one woman felt."*
>
> *When I told them that every soldier was my brother, I saw students nod. They could relate to that. . . .*
>
> *I said, "When I came back, I didn't have to feel bad that I'd killed someone, but I felt terrible about the soldiers I'd been unable to save. My experience was totally different from a soldier's, but it was just as painful, and it needs to be healed just as much." . . .*
>
> *As I was leaving a lot of the young women came up to thank me. The very last one, a petite student with long curly hair, had been crying. She said, "I'm only 21 years old, but I would have welcomed you home." Well, I started to cry then too. I said, "Thank you. For the first time, I feel welcomed home." And I did. (Meeks, 1994, pp. 50–59)*

Edie McCoy Meeks has finally begun to reach resolution and to communicate with her family about her Vietnam experience. Similarly, many

Vietnam combat veterans blocked out their feelings for a decade and only began to address their experiences in the 1980s. The Vietnam Veterans Memorial, which was completed in the early 1980s, has greatly facilitated their grieving and work toward resolution.

Laurie Palmer's poignant book, *Shrapnel in the Heart* (1987), tells the stories of the survivors of individuals killed in Vietnam who have left notes and personal memorabilia at the Wall. These survivors have written messages in an attempt to release their feelings and to make sense out of something that is essentially senseless—the loss of tens of thousands of young soldiers and innocent Vietnamese citizens. In large measure, the Wall has made it appropriate to be expressive. As Palmer said after she had tracked down a sample of people who had left memorabilia:

> *People, I found, not only want to talk about the person they lost in Vietnam, they need to talk. It is a deep yearning in many, suppressed because of the wildly erroneous notion that by now they should be "over it."*
> *(p. xiii)*

The Wall represents a nation's official homage to its fallen sons and daughters. It stimulates expression because it expresses grief itself: in the enormous numbers of names of those who died, in its blackness. But it also expresses hope as it rises out of the earth. The Wall provides a place for those who grieve the losses of the Vietnam War to share with others who grieve and for all to come and stare in sadness and awe.

The third illustration involves short-story writer Raymond Carver, who died in the late 1980s at the age of fifty. *Esquire* magazine invited writer Tobias Wolff to discuss Carver's human qualities and his body of work. Wolff and Carver had been close for many years. In his article, "Raymond Carver Had His Cake and Ate It Too" (1989), Wolff describes how huge disappointments and grief became a focus in much of Carver's writing and how these experiences energized his work. (Note that Tess Gallagher, a well-known writer and poet, was Carver's longtime companion.)

> *When Fitzgerald said there are no second acts in American life he was thinking about success, and a particular kind of success, the celebrity that arises not from talent alone but also from glamour and youth, and is therefore fated to pass and impossible to recover. In that sense he was right. But otherwise he was wrong. If we keep our eyes open we will all witness astonishing second acts, maybe even have one of our own. I've seen more than a few, and Ray's was among them.*
>
> *He used to love to tell the story of Dostoyevski's last-minute reprieve from the firing squad: the condemned men weeping and embracing as the soldiers took up their positions, the officer calling out the last orders just as*

the czar's messenger rode up with the pardon. How one of the men was beyond the reach of mercy, having gone hopelessly mad under the strain. This episode later became the central moment in a movie script Ray wrote with Tess Gallagher. It interested him so much, I think, for the simple reason that he had been there himself, and in more ways than one. He had come very close to suffering not only physical death but also moral and spiritual annihilation. As he wrote in Fires *[a partial autobiography by Carver]: "The time came and went when everything my wife and I considered sacred, or considered worthy of respect . . . crumbled away."*

Ray had been to the brink, and he had been spared. His consciousness of that release, and of its provisional nature, inclined him to view life with amazement. He took nothing for granted. Every moment with friends, every fresh story and poem was a gift he hadn't counted on. The loving life he shared with Tess Gallagher, the respect his work inspired in all kinds of people—to Ray, these were miracles. He wore his honors more lightly than anyone I've known, and not by pretending they weren't there, or that they didn't matter to him. They did, very much. . . . (When I ran across a good review of his work that he hadn't yet seen he would ask me to come right over with it, then tear it from my hands. If he was out of town he would beg me to "Fed-Ex" it to him.) He wasn't particularly modest about his work either; he knew he was something special, had to have known it or he couldn't have survived all those years of almost nobody else knowing it. What made Ray's success so easy for others to take was the kindness it inspired in him. He was always trying to help someone find a job, or win a fellowship, or get a book into print. I never knew him to do a mean thing. Not once. . . .

At moments of particular happiness he would look around with pure wonder. "Things could be worse," he'd say.

He was right. Things could have been worse. And they got worse. But as bad as they got, he did not lose his sense of privilege at finding himself alive at all, and not only alive but blessed. The last poem in his last book, A New Path to the Waterfall *is an act of insistence of his right not to be pitied [as he knew he was terminally ill with cancer]:*

> Late Fragment
> And did you get what
>   you wanted from this life, even so?
> I did.
> And what did you want?
> To call myself beloved, to feel myself
>   beloved on the earth.

(pp. 240–248)

Isn't it interesting how Raymond Carver and Barry, the single parent from the first example, despite different situations involving devastating loss, converge on the recognition of the blessing to be alive and the importance of invigorating our moments alive with that recognition?

The final example is brief. It tells of a type of loss that occurs every day in the large cities of America. It is the loss of our children. In 1993, the *Chicago Tribune* ran a series describing the events surrounding the violent deaths of sixty-one children under the age of fifteen in that year alone. The following letter was reported by Jan Crawford. It was written by David, age thirteen, after his classmate Shaun, age fourteen, had been shot on Halloween night—the fifty-fifth child killed in Chicago in 1993. Shaun was a popular football star, who happened to be in the wrong place at the wrong time when a gunfight between gang members broke out. His death crystallized the fears of violence held by his classmates at Holy Angels School in Chicago. In writing their essays, Shaun's classmates were trying to express some of their frustration, fear, and grief. In his essay, David said:

> *I feel great remorse for what has happened to him. He didn't deserve to die or any other kid. You really can't stop the gang violence uprising in the country. You cannot stop the gangs without fear for your life and your family. This gang violence is really getting out of hand and it must be stopped before there are no kids left. Innocent kids are being killed for unnecessary things like not being able to throw up a gang sign or because you have on certain colors. It's wrong and they need to put a stop to this. (Crawford, 1993, p.)*

David's letter speaks a truth that is overpowering in today's world. It is unclear how children subjected to almost daily violence in their neighborhoods and schools will be affected in the long term. Whatever the effects, they are not likely to be beneficial to the children. It is equally unlikely that the emotional scars will heal soon for the parents and relatives of the thousands of children who have been slain in the 1980s and 1990s in America's cities. Chapter 6 focuses on the special qualities of loss as a consequence of violence.

WORDS FOR SILENCE

As I argued at the beginning of the chapter, the meaning of loss may sometimes be found in images and silence. When Holocaust survivors' narratives of their incalculable losses in concentration camps become stares into space, their silence is flooded with meaning. While the traumatized survivor may search for meaning in the form of words, he or she may find words unable to convey the sense of the memories that exist. In his book, *A Jew Today* (1978), Eli Wiesel, the writer and Holocaust survivor, has said of some survivors' memoirs:

> *Their sentences are terse, sharp, etched into story. Every word contains a hundred [memories], and the silence between the words strikes us as hard as the words themselves. They wrote not with words but against them. (p. 200)*

Fortunately, as many Holocaust survivors have discovered, recounting experiences may be a way of achieving greater meaning and of countering traumatic silence with active communication to others who care about them and their experience. Many survivors recall a period immediately after liberation when they felt compelled to communicate what they had witnessed. Greenspan (1992) describes one such survivor, Paula, who had been imprisoned at Auschwitz-Birkenau. She confided in her journal on her first day of liberation:

> *Up until the last minute, the crematorium is our nightmare. We are telling everybody about this, whether we want to or not. Our stories are only about the crematorium, whether we want to or not. (p. 147)*

Thus, telling about the losses of close others in the fires of the crematorium and about fears of dying that way was a necessity for many survivors. Telling it conveyed meaning to the meaninglessness of the destruction that surrounded them. Wiesel's *Night* (1960) powerfully conveys his feeling of having died during the Holocaust even while continuing to live. Only through expressing some of the pain of the unspeakable losses can he resolve this paradox. Essentially, as suggested by a journal of thoughts kept by Herbert Kramer in the final year of his life, all survivors retell the death that lives on in their awareness.

> *The life story of every human being is a variation on the theme of loss through death—of every pet, every friend, every loved one, until, sooner or later, the self, too, is taken.*
>
> —Herbert and Kay Kramer

4

LOSS OF CLOSE RELATIONSHIPS THROUGH DEATH

We are healed of a suffering only by experiencing it to the full.
>   —Marcel Proust

One must go through periods of numbness that are harder to bear than grief.
>   —Anne Morrow Lindbergh

ON TYPES OF LOSSES

At some point as we mature, we discover that one of the most devastating types of losses we can experience is the death of a close other—whether relative or friend. These losses are almost always psychologically devastating. Consider, for example, a happy and growing young person who loses her mother at age twelve, parents who lose a child to an automobile accident at age eighteen, or a happy, successful middle-aged couple broken apart by the death of the husband just when they had grand plans for the second half of their life together. The death of a twin can be equally as devastating. As one incurs a fatal disease and begins to die, the other one may sink into a period of despair and depression so great that only suicide seems to offer an antidote.

A number of prominent psychological analyses of what makes people happy have noted that having close loved ones is critical to a feeling of happiness and a belief that life is personally meaningful (Baumeister, 1991; Myers, 1992). Thus, when a close loved one is taken from us—especially at a relatively early age and unexpectedly—our grief, mourning, and sense of despair may be profound and long term. There simply is no substitute person for those closest to us. The deceased related to us in a unique way that greatly contributed to our satisfaction with life and feelings that we were blessed.

The stories that are in this chapter are of the early period after the loss of a loved one. Chapter 12 focuses on the period at which healing begins to occur and the dynamics of that healing process. For some, though, healing takes an exceedingly long time or does not fully occur at all. This chapter centers on people living such stories. They are parents, spouses, romantic partners, and sometimes just best friends of the deceased.

Although grief literature tries to classify degrees of grief associated with different types of losses, I make no attempt to specify which type of loss typically wreaks the most devastation. I do know that the continuum of types of losses through death is a long one. For many survivors, no matter what type of loss—the loss of a child, the loss of a friend, or whatever—the loss falls at the far end of the continuum, indicating great pain, feelings that life is not worth living, and a long period of mourning and attempted recovery. Surely, the types of deaths that stun us terribly and that Anne Morrow Lindbergh (whose young son was kidnapped and killed in one of the most well-known and publicly enraging cases of this type of crime) was referring to in the opening quote all fall at this end.

In recognizing that any type of loss may lead to great pain, I speak from experience. Many years ago, a four-week-or-so-old cat, white, blue-eyed, named Gracy (actually a boy cat named for Princess Grace Kelly of Monaco who had just been killed in an automobile accident that week), came trotting along behind me and ensconced himself into my life. He was with me every day for three years, going to the office with me and sleeping in the out-basket. He went with me on trips, and we each took turns following one another on hikes through the neighborhood. You guessed it. He was killed at age three on a not usually busy street while we were visiting relatives. As I wept and felt totally crushed, I dug the grave and buried Gracy. I then went into an extended period of missing him and becoming intensely alert to all of the shades of white cats that exist on earth. Over at least a year, I grieved the loss of that cat and still do. He added important meaning to my life. Maybe he did not understand my human ideas about his value, but he sure acted as if he did. He was a companion and friend whose loss sent me stumbling along and affected what I did—even big decisions—for months.

I do not tell the Gracy story to suggest that the loss of a pet necessarily is as devastating as the loss of a close human loved one, but it may be. *The survivor's perception and imputed meaning count most in our understanding of the nature and extent of loss. The survivor defines the power of a loss in his or her feelings of devastation and extent and depth of mourning.*

What is clear for all who must endure such pain and mourning is that love is the original condition for its ultimate occurrence. As Robert Weiss (1988) argues, it is only the loss of relationships of deep, close attachment that triggers powerful grief. There is an irony in the grief to be reported here. It is that such grief can occur only when people love and develop an extraordinary bond of closeness. What, then, is wiped away through death is the continuity of that bond, which in large measure is composed of people's memories of being together: of the beloved's smile; tender, comforting touch; particular mannerisms and expressions; and voice. These countless memories continue to exist and sometimes bubble up into the consciousness of the survivor. The survivor, then in some sense, is really the victim. He or she will continue to experience these wonderful memories of a past love for which no further memories can be created.

MAJOR TYPES OF GRIEF

I not only live each endless day in grief, but live each day thinking about living each day in grief.

—C.S. Lewis

In grief literature, *grief* is defined as a person's emotional reaction to the event of loss (DeSpelder and Strickland, 1992) and as a "process of realization, of making real inside the self an event that has already occurred in reality outside" (Parkes, 1972, p. 56). As Lewis implies, it is a type of experience that most people anticipate with dread. But in principle, grief is an adaptive reaction that is essential to recovery. Working from a combined biological and psychoanalytic perspective, John Bowlby (1960, 1979), the late English psychiatrist, made important contributions to our understanding of grief. Bowlby argued that grief instinctively occurs and is focused on resolution and adaptation. Bowlby conceived a developmental theory of attachment based on his research with children and their mothers. He framed his analysis of grief within the context of the mother–child relationship. In this scheme, the child has great fear of being abandoned by the mother. Both crying and anger were once useful in this relationship to get the mother to return. When the loss is permanent, however, crying and anger do not work. Depression soon occurs, as does an inability to initiate and maintain action. This early stage of shock and numbness eventually is replaced by detachment from the loss. Bowlby viewed this detachment as an essential step for reorganization of one's life in the absence of the deceased close other. Reorganization then leads to new attachments. Grieving is the process that permits the detachment, reorganization, and new attachments to occur.

Bowlby (1980) concluded that there are two forms of pathological mourning. Both can reach various degrees of severity; less severe instances are difficult to distinguish from so-called normal grieving. The first category of pathological mourning is chronic and characterized by intense and prolonged reactions to loss, as if the mourner is on a constant emotional adrenaline kick. According to Bowlby, the second form involves the prolonged absence of conscious mourning. This delayed form of mourning has been described extensively by counselors who work with the bereaved. The person suffers vague physical and psychological symptoms (e.g., headaches, tension, insomnia) but does not readily relate them to the loss. It is as if this mourner is numbed, or in the early phase of grief. Such a mourning pattern also frequently involves zestful cheerfulness by the mourner that seems exaggerated to the outsider. Wortman and Silver (1989) have contended that this latter type of behavior may not signify mourning at all. Rather, these people may show an absence of grief because they feel no distress. Kleber and Brom (1992) suggest that both schools of thought may be correct. Some indeed may have no distress and show no mourning—however devastating the loss. Others, possibly the majority of those who show delayed mourning, may be kidding themselves and trying to kid their friends and associates. They often do not even accept sympathy and compulsively try to take care of others who are encountering various types of difficulties.

Bowlby's theory of attachment has proven to be one of the most useful stimulants for contemporary theory and research on grief (see, for example, Cochran and Claspell, 1987). His ideas have also been influential in investigations of adult attachment in close relationships (Hazan and Shaver, 1987). Presumably, people who have secure attachments in their adult close relationships have had secure relationships with their mothers. Those who are insecure or avoidant, however, probably have encountered ambivalence or abandonment in their relationships with their mothers.

An argument that I return to in Chapter 9 is that all of us probably will experience unresolved degrees of grief throughout our adult lives. We incur too many losses not to have lingering feelings and issues. While researchers have tried to determine what is an abnormally long period of grief, it seems that they cannot easily answer this question. It is clear that the first year after a death, especially an unexpected death, brings many reminders of the loss to survivors. Holidays, birthdays, and other special days often are times of acute anguish for survivors. Extended, deep grief is a problem when it interferes with a survivor's need to move on with life. The survivor must try to get to a point at which he or she can remember regularly and positively the lost other while taking constructive steps toward establishing a new life without the personal identity that was attached to the other. Often, the survivor needs to recognize that the deceased person would want her or him to achieve this new identity.

As many scholars have noted, different types of losses affect directly the length and depth of the grieving experience. Fulton (1979) makes a distinction between "high-grief" deaths and "low-grief" deaths. A high-grief death is characterized by intense emotional and physical reactions to loss. A low-grief death is less affecting emotionally, and the bereaved is able to cope more readily. Consistent with the delineation of types of losses in Chapter 3, the death of a child would be the classic high-grief death; the death of a person who had reached a quite advanced age and who had lived a long and fulfilling life would be a low-grief death.

Another type of grief, "disenfranchised grief," has been posited. Orbuch (1988) includes the end of nonmarital relationships in this category, and Savage (1989) includes the death of an unborn or a stillborn child. As a society, we do not typically provide the same types of social supports for people who experience these losses that we do for people who experience marital dissolution or the loss of an infant. In a certain sense, loss is loss, and each loss deserves due consideration of its meaning in the life of the survivor and requires a time for healing.

Researchers have argued that people need to be able to vent their emotions and mourn publicly their losses. I will have more to say about the power of telling one's story to close others as one avenue of public mourning in Chapter 12. We need to recognize that many people experience a somewhat disenfranchised grief because, for various reasons, they lack a community of close, caring others. Early in the AIDS epidemic, persons dying of AIDS often underwent this type of grief. In recent years, various communities have been diligent and effective in addressing the mourning needs of persons dying with AIDS and their survivors. Still, for many, an AIDS death is a stigmatizing type of death. There are many others, including the homeless, who silently experience disenfranchised grief. Because some people have become alienated or isolated from close others in one way or another, there are probably millions of people who experience unrecognized grief and anguish, and that is *in addition to* the normal grieving we all regularly experience.

Anticipatory grief is yet another type of grief. According to Schoenberg and colleagues (1970), anticipatory grief refers to knowledge of an impending death. With such knowledge, the survivor may be better prepared psychologically for the death. While anticipation probably does reduce the initial shock, that may be the extent of its ameliorative power. The survivor still may have to deal with substantial issues pertinent to the relationship that has ended and to the new life that he or she must develop.

One of the most sophisticated longitudinal studies of grief was carried out by Parkes and Weiss (1983). They studied 70 widowers and widows, interviewing the survivors at two weeks, eight weeks, thirteen months, and two to four years after the spouse's death. Parkes and Weiss identified several types of grief: (1) unanticipated, in which the survivor has great difficulty in moving on and often shows avoidance, self-reproach, and despair; (2) conflicted, in which the survivor goes up and down feeling ambivalence toward the loss of the loved one; and (3) chronic, in which there is a long-term intense yearning for the deceased loved one, especially among those who had been quite dependent on the loved one, that leaves the survivor with little idea of how to reestablish his or her life.

Do we grieve in the same ways in the 1990s that we grieved in the nineteenth century? A valuable book by Paul Rosenblatt entitled *Bitter, Bitter Tears* (1988) provides some insight into this question. He examined hundreds of tattered, dusty diaries written by persons who had remained behind in the eastern United States when their loved ones went West looking for fortune. Many of these adventurers died or disappeared and often left behind young widows. Rosenblatt found that the grieving processes of these survivors were similar to what people have shown in the twentieth century. Depression, despair, and a sense of hopelessness are frequently displayed in the diaries, which the survivors used for venting feelings and trying to resolve the different meanings of their losses.

A view that is often expressed in grief literature is that grief can be the prelude to positive developments in a survivor's life. C.S. Lewis said, "Still, there are enormous gains" (1961, p. 49). Cochran and Claspell (1987) eloquently argue that a key activity of grieving is a search for meaning that leads to insights and clarification of our philosophies of living and provides a more mature view of ourselves and other people.

SURVIVORS' REACTIONS TO THE GREAT LEVELER

He was my North, my South, my East and West,
My working week and my Sunday rest,
My noon, my midnight, my talk, my song;
I thought that love would last forever: I was wrong.
—W.H. Auden

Death and the loss of love are called the great levelers. They are so called because, regardless of our eminence in life, they can reduce us to feeling as if we are victims or survivors in a moment. Indeed, they can reduce us to a state in which our status and achievements matter little if at all. Auden's beautiful lines are haunting because they reflect how much of our being often is intertwined in our closeness with another human being. To lose that closeness is to lose a major part of ourselves. Our grieving in such situations may be inconsolable, insuperable, beyond words, expressible only in a crying out of the soul that mirrors Auden's verse.

When is a grieving reaction, whether in the form of crying out, depression and despair, or running fast to avoid thinking and feeling, so prolonged or intense that it is considered abnormal? That question is exceedingly difficult to answer in the abstract. People grieve in disparate ways. Common sense tells us that when a person feels that he or she is not able to get on with life because of grief, then the person needs to get help. Sometimes, however, people cannot see that grief is impairing them (see quote from Bill Moyers on page 48 regarding his father's grief). On those occasions, it often is the responsibility of close relatives and friends to encourage the individual to seek help.

The usual early reactions to the death of a loved one are shock, feeling numb, denial, and usually a lengthy period of highs and lows—with the lows including their own various degrees of depression and inertia. After the loss of her husband at age thirty-four, one woman reported, "When he died, I just felt empty, numb. I was in a fog."

In a moving and inspirational account of the sudden heart attack and death of her husband, who was in his forties, Elizabeth Neeld (1990) describes vividly her own early reactions at a memorial service for her husband:

> *The congregation is now beginning the final hymn: "Amazing Grace. . . ."*
> *I listen, but I am not present at a memorial service on July 4. . . . I am far*
> *away. . . . In a big white room in a house in Texas. . . . It's Sunday, and the*
> New York Times *covers the floor. . . . Greg [her husband] says, "Hey, I*
> *haven't heard our concert this morning. Isn't it about time?" And I go*
> *over to the piano I've had since I was a little girl and begin to play, "Amaz-*
> *ing Grace, how sweet the sound. . . ." (p. 18)*

Neeld suggests that this scene was typical of the many scenes she had of times of intense closeness in the early days after her husband's death. She was experiencing the "missing" state that was described in Chapter 3 as at the core of major loss. She continues:

> *In the days and weeks following, I must have told the story [of her hus-*
> *band's unexpected death] a thousand times. . . . I took little notice of the*
> *strange things that were happening to my body—or to my mind. My ap-*
> *petite disappeared. For days I felt no hunger. It was more than two weeks*
> *before I remembered that there were good things in the world to eat. . . . I*
> *lay awake for hours when I went to bed. (p. 19)*

Neeld's reactions are similar to early reactions of many individuals when faced with the sudden loss of a loved one. Neeld became seriously depressed and hopeless in the summer that followed her husband's death, which is common in such situations. As Meg Woodson notes in *The Toughest Days of Grief* (1994):

> *The smell of hopelessness and helplessness pervades the bog of our grief. Difficulties loom in the darkness as impossibilities. Taking initiative comes hard; being sucked into thick, clinging depression doesn't take initiative. (p. 30)*

Neeld's book reports a number of symptoms that, according to psychologists, often go along with depression after the death of a loved one (see, for example, Rando, 1993). These symptoms include:

feelings of sadness and hopelessnes
insomnia, early wakening, difficulty in getting up in the morning
thoughts of suicide
restlessness and irritability
guilt
eating disturbances and fatigue
loss of sexual drive
inability to concentrate

In most instances, the symptoms leave when the depression finally recedes to a more normal level (which may involve short bouts over some days, especially when the deceased loved one is strongly on the mind of the survivor).

In her classic book *On Death and Dying* (1969), Elizabeth Kübler-Ross describes the stages of denial and isolation, anger, bargaining, depression, and acceptance that frequently affect people who know that their death is imminent. Certainly, these responses occur as part of the experience of grief. Grief theorists have suggested a number of other phases of grief as well, including disorganization, undoing, guilt, acceptance, and integration. Stage, or phase, theories of grief have been criticized for implying lockstep sequences of experiences and suggesting that deviations from these sequences are abnormal (DeSpelder and Strickland, 1992). In fact, however, people's grief reactions are variable, sometimes involving only a small subset of the aforementioned, and may occur at any point during the grieving process. In her memoir of her husband, "Martin, What Should I Do Now?" (1990), former New York congresswoman Bella Abzug notes, "I still have tremendous pain. . . . I haven't found any five stages, just tremendous sadness" (pp. 95–96).

In the following sections, I consider some of the particular reactions associated with different types of losses. For example, a common reaction on the part of parents who have lost a child is a feeling of guilt and responsibility—even when there is no way they could have prevented the death. A principle that runs through this chapter on the loss of a close relationship through death is that universals are associated with every grieving reaction. The idea of "missing," which I have frequently mentioned, is one such universal, as is the idea that powerful grieving irrevocably changes people in some significant ways. At the same time, each loss is special and different, each grief reaction bears the individual's own idiosyncratic stamp of personhood.

LOSING A CHILD

> *"Hi, I'm Meg Woodson, and my son Joey just died," I said to strangers on elevators when I went alone to a conference.*
>
> —Meg Woodson

> *We miss hugging him . . . basking in his radiance. . . . He is missing everything life had to offer.*
>
> —Linda Corwin

A parent's grief is probably the most inconsolable, incurable of any kind of grief. Parents expect to outlive their offspring. They usually imbue their children with many plans and hopes, some of which they may once have had for themselves. The loss of a child dashes the expectations that the child will live a long, normal life and accomplish much—including continuing the blood line with her or his children. A frequent reaction of parents to the loss of a child is that of survival guilt: "It is not fair that she died before me." As discussed by Corr, Nabe, and Corr (1994), other types of guilt include death causation guilt (that they had a role in the death); illness-related guilt (that their neglect led to the child's fatal disease); and moral guilt (that the loss of the child is punishment for the parents' moral transgression). In light of the idea of survival guilt, consider the following comments by David McLemore, a *Dallas Morning News* columnist who wrote this Christmas essay about his daughter, Darshana, who was killed in a 1990 house fire:

> *Grief is hard. A great hole is ripped in your life. Perhaps the hardest thing, what keeps hammering away in my head, is how perversely the natural cycle is disrupted with her death. Children are supposed to be safe at home. Children are supposed to outlive their parents. There is nothing right about losing Darshana so young.*
>
> *She will always be 18, always on the threshold of life. We can never see her grow and change into a woman I caught a glimpse of [when he visited her on her college campus shortly before she died]. We will never see her grow as a woman. Never smile at her successes or weep with her over life's*

inequities. Never see her fall in love; never meet her husband for the first time. Never hold her child. The circle is broken. The pain is only heightened by the knowledge that those truly are not our losses. They are hers. (1993, p. 50A)

As part of coping with major loss, some people may be creative and contribute to others' welfare (similar to the idea of giving to future generations). Many parents who have lost children have expressed their grief in positive artistic and scholarly works. Indeed, I view the essay David McLemore wrote about his daughter as a wonderful creation to all who read it. These are precious gifts to us who are alive.

Along this line, there is a particularly touching project that I would like to describe. In 1988, Pan Am Flight 103 exploded over Scotland on a flight from Germany to the United States. The explosion was caused by a bomb, allegedly planted by two terrorists who now are hiding in Libya. Many of the individuals killed on this flight were Syracuse University students returning from Europe. The parents of these students have formed one of the most powerful special-cause lobbying groups ever established as a result of a tragedy. Not only have the parents been effective in urging the U.S. government to find and indict the persons who perpetrated the bombing, but they have also contributed many beneficial works in memory of their young, talented daughters and sons who perished. For example, a scholarship program was created in honor of the Pan Am 103 students. In 1994, the program funded its first group of scholars.

The most gripping work by the Pan Am parents has been a sculpture project started by one of the mothers. Susan Lowenstein, a gifted sculptor, has created a number of bronze figures of women and placed them on the Syracuse campus as a memorial to the students. The women who served as models for the figures are the mothers of the children who died. The expressions they show are those of their inconsolable grief at the very moment they heard about their children's deaths. In the pieces that make up this sculpture, called *Dark Elegy*, the figures kneel, lie, and stand while they weep, shout, and try to shrink away from the darkest moment of their lives. As I viewed these figures, I felt that no greater testament to the loss of these young persons could have been created. It is a monument to their parents' undying memory of and love for them. It is a place where generations of students, parents, and others will stand and shed their own tears.

"Haunting" is a theme among many parents who have lost children, including the Pan Am parents. As I note in Chapter 9, writers such as David Morrell, who created the Rambo series of novels and movies, have devoted parts of their lives and careers to their deceased children. Morrell's book *Fireflies* (1988) describes the death of his son Matthew to cancer at age fourteen. Matthew was very special to his father. The boy had great sensitivity, was a budding musician, and brought many friends to his parents' home. For Morrell, Matthew's death was staggering. Although the Rambo books were bringing Morrell fame and wealth at that time, without Matthew, the writer notes, these were unimportant.

Fireflies refers to a possibly hallucinatory experience Morrell had a few months after Matthew's death. Matthew appeared to Morrell as one of hundreds of fireflies and told Morrell to reestablish his hope, begin to contribute to others who have lost children, and thereby give Matthew's life and death greater meaning. Writing *Fireflies* and contributing as a speaker to organizations for grieving parents were Morrell's ways of working on his grief, finding the energy to move on with his work and relations with his family, and honoring Matthew.

A similar passage was experienced by Christa McAuliffe's mother, Grace Corrigan. McAuliffe was a social studies teacher who was NASA's first designated teacher in space. She was killed in the explosion of the *Challenger* space shuttle in 1986. Her mother and her father, who died in 1990, witnessed the explosion. Since her husband's death, Grace Corrigan has been a frequent speaker about her daughter and the *Challenger* disaster. In an interview with the *Boston Globe* on September 12, 1994, she said:

> *The important lesson we can all learn from Christa is to do what you want to do and do it as well as you can. . . . I could have done without the losses in my life, I guess. But everyone suffers some loss along the way. You cannot escape it. Who promised us a rose garden? (p. 13A)*

A particular kind of loss occurs when an only child dies and leaves a single parent. Evelyn Gillis (1986) was the single mother of a twenty-two-year-old daughter who was killed in an automobile accident. She notes some of the special deprivations that resulted from her daughter's death:

> *[W]e face the absence of support from another adult who would share the same feelings of loss and grief. . . . We alone carry the responsibility of the funeral arrangements.*
>
> *After the funeral, when other people return to their own homes and families, we are left to face the reality of the child's death, alone in a house that offers nothing but silence. . . . We cry out to have another person alongside who knows, really knows, what the death of the child means, someone who shares those special memories of how our family once was. (p. 315)*

Gillis indicates that getting on with her life took years. She often would grieve for hours at the grave of her daughter, and then not have the energy to drive away. She knew that to change her absorption in her mourning, she would have to give of herself to others. However, she felt it was better no longer to love or give, lest she again lose someone she loved deeply. She finally began to recover with the aid of a chapter of the Compassionate Friends' organization, which focuses on helping bereaved parents. Eventually she worked as a sibling leader in her group.

Unfortunately, many who lose a child go into a shell and seldom show the depth of grief that resides within them. Bill Moyers, the journalist, described the torturous grief that his father kept inside himself and what Moyers believed were the physical effects of that grief:

> *When my brother died of cancer in 1966 at age thirty-nine, my father began a grieving process that lasted almost twenty-five years. During that time he suffered from chronic, debilitating headaches that could not be cured. At one point, a doctor tried to tell him that his headaches were related to his grief, but he persisted in treating the pain as a medical problem, and the torment continued. After my father's death at eighty-six, I thought about how he could have been helped. (Powell, 1994, p. 42)*

LOSING A SPOUSE OR CLOSE, ROMANTIC OTHER

Tender Words on Paper Possible Legacy of Crash

This headline of a newspaper article, appearing on April 7, 1977, in the Nashville *Tennessean*, concerned a letter, apparently written by a young woman, found at the crash site of a Southern Airways DC-9 that crashed near New Hope, Georgia, killing sixty-four of eighty-five persons on board. The partially complete scorched letter said:

> *I'm sorry for hurting you. I didn't know you felt that strongly about me. I thought you were just another guy. . . . But I realize I was wrong. I don't know what else to say because whatever I write down, you won't believe it.* (Tennessean, 1977)

The letter ended abruptly, as apparently did the life of the writer. For some of us, close relationships end through dissolution or death while we still have substantial feelings of ambivalence about the nature or degree of our closeness. Such appears to have been the case for this writer. At least this person was trying to express her confusion to someone who was special in her life at the time of her death.

Reactions to the loss of a spouse or romantic partner can vary, but certain factors can make the devastation severe. As described earlier, Eliza-

beth Neeld's grief when she lost her husband suddenly was wrenching, because they had such a close, long-term relationship. The unexpectedness and suddenness, the relative youth of the victim, and the closeness of the bond all appear to contribute to the extent and depth of the grieving experience.

Joie White, whose husband Jason was killed while on duty as a police officer in Washington, D.C., in 1993, is another widow whose grief is almost overpowering. White, who is thirty, was described in a March 20, 1994, *Washington Post* article as embracing the memory of her husband by totally immersing herself in the trappings of his life. In effect, as described in Chapter 9, she is haunted by his loss. She notes in the article that for a long period after her husband's death, she waited by the front door for him to return at his normal 11 P.M. time. Because she was in total denial, she told people that her husband hadn't died. It finally hit her when she was filling out an application to return to school soon after the funeral. She is quoted in the article as saying, "I thought I was going to have a nervous breakdown, because that was the first time I actually had to state that I was a widow." Unable to do so, she wrote that she was married. Soon, though, her denial gave way to anger. About six months after the loss of her husband, she began seeing a therapist in order to begin the process of creating a new life and identity apart from those she shared with her husband. Her road back may be long.

The effects of losing a close relationship in early or midlife can be staggering for the survivor, who may grieve profoundly for years. Raphael (1983) reviewed evidence suggesting that continued intense bereavement may contribute to early death. One indicator is an increase of almost 40 percent in the death rate of widowers over the age of fifty-four during the first six months of bereavement. Suicide also is a peril during this very early stage. Raphael reported evidence indicating that the suicide rate among a large sample of widows and widowers was 2.5 times higher in the first six months after the loss than in the fourth and subsequent years. Short of death, a survivor's mental and physical health often are impaired during this intense bereavement period, which usually lasts for months but can last much longer.

The loss of a spouse or romantic partner through death is one of the most studied topics in the grief literature. Particularly valuable discussions may be found in Glick, Weiss, and Parke's (1974) research and analysis of the first year of bereavement and Shuchter's (1986) analysis of the dimensions of grief.

Glick, Weiss, and Parkes followed a group of forty-nine widows over a period of years and developed this conclusion about recovery after the first years of bereavement:

> *Most components of the grief syndrome—feelings of shock, of abandonment, and of loss of part of the self, for example—seemed to be a response to the loss of the husband, and so too have faded as the loss receded into the past. Loneliness, however, seemed to be a reaction to the husband's absence. . . . It did not fade with time.*
>
> *By the end of the first year . . . some widows were dating, generally without the emotional reliance on the man or men they were seeing who would have allayed their loneliness. . . . The follow-up interview, held two, three, or four years after the death of their husbands, revealed however that a good many were engaged to remarry or had already remarried. None of these described themselves as still lonely, although most continued to sorrow for their loss of their husband. . . .*
>
> *Sometimes when widows looked back on the first year of their bereavement they could single out events they felt had special significance for their recovery. Some spoke of incidents in which they asserted for the first time that their lives must continue and that they must look forward and not back. (pp. 212–213)*

Shuchter (1986) interviewed widows and widowers as well as others who had lost close loved ones. In considering the renewal of romantic relations after losing a spouse or lover, he notes:

The widowed person who has begun to expose his or her vulnerability and opens up to someone else carries a whole set of emotional responses that have been associated with being in love, making falling in love easy once the barriers are down. (p. 245)

He also describes a woman who fell in love a few months after her husband's death. She said that the chemistry was there when they just said hello and that she decided she would marry him and learn a lot more about him later. Shuchter notes that this couple may be in for difficult times as it is likely the woman has barely begun grieving. It is probable that she often will have experiences with her new husband that initiate strong feelings of loss. Possibly without recognizing it, she may associate events and cues in her new family with her deceased husband and be thrown into pangs of missing him. Furthermore, the woman probably will make some invidious comparisons between her new husband and her deceased husband. In many ways, these difficulties are the same found by people who divorce after long marriages and then remarry quickly. The situation is not hopeless but must be approached by both partners with patience and respect for the continued grieving process. To the extent that the woman in this example does not recognize and affirm her grieving, it is likely that she and the new relationship will be troubled.

One of the most interesting findings that has emerged in the last decade is that widows' and widowers' immune systems apparently are affected by loss and grief. Schleifer, Keller, and Stein (1979) have found that bereaved husbands' lymphocyte responses became less effective two months after their wives died from breast cancer. Why would a person's immune system be less able to cope with potential threats after the death of a spouse? There probably are many reasons, but the roles of depression, loneliness, and social support may be involved. Depression and loneliness are common experiences for the survivor after a loved one has died. Social support may buffer the survivor somewhat against the potential for physical disease. As discussed in Chapter 12, there appears to be great value in having a confidant(s) in such situations.

I conclude this section with an excerpt from Herbert and Kay Kramer's *Conversations at Midnight* (1990), which will be discussed again in Chapter 11. The Kramers wrote this book about death as Herbert Kramer was dying of cancer. It is a valuable book for anyone who is close to death and for that person's loved ones. Much of our life with our closest loved ones survives in the form of images and memories after our deaths. The following excerpt reveals the poignancy and vividness of some of these images. It is a narration written by Kay Kramer after she has watched the undertaker remove her husband's body from their home soon after his death:

> *Leaning against the porch pillar, I wept as I remembered the sight of him the first time he appeared at this door, the romantic arrivals during our brief courtship, the evening he arrived for our marriage ceremony, and all the times he left, usually racing at breakneck speed for Mr. Duncan's cab— coat, hat, and bag already airborne for his trip to the airport—and on to Washington in the early morning hours before the rest of the street was awake. I could see him running out the door to ride the new bike I got him on his sixtieth birthday, and the surprise on his face the time the white limousine came to pick him up for a Father's Day picnic at Gillette Castle.*
>
> *It felt as if my heart were breaking as I watched him leave this street for the last time, this street he loved, that looked so good to him each time he returned to it after every journey, this street that was home to him since 1953. (pp. 226–227)*

While Kay Kramer's memories reveal great pain, the book and their act of writing it in the last year of Herb Kramer's life were healing and uplifting experiences for both of them.

LOSING A PARENT

> *[I]t's very important for us—all of us baby boomers, who grew up in the biggest group in American history—to give our parents the dignity of living lives as whole as possible as long as they can. . . . Honor your parents and live without regret when they're gone.*
>
> —President William J. Clinton

This quote reveals President Clinton's feelings in particular about his mother, Virginia Kelley, who died at age seventy early in 1994. Clinton was very close to his mother, who had raised him by herself after his father died early in his life. She had an enormous influence on Clinton's accomplishments, including his political career. Clinton reflected on how, in the middle of a hectic life, he had tried to take some time to grieve soon after his mother's death:

> *I have literally signed thousands of letters to friends of hers and friends of mine who wrote me to say they were sorry she'd died and with some reminiscence of her. . . . Signing the letters, and being able to read them, was just a way of reconnecting with my mother.*
>
> *It was a way of grieving that even a workaholic could understand. I've got all these things around here I've got to do. I said, "I'm going to sign*

*these letters." So sometimes I'd sit in here [the Oval Office] by myself for
an hour and read letters, or do it at night. I'd cry and laugh and do all the
things you want to do. It was a way of being alone, doing something I
ought to be doing anyway, and then just kind of having images of my
mother flash before my mind. It helped me to deal with it. . . .*

*Yes, I think I have a pretty tough time on Mother's Day. . . . I recall the
first time I realized she was gone. I used to call her every Sunday night.
. . . So I came in on Sunday night from my trip to Europe [that occurred
soon after Ms. Kelley's funeral] and I was in the kitchen and all but had the
phone picked up before I realized: "My God, I can't do it."*

One theme that occurs throughout people's accounts of their parents'
deaths is the regret of not having shared more emotionally and cognitively
with them while they were alive. The lyrics from "The Living Years" (1988)
by B.A. Robertson and Mike Rutherford express this theme:

*Every generation
Blames the one before
And all of their frustrations
Come beating on your door.*

*I know that I'm a prisoner
To all my father held so dear
I know that I'm a hostage
To all his hopes and fears
I just wish I could have told him
In his living years.*

*Say it loud, say it clear
You can listen as well as you hear
It's too late when we die
To admit we don't see eye to eye.*

Or, as Willy Loman said about his father in Arthur Miller's *Death of a
Salesman* (1958), "I never had a chance to talk to him and I still feel—kind
of temporary about myself" (Act I). The loss of a parent also can mobilize a
person, even an adult, to alter the course of his or her life. Consider Michael
Jordan, the incomparable basketball star and leader of the three-time world
champion Chicago Bulls. Jordan shocked the sports world in 1993 when he
announced his retirement from basketball at the age of thirty. He further
shocked people by beginning a professional career with the Chicago White
Sox baseball team in 1994, playing with their Double A Birmingham team.
Why such drastic changes so quickly? Some sports analysts have suggested
that Jordan's retirement from basketball was directly related to the murder

of James Jordan, his father, in the summer of 1993. Jordan and his father were very close, and Jordan relied on him for advice and wisdom. The media focus on Michael Jordan has always been extreme. As Bernie Lincicome noted in an article for the *Chicago Tribune* on August 16, 1993, "Even cruel and undignified death [referring to his father's murder] cannot earn him the right of private grief but is illuminated by the same bright light as an underwear commercial" (1993, sect. 3, p. 1). I would guess that Jordan's retirement (which lasted less than two years) and the assumption of still another life challenge in baseball had a lot to do with his intuitive feeling of a need to get away from some of the limelight and to heal his grief.

In 1995, Jordan returned to professional basketball in time to lead the Chicago Bulls into the playoffs. In returning, he indicated that he felt he had gone as far as he could in his season plus of baseball. In effect, he seemed ready to return to the prime time and adulation of his countless fans.

Some observers may feel that an adult's loss of a parent has less impact than the other types of losses described in these pages. This may be true when the parent has lived a full and satisfying life and when the adult child has had much opportunity to be close to the parent. However, we all have loose ends, unfinished business, with our parents when they die. It has been reported that in the months following the loss of a parent, surviving adult offspring show greater incidences of spousal abuse, drunkenness, and extramarital affairs as well as conflicts among siblings (Ackner, 1993). The conflicts among relatives are quite common—even at the time of the funeral and especially at the time of the reading of the will. Death forces survivors to be more honest in how they perceive and really feel about one another. More generally, why might such patterns be associated with a parent's death? Probably the best answer is that the death causes the person to feel that he or she no longer has an anchor. This type of feeling may be particularly strong when parents are close to their children (e.g., the relationship of James and Michael Jordan).

A young child who loses a parent may have a sense of incompleteness as an adult.

> *Theresia [who died at age thirty-two] was a loving, caring and sensitive person. Her whole life was devoted to her young son and her dreams for his success in school and baseball. She will be missed beyond words by her son Chad.* (Cedar Rapids Gazette, 1993, p. 14A)

Chad's grief may always defy words. As a college teacher, I can attest to the grief frequently shown by students who lost parents when they were still young children. It is often a bitter, angry feeling that they were dealt a terrible injustice by life. The fact that they may not have known their dead parent does not ease their pain but rather causes them great consternation.

You can go to the Vietnam Veterans Memorial in Washington, D.C., and readily find the grieving adult children of soldiers who died when the children were infants or very young. An incompleteness follows these children throughout their lives. The agony of children who lose their parents when the children are still young seems to be intensified by the feeling of having known a loving parent for a short, inadequate time.

Quite young children may harbor feelings of unreality for a long time after a parent's death (Sanders, 1980, 1982). It seems impossible to them that their parent could die or leave them, and they may perceive the act as having been chosen by the parent. Some have argued that this is one of the main reasons young children need to be involved in funeral or memorial services for their deceased parent (Leash, 1994). Such involvement may help them accept reality. Sometimes later in life, children indicate that they felt cheated when their parent died because those attending them were not truthful with them and did not involve them in the formal plans for grieving. Over a long period after a parent's death, young and teenage children can be expected to grieve the loss, both explicitly and implicitly. The implicit type of grief may come through in their dreams, relationships with others, and actual physical and psychological health.

I end this discussion with excerpts from a journal essay a student, age twenty, wrote for one of my classes. She poignantly reveals the depth of closeness that can be achieved between a father and a daughter and how difficult life can be when that bond is broken:

> *My dad [who was in his forties] passed away over a year ago. It seems a lot longer though. I feel like I haven't seen him for ten years. I think about him every day. Nothing is the same without my dad. He was (or is) the inspiration in my life. . . . There are so many questions I'd like to ask him. He always had the answers. . . . It's hard for me to date people who didn't know my dad. I just wish he could meet them. No one understands how important he was to me. . . . I respect him so much and I was always so proud of him. Life just isn't as fun without his laughter. . . . It's so hard to write about all of this because he was such an enormous part of me and my thoughts. I just miss him so much.*

A PILE-UP OF LOSSES

Julie Hanson died of leukemia three years ago. She and John were college sweethearts who'd been married five years. . . . John Hanson's early shock was tempered by the six months the family had spent with Julie as she went through diagnosis and a bone marrow transplant. Then a month after her death, his father drowned. . . . "It was a year no one should have. . . . To lose my wife and then my dad? I was in a fog of misery. I went through the motions, I had to be there for the boys [his sons]. My only peace was that . . . we [he and his wife] had time to say goodbye, and the boys were able to be with her." (Reiner, 1991)

Probably the most difficult loss experience involves a succession of major losses within a short period of time. It is as if *losses beget losses*. This book includes many stories of people dealing with multiple, simultaneous losses. I mention one at this point because it provides perspective on how taxing these situations can be and how courageous some people are as they struggle with cumulative losses that would break most people's will to struggle on or even to continue living.

Elizabeth Glaser died on December 3, 1994. She and her family faced staggering losses during the last fifteen years of her life. In 1981, as a young woman of thirty-three, Elizabeth was infected with the AIDS virus through a tainted blood transfusion given to her when she gave birth to her daughter, Ariel. For several years, she was unaware that the transfusion was tainted. Ariel then developed the virus at age four. A son, Jake, born in 1984 also was affected by HIV, but he has not developed AIDS. In 1986, Elizabeth, Ariel, and Jake were diagnosed with AIDS. Her husband, Paul, a successful actor and director, was uninfected. After fighting the disease for four years and growing weaker with each passing day, Ariel died at age six in 1988.

In that year, after years of fighting to maintain secrecy about their HIV status to protect their children and Paul's career from discrimination, the couple revealed their situation to the public. Later, they appeared on the television program *60 Minutes*. After her daughter's death, Elizabeth publicly led what interviewer Kristin McMurran from *People Weekly* referred to as a call to arms in fighting AIDS at the national level. In describing her work on behalf of children infected with the AIDS virus to McMurran for the February 4, 1991, edition of *People*, Elizabeth said:

> *But as helpless as it felt at those moments, I knew that the next day might not feel hopeless at all, so I made the decision to choose to live.*
>
> *But after Ari died, I felt dead too. I spent a lot of my time lecturing myself, saying you've got to move forward, but I could no longer see any beauty in the world. . . . (McMurran, 1991, p. 94)*

At the 1992 Democratic convention, Elizabeth Glaser gave an impassioned speech on behalf of persons suffering from AIDS. She said that her daughter had taught her how to stop being bitter about her fate and to reach out to others suffering from this tragic disease. As quoted in her obituary in 1994, Glaser said of her daughter: "She taught me to love when all I wanted to do was hate; she taught me to help others when all I wanted to do was help myself" (*Des Moines Register*, 1994, p. 2A).

One of Elizabeth Glaser's major achievements was the cofounding of the Pediatrics AIDS Foundation with her friends Susan DeLaurentis and Susie Zeegen. It was launched in 1988 with a $500,000 donation from Paul's aunt, Vera List, and now has a very active board of directors and group of support-ers. It funds research on the cure of HIV, especially in children, and on ways to prevent infected mothers from passing the virus to their unborn babies.

Elizabeth said that her drive to see progress made in the cure of AIDS was fueled by thoughts of her daughter and buoyed by Ari's presence in her dreams:

> *At times when I'm not feeling strong enough to meet all my challenges, I want to be someone of whom Ari would be proud, because I was so proud of her. She would settle for nothing less than my best effort because that's what she gave. So in my weaker moments, I think about her, and I say, "Okay, Ari, you're right. I'm going to move on." And who knows what tomorrow will bring? I've always been someone who fought for a happy ending. Even though I cannot erase the death of my child . . . all I'm doing right now is giv-ing my best shot at fighting for a happy ending. (McMurran, 1991, p. 96)*

Glaser also wrote a book with Laura Palmer entitled *In the Absence of Angels* (1991) that documented the story of her family's tragedy and battle against AIDS. Her love and grief for her daughter pervade the book along with her determination to find hope for others facing AIDS.

The Glasers are great inspirations for people facing multiple losses. Elizabeth Glaser's will to go on and accomplish was derived from the social support of many influential, close friends who have stood by the family during their difficulties. We may wonder about all those people who face their own insuperable losses without good support systems. Can they, too, find such courage not only for their own battles but also for those of others who are facing similar difficulties?

STEPS TOWARD HEALING—EMBRACING THEIR MEMORY

> *Only the weak are afraid of emotion, vulnerability, and display of their own humanity.*
>
> —Taylor Caldwell

> *A friend wrote this to me [at a time] when I was so devastated: "They are never gone unless you forget."*
>
> —Evelyn Swanson

In this final discussion, I consider briefly the healing that occurs after the loss of a close relationship through death. The topic of healing is considered more broadly in Chapter 12. At this point, I emphasize again the value of public storytelling and both public and private reminiscences about our departed loved ones. These acts of embracing their memories connect past and present and give continued meaning to people's timeless contributions to one another. They also provide perspective and sometimes give direction and momentum to those who suffer similar losses.

As she began to heal, Elizabeth Neeld (1990) used the turning point of her husband's death to make key changes in her life, including giving up her college teaching job and becoming a full-time writer. She took this step with little money saved and few solid prospects for publication. Nevertheless, the decision was part of a set of steps that she feels are necessary for many people when they are recovering from tragedy. It is necessary, she believes for the individual to take risks, to come back from failure, to reinvent himself or herself, to reexamine assumptions, to self-manage, and to find new solutions. Neeld's commentary is eloquent in its treatment of the need to "find a comfortable place in your thoughts for the lost person" (p. 20) and to accommodate recurring grief. Ultimately, she found both in her life. She also found success as a writer and in a second marriage. In the end of her story, Neeld emphasizes the value of making time for thoughts and feelings about the lost person, to maintain an inventory of key images of ourselves from the past, and therefore to keep a critical thread of continuity with the past.

Anne Loew, age twenty-seven, wrote in the May 2, 1993, *Parade Magazine* about losing her father when she was seventeen:

> I remember telling myself, "I can't deal with these feelings now. I'll figure it out when I'm older." I wish I had let myself feel those healing feelings.
> His death left an empty place in my life, which I now try to fill with memories and personal reminders of him—he was from Texas, so I buy a yellow rose of Texas each year on his birthday. Many entries in my diary start, "Dear Dad." It's a way of sharing my life with him. (1993, p. 18)

Deborah Davis, in her book *Empty Cradle, Broken Heart* (1991), makes several suggestions for positive grieving for the loss of a young child that I have modified to include the loss of any type of close relationship through death:

1. Resolved grief will be marked by acceptance and integration of the loss into our lives. With gentleness, we can keep the past alive but be fully committed to the present.

2. Resolution includes sadness, love, and remembrance.

3.   Unresolved grief is accompanied by an inability to accept your loss, repression, or avoidance of it.

4.   Whether or not your grief is resolved, there probably will be anniversary reactions to the losses for which you grieve. Accept them. Plan to be with close others around those times. Do not hesitate to talk about your feelings regarding your memories and thoughts of what might have been. They count and deserve a place of honor in your mind. Yet, you owe it to your lost love and yourself to dedicate yourself to the present and to commemorating your loss in your life's work and contribution to others.

Guilt frequently accompanies major loss. Whether or not our behavior had any conceivable association with the loss, we may feel survivor's guilt. This type of guilt, discussed more in Chapter 9, can wreak havoc on a person's adjustment if it continues over time. As one parent said about her daughter's death:

> *I think that you feel out of control with almost any death, when you realize that you don't have control. . . . I go back and forth on that [whether or not she had any control]. Right after Heidi died I'd been confronted about my guilt over her death, and I go back and forth between wanting to take responsibility and saying, "Hey, come on, I did not cause this, this cannot be my responsibility." (Davis, 1991, p. 73)*

Ultimately, after a close loved one's death, we must let ourselves off the hook. We must recognize that we had nothing to do with the death. We must realize that we cannot always prevent bad things from happening. For example, when a child dies, we must acknowledge we did the best we could to find timely, expert medical help for him or her. We need to tell others our story and especially confide our feelings of guilt to people with whom we have close, confiding relationships.

Relatives and friends do survivors no service by pointing out that they should have stopped grieving months ago or by telling them that they should rejoice since their loved one is in heaven (Richards, 1994). Each grief has its own course or journey. By just saying "I'm sorry" and offering to listen if they wish to talk about it, we take acts that are helpful and remembered with warmth and thanks by survivors.

Patricia Weenolsen (1988) offers these words that summarize the importance of survivors' embracing their memories of their lost close relationships:

> *We can never completely "get over" a major loss in the sense that all its effects are negated, that it is "forgotten." Our losses become part of who we*

are, as precious to us as other aspects of ourselves, and so does the transcendence of those losses.

Precious memories
How they linger ever near me

. . . .
In the stillness of the midnight,
Echoes from the past I hear. . . .
In the stillness of the midnight,
Precious sacred scenes unfold.

From the gospel ballad, *Precious Memories*

5

LOSS OF CLOSE RELATIONSHIPS THROUGH DISSOLUTION OR DIVORCE

He told others he had never loved me. The years we had
spent together, what meaning did they have?
—Librarian, Age Sixty-two

The sorrow of the lover is continual, in the presence
and absence of the beloved: in the presence for fear of
the absence, and in absence in longing for the presence.
The pain in love becomes in time the life of the lover.
—Sufi Master Hazrat Inayat Khan

A TIME OF PARTICULAR SORROW FOR LOVERS?

Stephen Holden, of the *New York Times*, once reviewed a movie called *The Lost Words*. The review was headlined "How's love in the '90s? Depressing" (1994, p. 3). The movie portrays the rather dreary love lives of a group of young, supposedly sophisticated New Yorkers in their late twenties and early thirties. In essence, the movie blames the male characters for most of the domestic tumult it depicts. This tumult may or may not mirror the real lives of many people in that age range today. The male characters are whiny and insensitive to their partners' interests and use bravado to cover their anxiety about close relationships. The movie declares that love in the 1990s can best be summed up by five words: *discord, suspicion, anger, disappointment,* and *sex.* That summary does indeed add up to *depressing* and implies that there is a lot of grief in the divorcing and separating world of the 1990s. As discouraging as it may seem, there probably is a grain of truth in the movie, which we can recognize when we consider the number of people looking to therapists, support groups, and self-help books for solutions to anguished relationships.

Americans are a marrying and divorcing society. As we approach the twenty-first century, the divorce rate has risen to 50 percent for recent marriages, those that began in the past ten to twenty years. Our attitudes about divorce have tilted toward believing that divorce often is the answer to marital problems. In the 1990s, the stigma of divorce is mostly gone.

We will all probably lose a close romantic relationship at some point due to death, drifting away, moving away, dissolution or divorce, or a mutual parting of ways. We may lose many romantic relationships. Although not all of us will experience divorce personally, in light of the frequency of divorce, most of us will experience it at least indirectly through others close to us. We may become a child of divorce or a parent who must watch our sons or daughters encounter the pain of dissolution.

People of marrying age today often have had several close relationships or a long-term close relationship prior to marriage. On the one hand, such close relationships can provide valuable perspectives about other people. On the other hand, extensive experience with dating, separating, and dissolving means that the individuals involved may become somewhat cynical about the durability of close relationships. If they marry, divorce, and begin another dating period, they are likely to experience still more losses of this nature.

Not every individual may immediately process a succession of lovers as losses. Individuals may feel as if they are having the time of their lives. As time goes on, however, these individuals will find that people who were meaningful will come back to them in their memories. Over time, the dissolution process may exact a heavy toll in psychological pain and possibly in physical and practical devastation (e.g., reduced financial health or career losses). Thus, the words of Hazrat Inayat Khan at the beginning of the chapter are applicable for most types of major losses through death, dissolution, or divorce.

For many, the loss of a love through divorce or the dissolution of a non-marital relationship can lead to the same symptoms of loss described in Chapter 4: numbness; feelings of helplessness and hopelessness; thoughts of suicide; inability to concentrate, work, sleep, or eat; loss of sexual drive; guilt; depression; and loneliness and despair.

Even a friendly divorce can have many of these debilitating effects. The following excerpt is from Rheta Johnson's poignant essay on the end of a marriage, entitled "Only Scars Are Shared in a Friendly Divorce" (1993):

Half of everything they owned isn't that much. There are obvious gaps in his new household. A couch, but no table; books, but no shelves; and, where the china used to be, an eight-place microwave-safe set of dishes from K Mart.

Their possessions made a much more respectable showing as a whole, artfully placed as she'd had them in a home they built themselves on a large wooded lot.

There had seemed to be more, too, when the U-Haul was backed up to the house and helped load her share of 12 years into it. She had pulled out of the driveway and their marriage without looking back.

Now he sits sorting his memories along with his half of the furnishings. . . . They threw out each other's familiar features with yesterday's garbage, those grinning 8-by-10s signed by Olan Mills and paid for with money due the utilities. Like a garage sale where everything's free, they packed and chose over memorabilia that no longer had much meaning. The residue of marital bliss.

Their last night together was like any one of a thousand others, in many respects. He set the alarm, and she put out the cat. There was the sudden compulsion to reconsider. They found themselves standing at the top of a high dive, scared to jump off and too tired to climb down. There were others lined up behind, pressing and nudging, making the leap seem inevitable.

There on the purgatorial platform, they clung to each other for the last time. It had never seemed so important to be together. (p. 3C)

A TIME OF CRAZINESS WITH LOSS AND GRIEF AS SUBTHEMES

The divorcing time is, as Robert Weiss (1975) suggests, a time of craziness. For instance, there is a tendency for these sometimes tormented individuals to have sex regularly during their separation. Weiss found this activity to be common among his sample, regardless of level of hostility in the separation. Sexuality, presumably an act of kindness and care for another, occurs at such a time mainly because the two people have been sex partners. In fact, they may have liked the sex part; they just couldn't stand each other on other grounds. At the time of a divorce, weaning oneself from sexual activity is difficult, but it may be difficult to find a new sex partner quickly (although that is commonly done). Thus, the otherwise hostile and rejecting partners may find that they still have this common need.

The instability (a type of loss itself) caused by the deluge of divorces in American marriages is merrily captured by poet Judith Steinbergh in the following poem, entitled "There Are No Rules" (1988):

[A]nd my ex-husband on his fortieth birthday shows up to pick up his sister who is visiting me and brings his girlfriend who is still in college leav-

ing her on my front porch to chat about her major while he runs upstairs to shower and my lover comes to observe my daughter's classroom with his ex-wife who is not even his ex-wife yet while I am there visiting and we are cordial, we are more than cordial, we are intimate in this irony. You think everything is set, maybe no one is speaking and lawyers are handling it all when the rules change: my ex-husband's second wife leaves, my ex-husband calls for a date, my ex-husband invites my lover and me to a hot tub party, we are all in the steam together eating olives and drinking beer and talking about real estate development. Who knows what to expect next. Even Neptune switched orbits with Pluto and Mount St. Helens, dormant for centuries, bellows fire again. . . . Stable is a word we've invented so we can sleep. (1988, p. 18)

Perhaps the divorcing experience is not as frenzied for everyone as it seems to be in Steinbergh's work, but it often is convoluted and involves many steps, including shock or surprise at the decision to end a relationship; denial that it is happening; rushing to find a new mate or indiscriminate, frenzied dating for a period; and gradual adaptation to either a new relationship or a less hectic single life. In any type of loss circumstance, adaptation occurs only after the mind and body have had time to regroup. It is facilitated greatly by the diligent effort to combine staying hopeful and active with a review of the major aspects of the relationship: what went wrong, what to do now, and what to expect the next time.

In one of the first comprehensive treatments of the effects of divorce, sociologist Morton Hunt (1966) interviewed people who were recovering from divorce and slowly beginning to establish new relationships. He describes their pilgrimage in almost poetic terms, and his points are as relevant in the 1990s as they were in the 1960s:

The course of true love never did run smooth and, as we have seen, it is especially bumpy for the Formerly Married. Unlike the young, who come to each other relatively empty-handed, the divorced man and divorced woman come with all the acquisitions of the years—their individual histories, habits, and tastes, their children, friends, and chattels. Love can be a rickety vehicle, loaded with so much of life's baggage, and the trip back to the world of the married is often interrupted by slow-downs, halts, and backsliding. (p. 269)

A typical remarriage couple, as Hunt suggests, may have a particularly rocky road because they may become involved before they are ready for such renewed involvement. Each person's self-esteem may have been shattered in the previous relationship—whether or not the relationship involved marriage. Each individual may be lonely and very eager to remarry but at the same time feel that options are limited. This perception may be especially true for middle-aged individuals who do not have ready access to single persons of a similar age. They may feel less valuable in the "dating and mating market" than they did when they were younger. Single people with custody of their children may also experience a disadvantage because children limit their freedom. They also may feel having children makes the process of selecting the right partner for potential marriage more important than for those without children but also more frustrating as some of their prospects may not be very well qualified to be parents. Finally, people who are "recycling" may have leftover emotional problems that require professional attention but cannot be readily addressed because of a shortage of time and money. Thus, when these individuals remarry quickly, their new relationships may be time bombs just waiting to go off when enough pressure is applied.

Many distinctions could be drawn about the nature of the dissolving experience for different couples. Some may experience little stress and may in fact move on to other apparently happy relationships soon afterward (or even before if they have been having an affair). I use the word *apparent* because I do not think that we can easily escape doing some degree of emotional work to get beyond a major loss. Those who move too quickly will have to come back and deal with the loss later—or the loss will likely deal with them in the form of psychological or physical difficulties at other points in life. In the end, I suggest that loss and grief are what might be called significant subthemes for this period. Just as a person who loses a close relationship through death must spend a considerable time in grieving and recovery, so must a person whose relationship ends through dissolution or divorce.

THE PROGRESSION TOWARD DISSOLUTION

There are at least as many scenarios that eventuate in the dissolution of a close relationship as there are people who have encountered dissolution. In some instances, the deterioration of the relationship is slow and halting. In others, the progression of the dissolution is up and down, including periods of separation and periods of living together or being a couple. In still others, the progression is as swift as a bullet. This latter type is most interesting because it is most puzzling, at least to the person being left. It is as if, out of the blue, one partner in an otherwise functioning, satisfactory relationship decides that she or he wants out and promptly takes the steps to get out. Of course, this particular type of progression may seem as if it is out of the blue to the person being left; but to the other partner or a knowledgeable outsider, the progression may have been more gradual and systematic. If the couple could communicate about problems, such an event would not come as a surprise.

Based on her years of clinical practice, Kessler (1975) divided the typical psychological process involved in dissolution into seven emotional stages, as follows: disillusionment, erosion, detachment, physical separation, mourning, second adolescence (i.e., starting to go through the rituals of dating again, just as one did as an adolescent), and exploration and hard work (which refers to the steps toward establishing a new identity and possibly a new close relationship). Kessler stresses that different people experience these emotions in a different order, that the start and end points are unclear, and that the duration of these experiences differs across people.

Do couples often understand the progression toward dissolution as it is occurring? Some probably do. Many don't. Loss and mourning for these couples often are more intense because they were unprepared for the dissolution. Their unpreparedness sometimes is the result of their partners' highly different understandings of how stable and successful the relationship is.

In trying to pinpoint the progression of events toward dissolution, it is helpful to study the perceptions of both members of the relationship. Often there is a complex web of understanding surrounding a close relationship and the major events in its history. Within these understandings resides much of what determines the success of the relationship. My colleagues and I studied partners' perceptions of their problems in the mid-1970s and were struck by the divergence of those perceptions (Harvey, Wells, and Alvarez, 1978). For example, often the woman in the relationship would say that she was unhappy because her partner made no effort to understand how she felt about their emotional life. In contrast, the man would say that the woman was unhappy principally because he was not earning enough money. One woman participant said, "He never takes the time to learn what is on my mind and to share his feelings with me. He is always at work or too tired when he comes home." Her husband said: "She does not understand or appreciate how hard I work and how much pressure I'm under at work. If she did, she wouldn't be so demanding when I come home and then hurt when I don't have the energy to deal with her problems" (p. 250).

These are classic lines from which many a close relationship begins to unravel. More recent work (Holtzworth-Munroe and Jacobson, 1985) has painted a clearer picture of the importance of mutual understanding, divergences in understanding, and recognition of such divergences as powerful elements in conflict and eventual separation. An interesting finding in this research is that women regularly engage in considerable attributional analysis of what is happening in a relationship, but men engage in this activity mainly when the relationship is in trouble (see also Hill, Rubin, and Peplau, 1976, for similar findings from a sample of college students). In my own work on couples' attributions, I argue that if couples are flexible in their understandings, they are more able to revise misperceptions and converge on important issues that are key to whether the relationship survives (Harvey, 1987). They may not agree in their attributions and evaluations, but at least they will know more clearly how they disagree!

VAUGHAN'S ANALYSIS

Diane Vaughan (1986) collected reports from 103 women and men after they had separated or divorced; former partners of the respondents were not included in the sample. Across her sample, Vaughan found evidence for various stages in a relationship's dissolution. She proposed that "uncoupling" involves (1) secrets, or the breakdown of frank communication in at least one area of the relationship; (2) the display of discontent, whereby the initiator, in particular, begins to define negatively one or more aspects of the previously positive relationship; and (3) a transition from one's role as a partner to a more ambiguous role of independent person, while trying to cover up the leave taking. Because of the value of Vaughan's work as an analysis of the sequence of dissolution, let us consider the progression of uncoupling in more detail.

In the secrets stage, one of the partners, the initiator, develops a deep unhappiness with the relationship. This phase is rather quiet and involves only the initiator. The initiator broods a lot, goes through life mulling alternatives, and eventually begins to show his or her discontent. The initiator may not be able to articulate fully the major complaints with the relationship but begins to show anger, perhaps blowing up over small matters. The initiator also may show various forms of passive-aggressive pulling-away behavior such as perfunctory sexual behavior or forgetting to wear her or his wedding ring.

At some point, for some people, potential outside romantic relationships begin to develop. Indeed, potential romance may be the major secret that then leads to other stages in which the initiator makes an invidious comparison between the outsider and the present partner (e.g., how much easier it is to talk with the other person than it is to talk to one's partner). The outsider is a transitional other with whom the initiator may discuss the problems in his or her relationship and perhaps form some type of fledgling romantic relationship in its own right. In Vaughan's sample, respondents who reported such outside activities also sometimes reported guilt, which then often led to further passive-aggressive behavior toward the spouse or partner. Why? Because if one can make the partner take actions that clearly violate the relationship, then one can lessen one's own guilt about violations.

Vaughan's analysis of the reports shows that the initiator is in charge of the events unfolding. This person feels better about what is happening than the other—maybe not happy, but relieved that soon she or he will be free.

Vaughan's finding parallels earlier evidence presented by Hill et al. (1976), who studied the breakups of college student romances. Hill et al. found that the individuals who believed they had instigated the breakup reported less severe emotional consequences than did those who had not.

In Vaughan's sample, the initiator was already beginning to transform his or her identity from being part of a couple to being single or perhaps a member of a different relationship. The initiator also tended to make further moves toward what Erving Goffman (1959) once called "cooling the mark" (roughly defined as getting the person who is being left to accept his or her fate and not make trouble for the initiator). The initiator achieves this by (1) focusing on the negative qualities of the partner; (2) indicating a belief that the relationship has been unsalvageable for some time; (3) trying to convince the partner that the relationship was/is beyond repair; (4) telling other people the story of the demise of the relationship—making it public, thus strengthening the commitment to ending it; (5) possibly seeking a transitional partner(s); and (6) beginning the process of grieving or mourning. Anyone who has been in a long-term relationship is likely to mourn its loss. Initiators just start sooner, according to Vaughan.

Vaughan found that the person being left is often "out in the cold without a clue." The person's life is caving in, and she or he really does not understand why. Many of us have been in this position. It is one of life's worst conditions because we feel that we have no control over another's feelings and decisions about us. What we often do in such situations is to make it worse. We get angry and tell our partners to be gone right away; then we apologize and plead for our partners to come back; then we waver between bravado and pitifulness in our statements. The truth is we often are out of control: The control is sitting in our partners' hands. We may start to analyze and recognize aspects of the relationship that should have served as warnings, but that does not make us any happier. We still are losing, pardon the metaphor, our right arm, and there is no way to sew it back on. We feel abandoned by those to whom we are still strongly attached.

Robert Weiss (1975), in his classic study of separating and recently divorced people, has defined separation distress as, "a response to intolerable inaccessibility of the attachment figure" (p. 42). While it may be clear to friends and family who initiated the breakup and the initiator may catch more heat about why the relationship has to end, compared to the one being left, he or she still has a head start toward restoring self, establishing a new identity, gaining control over his or her life, and developing a new close relationship.

Vaughan's strong emphasis on the experience of the initiator versus that of the person being left probably does not do justice to the complexity of many breakups. As Weiss (1975) eloquently argues, based on his interviews with individuals in the organization Parents without Partners, the matter of who actually gets the dissolution ball rolling usually is a complicated matter:

> *There do seem to be differences in the impact of separation on those who define themselves as leavers and those who define themselves as left, but the differences seem to be more nearly in the character of the resultant distress than in its intensity [meaning that each will suffer more or less to the same degree]. In most separations . . . [the] marriage became intolerable for both partners; somehow one partner rather than the other decided finally to call it quits. Sometimes husband and wife alternated in the initiation of preliminary separations. . . . Sometimes a spouse who had been unwilling to accept responsibility for ending the marriage behaved so outrageously that the other spouse could not go on with it. And sometimes a husband or wife who had insisted on separation later had a change of heart and wanted to become reconciled, but the other spouse now refused. In all these circumstances the identification of the one spouse as leaver and the other as left oversimplifies a complex interactive process. (p. 63)*

Weiss notes that when there is a more clearcut leaver versus left in the breakdown sequence, the leaver may have some advantages but also incurs some major costs. Chief among those costs in Weiss's sample was guilt. These individuals may experience harsh reactions from outsiders such as friends of the couple that increase their feelings of guilt. Further, the leaver sometimes starts to question his or her own ability to stick to a commitment and to meet the partner's emotional needs.

GETTING DUMPED

The question of the impact of being the leaver rather than the left certainly applies to nonmarital dissolutions as well as to divorce. An experience many of us have had is that of being left by someone with whom we were having a close relationship. Feelings of lowered self-esteem, anger, self-reproach, and even helplessness or hopelessness are common in these circumstances, just as they are when a person decides to leave her or his spouse in a marriage.

Consider the following story, entitled "Being Dumped for the First Time Is No Easier for an Adult" (1993), from Cheryl Lavin's *Chicago Tribune* column "Tales from the Front," which presents stories about all aspects of relationships:

> *There are certain "firsts" we all remember. First date. First kiss. First love. First time we're dumped.*

Usually the first dumping happens early in life. There's the shock. The tears. The depression. Then slowly scar tissue forms. And life goes on. Until the next time.

Ellen never had that first dumping. Until now. After college, she had a string of relationships. None of them lasted more than a year. She ended every one of them. . . .

The dumper in this case is John. He's the one who has introduced Ellen to all those doubts and insecurities that are part of being dumped. . . .

Ellen and John met at work. "He wasn't handsome in a conventional way," she says. "But he was very charismatic and had a powerful personality. . . .

They hit it off right away and Ellen found herself relating to him in a way that was very unfamiliar to her. . . .

Ellen knew the relationship must mean something when she heard herself lying and saying she was free when she was really busy. She knew she was not her old independent self when she found herself turning up the volume on her answering machine when she took a shower so she could hear his voice if he called.

She was falling in love with him. And, she had every reason to believe, he was falling in love with her. He wanted to be with her all the time. He made those offhand, long-term plans: "Next summer we should. . . ." He came to her father's 60th birthday party. He introduced her to his brothers when they came to town. . . .

"Things were going great. . . . That's what I have to keep telling myself right now. . . . I was acting like a normal girlfriend in a normal relationship."

Then John went to Florida with a few friends for a vacation. When he came back, he was different. And he continued to act differently. And then he broke up with Ellen. It just wasn't working.

Huh?

Ellen was stunned. . . . It hurts!

She blamed herself. "What did I do wrong? Was I too available? . . . Should I have set limits, only spent one night a week with him, to keep up his interest? Did I stop trying to look my best?"

Lots of questions. No answers.

Ellen is taking the dumping very hard. (p. 3C)

It is easy to sympathize with Ellen. After getting her expectations and hopes up (and having so much evidence of John's involvement), only to be summarily dumped is the pits! This type of frequent experience in the dating and mating world is at the heart of the cynicism and negativity many people feel about the business of searching for close relationships today. They often start to feel that no one can be trusted and that it is critical not to get their hopes up early in a relationship. Such suspicions often affect the development, or lack thereof, of the next relationship. Thus begins a vicious cycle with both players experiencing the same apprehensions.

As I suggested in the opening chapter of this book, it is quite likely that underneath the heartache of persons who have been hurt in love is a deep grief, a grief born of the knowledge that the realities of life are at odds with the way they implicitly hoped their lives would turn out, a grief looking desperately for faith in a lover who will help them find the happiness and intimacy that they desire.

VICTIMS OF DIVORCE OR DISSOLUTION

On November 26, 1993, the *Washington Post* carried an article with the head-line, "900-Year-Old Letter Casts Light on Spurned Lover." This letter had been recently discovered in Russia and was written on birch bark. Its words spoke of a woman's grief at the apparent loss of her significant other's love:

> *I have sent to you three times. . . . What is the evil you hold against me, that you have never visited me this week?. . . Is it that I hurt you by send-ing to you, and you, as I see, do not like it? If you liked it, you would have broken free from [people's] eyes, and come.*

The article went on to say that the recipient had torn the letter in three, per-haps in anger or fear of discovery. The letter ended, "Even if I hurt you thoughtlessly, if you will begin mocking me, let God judge you, and my weakness."

Who are the victims of divorce, and why is divorce or dissolution so devastating? The victims include all persons who are very close to the di-vorcing process, the couple; their children, if any; their parents; and their friends. Often, a couple's parents and close friends feel as much loss and grief as the couple. Each of us believes our marriage or significant relation-ship will continue "until death do us part." Thus, divorce is devastating be-cause it robs the divorcing couple of their innocence and expectations about long-term bliss with their very closest other in life. The result is often a hard knock on one's self-esteem, sense of control over major events, feeling of competence, and overall feeling of hope in life.

We tend to compare ourselves with others whom we perceive to be en-gaged in solid relationships. Such social comparisons make more salient our loss and the possibility that we will never again experience such stabil-ity and hope. We often know about the world of the "formerly married," to use Hunt's term, and its perilous course. This knowledge may wither the early sense that the "grass is greener," or "anything is better than this relationship." The person who loses a partner may also lose the emotional support and companionship that usually go along with such relationships. Even in sadly deteriorated relationships, partners may not recognize the extent to which they have been attached and thus may be bewildered by their bereavement at the loss of this attachment. After all, many partners have been together since they were quite young. They often have gone through many adversities together, which create an attachment, even if the marriage is poor and becoming poorer.

There is a great loss of social identity attendant to divorce and dissolution. We have been known as "Joan's significant other," "John's wife," or "Mary's live-in partner" by our friends and families, and we and the outside world have to learn that these identities no longer hold. Depending on how much we wanted this role and want to continue in it, the change can be daunting—but it has to be done. The sooner the newly single person can recognize the need to change his or her life, perhaps by involvement in support groups and working on self-improvement, the sooner the adjustment will be well underway. The high frequency of divorce in our society has led to more sensitivity, or caution, in the way outsiders view close relationships. Too often, many of us have been shocked to discover that the long-term, seemingly well-functioning relationships of good friends or family suddenly no longer exist.

I end this section by quoting from "Here Lies My Heart," a poignant article in *Esquire* (1990), by the magazine's former editor Willie Morris. In this piece, Morris describes his marriage and divorce, which occurred twenty years prior to his writing the article:

> With divorce one gives up a whole way of life—friends, routines, habitudes, commitments. You are on your own again, and in diaphanous territory, and for a while your most fiendish habits may worsen. Then I told myself I could not afford to be deranged. I had a demanding job, after all, and scant choice but to function. The problems of real day-to-day life were easier to deal with than the imaginary ones; I willed my own salvation.
>
> For the longest time I thought I could never love again. I was wary and afraid and remembered too much. Yet as the days slowly pass, on into the years, you discover you can love again, and that, of course, is a whole other story. But I shudder now to think what my girlfriend of that time had to live with—and not merely the intolerable acrimony and spleen she was forced to share—for in the nature of it we all subconsciously compare our later loves with the first, no matter the wreckage and flaw. How could I have known then of the psychic hold she [his former wife] would have on me for the rest of my life? The wisps of memory, the dreams, the tender long-ago assurances. Her ghost would exist till I died. (pp. 174–175)

While Morris hit on many truths about loss in this article, in the end, he expressed a truth that we all should know about major close relationships that end: Psychologically, they never end. They live on in our memories, in our expectations about other close relationships, and in our subconscious views of ourselves and others. Indeed, at this psychic level, they do not die until we die!

THE CHILD'S GRIEF

Each divorce involves victims beyond the divorcing couple. However, no third party grieves as much as the child of divorce. In the 1990s, 50 to 60 percent of all children under age eighteen will spend some part of their childhood in a single-parent household.

Good scholarly research works and analyses exist on the effects of divorce on children. Two such works are Wallerstein and Kelly's *Surviving the Breakup* (1980) and Furstenberg and Cherlin's *Divided Families* (1991). These analyses point to varying patterns of reactions by children of different ages and genders. As the writers point out, there may be positive effects for children who are relieved from being in households in which marital conflict occurs, and children may learn to be more independent when their families break up.

Overall, however, many children suffer because of the turmoil surrounding divorce and its resulting discontinuities. They often grieve their parents' divorce for years, well into their adult years. I encounter many students in my college classes who have a great desire and need to discuss their feelings about their parents' divorces. It seems to be a fact of life that whatever adjustment the parents may have made, in most cases the children still are adjusting well into adulthood. For this reason, children-of-divorce support groups are becoming popular throughout this country. Listen to the following statement by one thirty-seven-year-old "child" of divorce who wrote his story as part of a study I did on the effects of divorce on children:

> It has been 20 years since my parents divorced. My father has remarried; my mother has been to the altar three times since then. But it is that initial legal proceeding two decades ago that still causes the pain. . . .
>
> I walked away from that interview [with a divorce attorney who was discussing the effects of divorce on children] realizing for the first time what my pain is about. It isn't that I want my parents reunited. As an adult, I can see quite clearly why that wouldn't work. My hurt comes from an underlying feeling that my parents did not love me, or my sister or brother, enough to put us first. Their own pain came first, and as a result, we were caught in the middle as one lashed out against the other.

My mother dealt with her pain by moving us thousands of miles away from my father. Clearly, she wanted to hurt him. Whether he deserved it or not is between them, but I know that we didn't deserve it. Children should, at the very least, have access to both parents.

How should parents interact with their children to lessen the negative impacts of divorce? The May 1994 issue of *Hemispheres* summarizes the following well-reasoned points by family counselor John Rosemond on how parents should deal with their children when they have decided to separate and divorce:

If at all possible, jointly parents should tell children about their impending separation and divorce before the process begins. Rosemond says that it is imperative in this discussion that the parents be declarative and not imply that they're asking for the children's views. Custody and other arrangements should have been worked out before the discussion and clearly communicated to the children. Rosemond advocates being clear and succinct in this conversation and not "beating around the bush" or talking as if the events might not occur. Further, the parents should state what will happen matter-of-factly without editorializing or trying to tell the children why the marriage is not working. In turn, they should be prepared for the worst possible reactions by the children, including that the children will think the split is their fault or that they are not loved anymore.

Rosemond goes on to advocate a flexible custody or visitation schedule, with a lot of care given to how custody will be arranged (e.g., whether shared, traditional, or whatever). He also stresses the importance of the parents' own effective grieving and adaptation as key factors in the children's eventual adaptation. Finally, Rosemond stressed the value of ex-partners' dealing with one another with professionalism and dignity. To the extent that this relationship is handled well and children are not put in the middle in continuing conflict, children can readily adjust and even prosper after their parents divorce.

GETTING OVER DIVORCE

Although Chapter 12 provides a general perspective and review of some specific approaches to healing from any type of major loss, there is a question that needs to be asked now: Are there tactics individuals can use to better deal with the particular qualities of divorce or dissolution?

One useful primer on getting over divorce is Kleinke's *Coping with Life Challenges* (1991). His advice is logical and direct. He says that overall, people have to learn how to let go. This involves accepting the fact that we cannot own or control others and their decisions. We often must accept and respect those decisions, even if they go against our desires and best interests. A specific tactic that Kleinke advocates is collecting all of the artifacts (e.g., letters, gifts) associated with our lost love and hiding them. He suggests that this step will help us to progress in our grief. Kleinke also offers these particular suggestions:

1. Accept a loss as worthy of grieving.
2. Be open to the experience of mourning.
3. Recognize the stages of grief work as tasks for which we are responsible (e.g., to stop denying, to move beyond anger and isolation).
4. Take time to accomplish the tasks of grief work, which include accepting the reality of loss, experiencing the pain and grieving, adjusting to a new life, and getting on with the new life.

I often hear people say that these kinds of suggestions are good but not easy to accomplish. I think that is true. Major loss is *major* because it staggers us in significant ways. We do not simply go out and find a new, substitute lover. We may try. But as many of us know, there are no substitutes. Each person is different and brings to a close relationship a whole set of new dynamics and issues. We do not move on easily and without a struggle of mind and heart.

Kleinke's suggestions involve a general strategy of actively confronting loss. I believe that most scholars and therapists in the broad domain of loss would endorse such a strategy. Naturally, people may try to avoid thinking about or having feelings about their loss. However, research by Daniel Wegner (1989) has shown that it is very difficult to suppress thoughts. In fact, the more we try to suppress them, the more we often obsess about them. We might as well have them out in the open and try to work with them. That is a critical step in confronting versus denying. In a 1991 talk, entitled "Fanning Old Flames," at the American Psychological Association meeting in San Francisco, Wegner said:

> *Ruminations about past loves can be painful and persistent. So people try to avoid them to gain immediate relief. But suppressed thoughts can turn into long-term obsessions that interrupt daily lives and hinder the ability to form new relationships. . . .*
>
> *Think hard about that old love. Come to grips with the pain of disappointment. Go ahead and get obsessed. Write a journal, talk to everyone about how you feel. . . . If you go ahead and think about it, it will be bothersome at first, but eventually you will get used to it. (p. 6)*

As articulated in Chapter 2, I believe that a combination of private work on one's own story of loss coupled with social interaction with or confiding in others is an approach to healing that embraces the value of the story or account that was discussed earlier and that Weiss (1975) emphasized in his study of marital separation. Mutual confiding in grief support groups appears to be a very constructive step toward healing (Wuthnow, 1994). While spilling one's soul to people with whom one is only generally familiar is a quite humanizing and humbling activity, it is also an activity from which we can learn a great deal about ourselves, relationships in general, and how to lean on others at certain times in our lives.

Weiss's research was done with the support group called Seminars for the Separated. This group devotes two hours per week to group discussion of topics designed to help newly separated and divorced persons manage the emotional and social challenges confronting them. The series of meetings may last indefinitely or for a few months at a time. There are literally thousands of support groups in this country, many of them dealing with loss and, specifically, separation and divorce. No one should feel reluctant to see if these groups have something valuable to offer. A person who desires to work hard on adapting to a major loss may benefit greatly from such meetings along with personal reading, reflection, and professional counseling.

Gradually, we all recover from lost love, however potent the mutual love may have been when it existed. In one of the most perceptive novels I have ever read on love won and lost, Alain de Botton (1993) tells the magical story of a one-year love affair between a young man and woman (Chloe) in London. Writing in the first person, de Botton tells how they felt that their meeting on a flight from Paris to London was so accidental as to be magical. They delighted in one another and in their passions and similarities for months until Chloe ran off with the narrator's friend. The narrator is crushed. After a few months of grieving, he finally begins to recover, which he recognizes when he feels guilty for not grieving:

Then, inevitably, I began to forget. A few months after breaking up with her, I found myself in the area of London in which she had lived and noticed that the thought of her had lost much of the agony it had once held. I even noticed that I was not thinking primarily of her . . . but of the appointment that I had made with someone in a restaurant nearby. I realized that Chloe's memory had neutralized itself and become a part of history. Yet guilt accompanied this forgetting. It was no longer her absence that wounded me, but my growing indifference to it. Forgetting was a reminder of death, of loss, of infidelity to what I had at one time held so dear. (p. 219)

GAINING PERSPECTIVE

There is much to be said for gaining perspective about the important events in our lives. Grief helps us achieve such perspective. Certainly, the endings of relationships with people whom we have loved dearly and been as close to as we have to any living being require an attempt to gain an overall, long-term perspective about what happened, why, and what it all meant. Willie Morris, whose article about his divorce twenty years earlier was quoted earlier, developed such a perspective that is epitomized in these lines:

> *All that was a very long time ago, and I see now that, as with much of life, this is really a little long-ago tale of time passing, and of vanished grief. So many of our friends of those days are dead now, and others have gone their own way. In the course of an existence, people move in and out of one's life. Often we do not know the whereabouts of those once dear to us, much less what they are feeling or remembering. Close relationships oscillate between tranquillity and destruction, between fire and ice. Old fidelities wither, and love dies as the lovers go on living. There are a few small islands of warmth and belonging to sustain us if we are lucky. That is how I wish to think of her now, in the days of our happiness.*
>
> *She became a respected feminist and writer. She subsequently married again, to a distinguished man and old friend. They, too, are now divorced. As for myself, a writing man, I never remarried, although I came close two or three times. . . .*
>
> *Yet the further I grew from those painful moments, the more the bitterness faded; one is left with a kind of mellowing sadness, and recollections of the beginnings of love when one was young, the heightened promise and trust. I also comprehend now that in many ways I grew and developed into the adult I am today, for better or worse, because of her, and of her values. Our son is now older than we were when we married, and I see her in him, in his courage and commitment. . . .*
>
> *In this moment I find myself driving in a Mississippi Delta twilight toward a warm new love, one that matters to me. All around are the landmarks of my own beginnings, the cypresses in the mossy ponds . . . the interminable flatness in the burnt-orange glow. The years are passing, and even in this rare twinkling of serenity and happiness and fulfillment I think of Celia, and remember her. (1990, p. 175)*

While much of this chapter has focused on the pathos of lost love, we need to keep in mind that there is an up side to these frequent losses: Humans learn through pain. There really is no other way to learn about the vicissitudes of the complex dating and mating practices in the 1990s. Through these sometimes intimate interactions with diverse other human beings, we become wiser about life and who we are. Unquestionably, younger generations are a lot smarter about the complexities of loving and losing love than were past generations—though, as we so often hear of violence associated with love lost, it is alarming how little that intelligence seems to guide conduct. Further, more people in these recent generations have *loved* than ever before. It is a sweet taste, especially for the beginning lover or the person long deprived.

> *Tis better to have loved and lost*
> *Than never to have loved at all.*
> —Alfred Lord Tennyson

6

LOSSES RESULTING FROM WAR AND VIOLENCE

The deepest grave on earth can never contain the violent death of a single decent soul.

—John Nichols

We are the shoes, we are the last witnesses.
We are the shoes from grandchildren
*   and grandfathers,*
From Prague, Paris, and Amsterdam,
And because we are only made of fabric
*   and leather*
And not of blood and flesh, each one of
*   us avoided the hellfire.*

—Moses Schulstein

This chapter is about the belief that losses and grief resulting from war and violence are unique and represent a topic for separate study. They are not necessarily more devastating than other types of losses, but they are different. They are also quite common in our world. The chapter will examine grief that is derived from the loss of loved ones in war, including the Holocaust, and in the daily violence that bombards U.S. citizens in their streets, playgrounds, homes, and businesses.

Many of the accounts reported in this chapter pertain to people's recall of events that occurred in the past. As we will see, some people report having highly vivid memories of events involving death and great fear. In Chapter 9, I discuss how some people who have had traumatic experiences continue for a lifetime to be haunted by their images of the loss of loved ones and friends. Salaman (1970) notes that these fresh memories often concern traumatic experiences that have been critical in defining who the survivor has become and represent critical transition points in the survivor's life. As Dostoyevski said about such memories, "They may be grave and bitter, but the suffering we have lived through may turn in the end into sacred things for the soul."

LOSS AND GRIEF RESULTING FROM WAR

Wars do not end when the shooting stops. They live on in the lives of those who are veterans of those wars. They live on in the lives of those who are the survivors and the dependents of those who lost their lives in war.
                                                                                    —Max Cleland

Loss and grief resulting from war can traumatize survivors, whether they are involved directly or are from families who have lost loved ones in war. In the wake of serving in combat, soldiers frequently experience posttraumatic stress disorder (PTSD). The symptoms of this disorder are numerous but include feelings, thoughts, and behaviors that are similar to those shown by persons exhibiting serious bereavement (Kuenning, 1990). Specifically, persons showing PTSD often report the following problems:

depression
anger
anxiety
sleep disturbances
tendency to react under stress with survival tactics
psychic or emotional numbing
emotional constriction
loss of interest in work and activities
survivor guilt
hyperalertness
avoidance of activities that arouse trauma memories
suicidal feelings and thoughts
flashbacks of war or death scenes.

These symptoms may continue for years, or they may abate some months after the experiences. Indeed, they may not begin to appear for months, or longer, after the traumatic event. For some, the memories will never fade. In some cases, the experience involved such great trauma that it is hard to imagine anyone surviving it. Y.C. Lindsay, a young soldier, was captured by the Japanese in 1941 when the 20,000 American troops defending the Bataan peninsula in the Philippines were overwhelmed by 150,000 Japanese troops. He then survived the 1942 Bataan death march, a forced march of prisoners that involved thousands of deaths. Later he and other prisoners were shipped to Japan. The trauma he experienced is comparable to the trauma experienced by Holocaust survivors. At age seventy-three, he vividly described part of his experience to reporter Mike Patty of the *Rocky Mountain News*:

> *They loaded 1,200 of us in the hold of this ship packed in so tight that one man couldn't sit down unless another man stood up. We were in that hold for 39 days. Eventually enough people died so that everybody could sit down, but there never was enough room to lie down during the whole 39 days. . . .*
>
> *An American torpedo missed our ship by about 9 feet, but you just didn't care. At night, it was so black down in the hold and you could hear the sonar ping against the hull, the torpedos going off and the Japanese dropping depth charges. We were only getting about a cup of water a day, and I hoped a torpedo would hit us so the cool water would come in. (Patty, 1994, p. 36A)*

As an example of the possible long-term impact of trauma and the environmental cues that can trigger reactions, Tick (1991) tells of a client who had not heard the Joe Cocker lyric "the great relief of having you to talk to" since his service in Vietnam. Twenty years later while he was driving down the road, he again heard the lyric, pulled over, and started to cry. That night he explained, "It was everything—the guys I left behind, the brothers I had over there who were the only people in the world I could talk to because the others would never understand" (p. 30).

It appears that troops who are most susceptible to PTSD symptoms often have been involved in the most gruesome experiences that can be encountered in war. For example, a telling experience for many combat troops landing at Normandy on D day in 1944 was the sight of countless corpses littering the beach and the cries of injured men in agony. These macabre experiences, which will be discussed later, were vividly recalled fifty years after D day, and the veterans reporting them indicated that they had spent a lifetime trying to deal with them—whether by trying to suppress their memories, by getting counseling, or by talking about their experiences with other veterans and confidants. A study by Sutker et al. (1994) found a high rate of PTSD shown by troops assigned grave registration duties (which involved handling the bodies of dead soldiers) during the Gulf War of 1991. Sutker found PTSD rates of 48 percent among those who had combat duties as compared to no symptoms among soldiers in a sample of veterans who were not deployed to combat.

The following poem by Bob Watts (1991) succinctly recounts a brother's trauma and attempts to cope when he came home from Vietnam:

Missing

My brother opened up the wound
Inside his head and pulled out jungles
He'd brought home as phantom souvenirs.
He dug them out as thick as dust
And laid them on our hills,
So that his head was empty,
A space he couldn't fill
Until he fed himself
The only hollow-pointed fruit
He'd ever grow.

Stories from Vietnam

There were over 58,000 American casualties and over 2 million Vietnamese casualties in the Vietnam War. The losses and grief resulting from the war are distinctive not only because of the magnitude of these losses but also because of the particular qualities of that war. It was not until the mid-1980s that many of the veterans, as well as many others, began to grieve openly. The catalysts for this grieving were the creation of the Vietnam Veterans Memorial in 1982 and late 1980s movies such as Oliver Stone's *Platoon*, which portrayed the terror of combat action and death in the Vietnam War.

As lucidly outlined by Kuenning (1990), the Vietnam War was different from other wars for a number of reasons:

1. *The average age of soldiers was nineteen, compared to twenty-six in World War II.*
2. *The largest segment of the troops in Vietnam came from working-class and poor backgrounds; African Americans served in Vietnam in numbers greater than their numbers in the general population.*
3. *Motivations for serving varied but often did not involve patriotism. It was unclear to many, both in the United States and Vietnam, why the war was being fought.*
4. *There were few, if any, front lines. Guerrilla warfare in miserable weather and under extraordinarily difficult conditions characterized much of the war.*
5. *A tour of duty was set at one year. This shorter length of time than in previous wars was designed to reduce the number of psychological casualties.*

6. *Troops usually did not go as a part of a unit that had spent quite a bit of time together and had formed close bonds. Soldiers went to war alone and came home alone.*

After returning home, soldiers were not given a period of decompression and debriefing. It was common for a soldier to be on duty in the Vietnam jungle early in the week and back in his hometown visiting with family and friends later in the same week. Such changes were mind-boggling and made the war and its psychic toll seem less than real to the young soldiers. These soldiers also encountered the American public's vehement opposition to the war—opposition that, in the later stages, included opposition to military personnel. Paulson (1991), describing his return home from the war, said:

> *I felt as if I had ruined my entire life, and I was only 22. I had nowhere to go, no one to explain what had happened to me, and no emotional support. I could only suffer and feel the pain, deep pain. It was not until ten years later, after much psychotherapy, that I could even begin to integrate my war experience positively into my life. (p. 158)*

Another veteran's experience, reported by Brende and Parson (1985), reveals the confusion and ambivalence that existed between families, loved ones, and the veterans about what they had done in Vietnam:

> *I got back about 6:00 in the morning. Everybody was asleep. They got up, welcomed me back. I got a few hugs and kisses. The whole scene lasted 15 minutes. . . . They went to bed. Next morning my sisters went to school as usual. . . . Everything seemed the same to them. . . . I felt nervous, tense, jittery. . . . So I walked down to the package store and bought me some liquor to help me out. . . . In spite of all of my efforts to avoid having anyone see me, a longtime friend saw me and really welcomed me home. It was really nice. Then, like out of nowhere, six guys showed up on the scene; I knew most of them. They wanted to know about the good dope in Vietnam. They also wanted to know what it was like having sex with Vietnamese women. One of them yelled out, "How many babies have you burned, man? Yea, you killers, man you heard me." Before I knew it the cops were there. I had beaten up four guys severely. . . . I had done a lot of killing in 'Nam; I just wanted to be left alone. (p. 50)*

A final set of factors that made Vietnam different and figured in the avoidance of recognizing the losses of the war were the atrocities that occurred. There were well-known instances of American troops slaughtering Vietnamese civilians (e.g., the My Lai massacre). Also, because civilians, in-

cluding children and the elderly, were often the enemy, suspected but innocent civilians sometimes were killed by American troops.

The U.S. military's practice of indexing its successes in terms of body
counts dehumanized the enemy and provided a crass basis for the promo-
tion of those officers who were involved in the greatest number of killings.
"Waste them" was almost an official policy term, which was applied to the
earth as well as the enemy, as Agent Orange and napalm were used extensively. Many veterans have expressed grief and guilt about their involvement in this policy. The American forces also used the term "waste them" in
reference to its own dead. Body bags were the order of the day after heavy
combat, and many a veteran still becomes terrified when remembering how
he put his friend's remains in a "baggie" or identified remains in body bags.
While soldiers may have found terms such as "baggie" and "waste them,"
which transformed the dead bodies of their comrades and enemy into piles
of waste, made it easier for them to deal with their losses, the losses were
real. Later, they could not so readily dismiss their losses and pass over their
grieving.

It is important to note that many veterans of this war never came home
in the sense of returning to the satisfying, secure lives they experienced
prior to going away. It has been estimated that as many as 30 percent of the
homeless in this country are Vietnam veterans (Kuenning, 1990). According
to Kuenning thousands of veterans have been imprisoned or are on parole;
tens of thousands have had or have serious drug or alcohol addiction problems; and thousands have committed suicide. Why? Compared to the veteran of World War II, the Vietnam veteran carries an immense burden of
guilt and feelings of unnecessary loss of friends, health, and time. Dealing
with this package has been beyond the resources of many veterans. In their
minds, homelessness, crime, and addiction have appeared to be the only re-
courses available to them. Many feel as if they were not welcome home.
Many others are still trying valiantly, sometimes unsuccessfully, to deal
with the residual horror of this war.

Many veterans encountered lukewarm receptions and rejection from
previous close others when they returned home. Brende and Parson (1985)
report the following fairly typical story told to them by a veteran:

> *After a short while, my girlfriend told me she didn't know how to relate to
> me; or how she really felt about me now. I had expected things to be the
> way they were; but they weren't. She said she thought I had been killed in
> the war, because I stopped writing to her. Honestly, I didn't know how to
> relate to her now either. I dreaded going to bed with her; I just didn't know
> how I'd do. She said that I wasn't the loving guy she used to know and
> love, that something horrible must have happened to me over there to
> change me so completely. . . . She said that the look in my eyes was the look*

of a deeply terrorized person. . . . She also mentioned that my frightened look . . . my aloofness, you name it . . . made her too uncomfortable to continue our relationship. She said that besides, she had found somebody else anyway. That really hurt me; it burned me up inside to hear this.

When it came to my family, my mother told me that I wasn't as considerate and sweet as I used to be. My dad felt I wasn't diligent and committed as he remembered me to be prior to Vietnam. I didn't know what any of these people were saying. I knew I was getting pissed off more and more by hearing all this bullshit, I know that. (p. 46)

Perhaps one of the greatest devastations for soldiers in Vietnam was being left by a lover back home. Tim O'Brien's book of stories about the Vietnam War, *The Things They Carried* (1990), contains several instances of this experience. In one story, O'Brien describes a young lieutenant, Jimmy Cross, who carries letters and photographs from his lover Martha. Upon receiving a "Dear John" letter from her, he burns the letters and photographs while crouching at the bottom of his foxhole. This narrative follows:

He realized it was only a gesture. . . . Besides the letters were in his head. And even now, without the photographs, Lieutenant Cross could see Martha playing volleyball in her white gym shorts. . . . He could see her moving in the rain. . . . In those letters Martha had never mentioned the war. . . . She wasn't involved. She signed the letters Love, but it wasn't love, and all the fine lines and technicalities did not matter. (p. 23)

O'Brien uses his stories to express his grief and as a method of healing. In one, he tells of his return twenty years later to Vietnam and how he experienced powerfully all that he lost there:

Below, in the earth, the relics of our presence were no doubt still there, the canteens and bandoliers and mess kits. This little field, I thought, had swallowed so much. My best friend. My pride. My belief in myself as a man of some small dignity and courage. . . . I blamed this place for what I had become, and blamed it for taking away the person I had once been. For twenty years this field had embodied all the waste that was Vietnam, all the vulgarity and horror. (p. 210)

The women who served in Vietnam—nurses and Red Cross workers—have only recently been given national attention. As the story of Edie in Chapter 3 illustrates, many of these women have experienced PTSD symptoms. They, too, were hurt, angry, and lonely and experienced little emotional support after their service in Vietnam. In 1993, a memorial in the form of a statue showing women assisting wounded soldiers was placed near the

Vietnam Wall in Washington, D.C. This recognition, along with the greater public acknowledgment of their role in taking care of the dead and dying, has contributed much to their recovery from this war.

Finally, although the losses from Vietnam continue to haunt this nation, Kuenning (1991) quotes Stewart Brown, a veteran center leader in California, who has this perspective on what that war may have given some of the combat veterans who returned:

> *I think Vietnam combat veterans are much more in touch with important issues of the human experience than the American population in general. This is because veterans experienced life and death in a magnified, graphic form. (p. 334)*

Stories from Normandy

> *No one was prepared for this scene from hell.*

> *German machine guns opened up on us when the ramp went down. Several men in front of me were killed. The water was bloody. It was bright red.*
>
> —Harold Baumgarten

Excerpts from stories reported to the author and his colleague Christina Davidson in June 1994 by veterans and family survivors of D day, 1944, the Allied invasion of France, help to sketch some of the feelings of horror and loss that were experienced by soldiers who were among the first to hit the beaches. Thousands of people from the United States (30,000 veterans alone), Great Britain, and all over the world assembled along the Normandy beaches in June 1994, to commemorate the fiftieth anniversary of D day.

Many of the veterans and family members were in their seventies and eighties. They were coming to Normandy for one final search for meaning in the most dramatic event of their lives. They were coming to grieve again and to try to attain completion of those events of five decades earlier. Many were coming to share their lifelong pain and sorrow, which usually had begun in their innocent youth and continued into their twilight years, with other people who had experienced a similar type of pain and sorrow.

It was reported on *Gettysburg*, a 1994 documentary, that in the early part of the twentieth century, thousands of veterans of the U.S. Civil War made a similar journey to Gettysburg, Pennsylvania, to commemorate the fiftieth anniversary of that deadly engagement between the Union and Confederate armies. As if to attest to the significance of this reunion and the psychological fulfillment and meaning it represented, many of these men died on their return home after the Gettysburg reunion.

The stories that we collected from Normandy veterans and family members of soldiers killed there contain a range of emotions. Almost all of them point to the necessity of the sacrifice of life to defeat Hitler. Many of them speak with great sadness and sometimes anger at the loss of thousands of young men during the early hours of the assault. Confusion and faulty planning led to many deaths. For example, many troops and tanks were put out of the landing crafts too far out at sea to make it to shore. Prior bombing of German installations, particularly above Omaha Beach, did not completely disengage machine gun placements, which took huge tolls on the early waves of landing troops. Warren Rulien, then a twenty-four-year-old private with the 116th Regiment of the 1st Division, said:

> *I was almost enthusiastic about hitting the beach. But as we got nearer to the shore, German bullets began hitting the sides of the landing craft. The ramp was lowered, and I stepped off into water up to my chest. I lost my balance and dropped my rifle. We'd been told the Navy Seabees were going ahead of us to get rid of the mines in the water. But the mines were still there, sticking six feet out of the water on steel rails, and there were Navy men floating dead in the water. I took one of the bodies that was floating— and pushed it in front of me toward the shore. I figured I couldn't do anything to help the poor guy and his body would stop bullets. Landing craft were continuing to bring in waves of soldiers and they were bunching up on shore, taking shelter behind a three-foot-high seawall. They were being slaughtered. (Harvey and Davidson, 1994)*

All told, the stories from World War II veterans reveal more acceptance and healing and less continuing turbulence than do the stories of many Vietnam combat veterans. Of course, World War II veterans are approximately twenty to thirty years older than Vietnam War veterans. However, compared to Vietnam veterans, World War II veterans had a strong sense of what they were fighting for (i.e., freedom and their way of life) and were given a very positive reception by the American public when they returned home.

This is not to say that World War II veterans escaped postwar adjustment problems and even PTSD-type effects. One Normandy veteran said, "I drank every day for 25 years. If I wanted to sleep, I'd go down to the bar and get drunk." Also, many could not hold jobs, and marriages suffered— although in that generation few divorced. One World War II veteran's son described his father as a brooding, guilt-ridden alcoholic who often woke up screaming and shut himself off emotionally from his children. This son said of his father: "He could never love again. He saw too much. His heart was dead."

Unlike many Vietnam veterans, World War II veterans frequently spent their time in combat with soldiers from their home city, state, or region. In fact, one of the hardest hit towns in the United States in 1944 was Bedford, Virginia, a city of about 4,000 people. Over 90 percent of thirty-five soldiers from Bedford were killed in the initial D-day landing. This large number of deaths from a relatively small town has been associated with an uncommon degree of mourning in Bedford—mourning that has reverberated over fifty years in the lives of the town's residents (Stone, 1994). One of the only survivors from the Bedford company of soldiers was Robert Sales. In the June 6, 1994, issue of *The Stars and Stripes*, he commented on the loss of so many of his friends from his home state:

> *You couldn't walk without stepping on a body. . . . It was so shocking to see the hundreds of men washing in the surf—men I grew up with, double-dated with, puffed off the same cigarette, drank out of the same bottle with—lying there dead. Stark faces with eyes and mouths wide open. (p. 8)*

Many of the men who had been among the first troops to go ashore indicated that they recalled certain events of that day quite vividly. William Isenberg provided a typical commentary about the early landing experience:

> *There was direct fire coming down at us. We suffered heavy casualties. There were a helluva lot of flashes, a lot of noise, a lot of people on the beach yelling. We were all scared and trying not to show it.*
> *I've tried to wash it all out of my mind. I saw a lot of people murdered that day. But I didn't come back to remember that. I came back to visit my brother's grave [his brother was killed in the invasion]. . . . There were a lot of guys who were heroes at D-day. (Harvey and Davidson, 1994)*

Jim Wilson was nineteen on D day and still vividly recalls what happened when he hit the beach:

> *We were all scared in the boat. For some reason I wanted to die on land. I thought to myself, "I'm a young man. What am I here for? I'll be wasting my life if I lose it." What we encountered when we reached the beach was ghastly. The shore was awash with corpses. Wreckage of war was everywhere. The place was blown to hell. . . . Many of the things you remember were bad. But there were some good things too. For example, we went to Paris. We had some good times in Paris. (Harvey and Davidson, 1994)*

The plethora of bodies and sounds of pain and dying were common themes in the stories of those veterans who were among the first units to

land on the beach. Hal Parfitt, then a twenty-two-year-old West Point–
trained officer, said:

> My strongest impression was seeing the bodies on the beach, and the havoc
> that was created by the defensive fire. It was shocking, appalling, to see all
> the bodies lying on the beach. Really, there wasn't time to do much for the
> wounded except get them to high ground. . . . My object was the same as
> everyone's—to survive. (Harvey and Davidson, 1994)

Another man, Jessie Gorman, who was a young infantryman when he
came ashore, recalled:

> It was terrible to think, but I thought that the dead and the injured were
> the lucky ones. Though physically unscathed, the soldier who must go past
> his dead and injured comrades is terrified. (Harvey and Davidson, 1994)

Gorman's experience that day had a major impact on his life. In his fifties,
he went back to school to earn a master's degree in psychology, specializing
in PTSD.

D day also had a lifelong impact on actor Charles Durning, now sixty-
seven, who was a seventeen-year-old infantryman in 1944. Some of his experiences remain too painful to him to discuss. He told *Chicago Tribune*
writer Kenneth Clark:

> There are certain things in your life you don't want to share. There are
> things I've never told my family to this day. . . . I thought Omaha Beach
> was the name of a town in France. . . . People say, "What was it like?" I
> don't know. I didn't even know where the shells were coming from. I just
> had this beach—with sand—and the guy next to me.
>
> Then we got inland, and after people would say, "What cities were you
> in?" And I'd say, "I don't know; I saw a building in front of me and I was
> trying to get through it." It was the same way with the enemy. (Clark,
> 1994, p. 3)

Durning experienced PTSD-type symptoms (then called "combat fatigue")
on his return to the United States. He said:

> I've had friends who committed suicide over it. I freaked out and went into
> the hospital. For years after I came out of the service, I couldn't walk through
> an open field because of [imagined] land mines. I can remember walking
> across a street in New York shortly after the war ended and a backfire went
> off. I went into a crouch at high port (rifle at the ready). I got to the other side
> of the street and a cop said to me, "You never get over it, do you?" (p. 3)

Durning cites two great blessings that have come into his life since that war:

> *The first is the gift of forgetfulness; you forget the pain, you forget the anger. The second is a sense of humor. Without that, you're lost. (p. 3)*

Still others who lost relatives or loved ones at Normandy spoke of missing them every day. A son who lost his father at Normandy spoke to an interviewer about his mother's death at age sixty-two: "My mother was very sensitive. She declined in health after [my father's] death, and I'm sure it was the grief" (Harvey and Davidson, 1994).

Fifty years later images of the horrors of war still haunt some Normandy survivors. One veteran who had been a prisoner of war told of a recent dream:

> *[I dreamed that I was back in Normandy] dodging bullets. . . . There was a guy in a foxhole a few feet away. I'm crawling, crawling, trying to get to him, and . . . I never get to him. (Harvey and Davidson, 1994)*

A former paratrooper who had come down in the small French village Ste.-Mère-Eglise spoke of the terror of hanging in the night air while being shot at by the Germans. He said that when he landed he saw three of his buddies with their parachutes ensnared, one on a tree and two on poles. Each had been killed while dangling in the air. He said the image reminded him of Christ on the cross. At the church in the center of this city, a model of paratrooper John Steele now hangs from one of the church steeples. When his parachute was caught there, he played dead and was later rescued by the American troops. With this vivid image, Ste.-Mère-Eglise now stands as a mecca of memory and healing for American and British paratroopers, a place that symbolizes great loss but also great courage.

> *He stands in the unbroken line of patriots who have dared to die that freedom might live and grow and increase its blessings. Freedom lives, and through it, he lives—in a way that humbles the undertakings of most men.*
> —A Scroll Presented by President Franklin Roosevelt to Mr. and Mrs. Joseph Shimon, Whose Son, Joseph, Jr., Was Killed in World War II

Holocaust Testimonies

> *The Holocaust defies literature. . . . We think we are describing an event, we transmit only its reflection. No one has the right to speak for the dead . . . . Still the story had to be told. In spite of all risks, all possible misunderstandings. It needed to be told for the sake of our children.*
> —Elie Wiesel

> *[T]he response to* Schindler's List *is proof that the most offensive word in any language is* forget.
>
> —Richard Corliss

"Holocaust memory is an insomniac faculty whose mental eyes have never slept" (p. 10). This is a quote from Lawrence Langer's *Holocaust Testimonies: The Ruins of Memory* (1991). The purpose of Langer's book is consistent with Wiesel's argument that the Holocaust story must be told. Langer explores how survivors of the Nazi death camps remember the horror of their experience. He argues:

> *A main effect of these testimonies (and, I hope, of this book) is to begin to undo a negation—the principle of discontinuity which argues that an impassable chasm permanently separates the seriously interested auditor and observer from the experiences of the former Holocaust victim. (p. xiv)*
>
> *Would silence be better? Perhaps for us, because it would spare us much pain; but because memory functions with or without speech, it is difficult to see how* not *telling her story could ease [the survivor's] distress. Memory cannot be silenced; it might as well be heard. . . . (p. 50)*

Langer's work is based on hundreds of videotaped interviews from the Holocaust Archive at Yale University. He refers to the type of memory under study as "deep memory," memory that tries to recall the self as he or she once existed, as opposed to "common memory," which attempts to link the self with the present. The stories Langer extracts show confusion, doubt, and moral uncertainty. There is survivor guilt: "Why did I survive when so many died?" As Charlotte Delbo's testimony about her nightmares of Auschwitz illustrates, there is immense bleakness:

> *The skin covering the memory of Auschwitz is tough. . . . Sometimes, however, it bursts, and gives back its contents. In a dream, the will is powerless. And in these dreams, there I see myself again, me, yes me, just as I know I was: scarcely able to stand . . . pierced with cold, filthy, gaunt, and the pain is so unbearable, so exactly the pain I suffered there, that I feel it again physically, I feel it again through my whole body, which becomes a block of pain, and I feel death seizing me, I feel myself die. Fortunately, in my anguish, I cry out. The cry awakens me, and I emerge from the nightmare, exhausted. It takes days for everything to return to normal, for memory to be "refilled" and for the skin of memory to mend itself. I become myself again, the one you know, who can speak to you of Auschwitz without showing any sign of distress or emotion. (pp. 6–7)*

As the 1994 movie *Schindler's List* vividly illustrated, fate and caprice were everywhere and often determined who went to the gas chambers. Langer reports Lena Berg's testimony about the terror of the selection procedure:

Every roll call was a selection: women were sent to the gas chamber because they had swollen legs, scratches on their bodies, because they wore eyeglasses or head kerchiefs, or because they stood roll call without head kerchiefs. Young SS men prowled among the inmates and took down their numbers and during the evening roll call the women were ordered to step forward, and we never saw them again. Maria Keiler, a childhood friend and schoolmate, died that way. She had a scratch on her leg and an SS man took her number. When they singled her out at roll call, she simply walked away without even nodding goodbye. She knew quite well where she was going, and I knew it, too; I was surprised at how little upset I was. (p. 164).

Liberation from the death camps brought little immediate psychological reprieve for some of the survivors. In his posthumous volume *The Drowned and the Saved* (1988), Primo Levi explored the darker side of this dilemma:

In the majority of cases, the hour of liberation was neither joyful nor lighthearted. For most it occurred against a tragic background of destruction, slaughter, and suffering. Just as they felt they were again becoming men, that is, responsible, the sorrows of men returned: the sorrow of the dispersed or lost family; the universal suffering all around; their own exhaustion, which seemed definitive, past cure; the problems of a life to begin all over again amid the rubble, often alone. Not "pleasure the son of misery," but "misery the son of misery." Leaving pain behind was delight for only a few fortunate beings, or only for a few instants, or for very simple souls; almost always it coincided with a phase of anguish. (pp. 70–71)

Philip K.'s testimony, reported in Langer (1991), provides a view of this experience that embodies the ambivalence that so many survivors have expressed:

I often say to people who pretend or seem to be marveling at the fact that I seem to be so normal, so unperturbed and so capable of functioning—they seem to think the Holocaust passed over and it's done with: It's my skin. This is my coat. You can't take it off. And it's there, and it will be there until I die. . . .

If we're not an eternal people before, we are an eternal people after the Holocaust, in both its very positive and very negative sense. We have not only survived, but we have revived ourselves. In a very real way, we have won. We were victorious. But in a very real way, we have lost. We'll never recover what was lost. We can't even assess what was lost. Who knows what beauty and grandeur six million [Jews who were murdered in the Holocaust] could have contributed to the world? Who can measure it up? What standard do you use? How do you count it? . . .

> *We lost. The world lost, whether they know it or admit it. It doesn't make any difference. And yet we won, we're going on. . . .*
> *I think there are as many ways of surviving survival as there have been to survive. (p. 205)*

DOMESTIC VIOLENCE: A CLIMATE OF FEAR

In September 1994, 38,000 pairs of shoes were placed along the Capitol's reflecting pool to symbolize more than 38,000 gun deaths in the United States in 1993. Shoes were chosen because they are smaller than coffins, according to one organizer, and more reminiscent of life. They are familiar, and they quietly caution that we all could walk in these shoes.

Now, near the beginning of the twenty-first century, Americans live in an atmosphere of increasing violence, particularly in cities and homes. Fear of crime and violence in many large U.S. cities has led to increases in police officers walking beats, the establishment of police substation operations in neighborhoods, increased use of private security forces, a growth in security alarm companies, increases in the purchases of firearms by ordinary citizens, and curfews for teenagers. In the early summer of 1994, 195 people in New Orleans had been killed since the beginning of the year. The city coroner's office had been overwhelmed, resulting in a pileup of dead bodies waiting for autopsies.

This atmosphere of violence affects our experience of loss and grief in many ways. It has been estimated by the U.S. Census Bureau that violence leads to nearly 2 million deaths every year in the United States. As many as 100 million Americans have been touched by violent crime—a vast army of victims who suffer long after official justice has been done, if it is done. We underestimate how long it takes people to recover from losses incurred in violent crime. As a national mental health problem, violent crime survivors' mental health is at the top of the list in the 1990s. Depression and anxiety about many aspects of daily life permeate the minds and emotions of these millions who have lost their loved ones to violence.

The American public may become inured to this vast sea of suffering and the factors that lead to it. However, a lifetime of pain and mourning awaits families and friends who are the direct survivors of victims of violence. Their pain is often increased because the deaths were so unnecessary and occurred at a point at which the victim had so much to look forward to.

There are numerous indices of our fear of violence. Steve Marshall (1994) reported in *USA Today* that people's shopping habits have been influenced by fear of crime and violence. People carry less money and use credit cards more. Fewer shop after dark, and more shop closer to home. They shop less at convenience stores and more in shopping malls. According to a Gallup poll, the number of Americans who worry about being murdered in the 1990s is almost double the number who worried in 1981. The mental costs of their fears are enormous. Many of these deaths haunt every day of a survivor's life. In an interview for the January 30, 1994, edition of the *Chicago Tribune*, one mother, age thirty-six, whose four children were killed in a fire set by her ex-boyfriend five years earlier said:

> *I'm trying to build a life, but there's still an empty feeling. I'm not complete because I don't have my kids and even if I get married and have more kids, the feeling will still be there that a huge part of me is missing. (Pop, 1994, sect. 6, p. 3)*

Another mother, whose twenty-three-year-old daughter was stabbed to death in 1986, said, "We will never be really happy again" (*USA Today*, 1993, p. 8A). How could she? Her daughter's death was unnecessary, a roll of the dice that has become part of living in many cities of America. Yet another mother, whose thirty-two-year-old daughter's throat was slashed in 1988, said, "I've aged 10 years. I have gray hair, my cholesterol is up and I have abdominal pains I never had before" (*USA Today*, 1993, p. 8A).

In an editorial for *Newsweek*, Adler (1994) noted that children in the United States experience directly or indirectly so much violence that they are growing up increasingly afraid. They see on television thousands of instances of violence. They may experience real violence at school and in the home, and many may experience child abuse. The whole nation grieved when twelve-year-old Polly Klaas was kidnapped from her own bedroom at night while playing with other children and later was found murdered. The man who took her had a habitual criminal record and only recently had been released from serving half of a sixteen-year sentence for kidnapping.

In 1993, the world shuddered to see videotaped evidence of two young English boys abducting a two-year-old whom they later murdered. There are so many manifestations of violence by young people and directed toward them that vast literatures of research and writing are now devoted to the topic. Children throughout this country know about these events, which produce fear as well as a sometimes blasé attitude about the frequency of violence. We can only wonder how this generation of young people will grieve these losses and be affected by them as they become adults and have children of their own.

One of the worst types of losses to violence occurs when the perpetrator is never found. Grieving cannot be completed when a killer is not found—or when a family never learns exactly what happened when their loved one died. In 1993, Tammy Jo Zywicki had car trouble while driving on the interstate from Chicago to Grinnell College in Iowa. Apparently, she was picked up by a truck driver. Days later her body was discovered 500 miles away in a ditch. Police officials, family, and her student colleagues engaged in an enormous search for her killer that so far has turned up only false leads. Such wanton killings are an increasing blight on the landscape of the 1990s in the United States. The injustice of so many of these killings is matched by the fact that only a modest percentage of the killers are captured by the authorities. The Zywicki story is one of immense sadness that has been well publicized because of the efforts of Tammy's family and friends and the particularly cruel nature of her death. Today, each of them tries to move on with life, but each still must grieve intensely and continue to search for any leads of who killed Tammy.

In an interview with Ron Arias for the August 23, 1993, edition of *People Weekly*, Tammy's father, Hank, struggled to find logic to explain the events surrounding her death:

> *Maybe if she had been more of a free spirit . . . she would have taken the first ride and got through the whole thing without a problem. That's what's so frustrating. There are prostitutes and other kinds of women in crazy situations, and they're still alive. Then there's a kid like Tammy, someone you protected, nurtured and guided. She worked hard, went to school on a scholarship, did all the right things. And someone takes her life. It's unfair, totally wrong. People talk about God and how He's controlling things. Well, why did He let this happen? (Arias, 1993, p. 39)*

In later chapters I tell the stories of several persons who have been motivated by the violent deaths of their loved ones to try to do something to stifle the flood of violence in this country. One such person is Victoria Crompton (1994). She tirelessly tells the story of her daughter Jenny's death at age fifteen at the hands of Jenny's nineteen-year-old boyfriend, Mark, to audiences around the country. I first became aware of Victoria's story when she took a graduate class with me.

The story of Jenny's death is often repeated in the romances of teenagers and those in their early twenties. It is the story of a tragic and undeserved early ending to a very promising life in 1986. It is the story of a first romance—in this case Jenny and Mark's. It is the story of Mark's attempts to control Jenny's life—from what she did and how she spent her time to her network of friends. It is the story of Mark's physical and verbal abuse of Jenny, both in private and in public. Ultimately, it is the story of Jenny's attempts to break the relationship and Mark's dogged refusal to do so. His refusal included such actions as obsessively following Jenny, surreptitiously watching her, breaking into her school locker, and finally breaking into her house and lying in wait to kill her. His dazed reasoning must have been that if he couldn't have her, no one would. He now serves a life sentence for murder in an Iowa prison. Victoria, Jenny's mother, continues her grief, as do Jenny's relatives and her best friend—a young woman who recently married. Their lives changed dramatically that day in 1986.

Compton's grief and resolve to give greater meaning to Jenny's life and death have led her to years of presentations about teen dating violence. She said in a paper presented in my class:

My life, since 1986, has been taken over by the topic of teen dating violence. I give approximately 500 speeches per year to high schools, church groups, and parent groups. After every speech I am approached by teens who tell me they, too, are being abused. I tell them what signs to look for, how to get out safely, and whom to contact for help. I can sense when a school has a problem, and I can usually identify the victims in the audience. (p. 7)

In another story of death that galvanized a survivor's resources to try to address a dreadful societal problem, Clementine Barfield began an organization called Save Our Sons and Daughters in Detroit in the late 1980s. She created this organization to mobilize neighborhood parents' efforts to combat the violence against young people that is a part of almost every sizable U.S. city in the 1990s. The support group meetings offered by this organization permit grieving mothers and fathers to tell their stories and offer support to one another. Ms. Barfield's sixteen-year-old son Derick was killed in 1986 by another teen who fired a gun into an automobile in which Derick and his brother were driving. They were shot because the killer believed that the brothers had wronged him and his friends in an earlier incident in the neighborhood. In 1986, 365 youngsters were shot, 43 fatally, in Detroit alone. Clementine Barfield said about her work to end youth violence:

This isn't just about me and mine. . . . I'm able to think of every child out there as though he were my very own. And I think that's what everybody is going to have to do to really change the way things are. You've got to look at all of the children and think of them as your very own. (Kaplan, 1993, sect. 6, p. 1)

FINDING PEACE FROM THE RAVAGES OF WAR AND VIOLENCE

My contribution might have been small, but I walked in the company of very brave men.

—Veteran of Omaha Beach

I'm all wept out. I can't weep any more.
—Veteran of Omaha Beach Who Later Wept
at the Vast Cemetery Overlooking the Beach

As we talked with Normandy veterans and family members of those who died on D day, it became obvious that this media-hyped, worldwide fifty-year anniversary was something that they valued greatly. So many spoke of the courage of their buddies who did not return. One veteran, Rene Dussaq, commented about the courage it took to continue moving up the beaches and cliffs straight into the teeth of enemy fire:

> *We were afraid but were able to overcome our fear because we knew we were doing something for a noble cause. . . . Thinking of another human being more than you think of yourself—that is courage—the capacity to give one's life for another. (Harvey and Davidson, 1994).*

The events that marked the anniversary have given younger generations a much better perspective of D-day's dreadful morning. The commemorations seemed to give new life, meaning, and hope to thousands of veterans, kin, and close friends who have grieved their losses—sometimes in obscurity—for half a century. These events, which included eighty-five-year-old former paratroopers again jumping out of airplanes to salute their fallen comrades, were cathartic, rejuvenating, and redeeming for many veterans and close survivors, and they served as a living statement that might have read:

> *We remember you gave your life for us. It is time to honor those who gave their lives and those who returned but who also gave much including a prime part of their youth for their country. We are grateful.*

Indeed, Normandy veterans and family survivors have their memorial now even more firmly in place than before. It is their image of those beaches, cliffs, bodies, and confusion. It is their image of our collective remembering. For those who returned for the anniversary and for those who remember, this was a rite of passage, a completion of their moment in destiny, not unlike the return of the Gettysburg veterans to that fabled battleground early in the twentieth century.

Vietnam veterans also are slowly finding more peace. Don Ross, *USA Today*'s copy desk chief, went back to Vietnam in 1994. He had served there as a young Marine in 1969. He said, "Nothing prepared me for the feelings I experienced on my return—the sights and sounds whipped my emotions from anger to compassion to pride in having served" (Ross, 1994, p. 1A). He told of his trip to find the so-called Valley of Death, the Khe Sanh combat base in central Vietnam, which had been embroiled in a savage seventy-seven-day siege during which 20,000 Marines were surrounded by as many as 40,000 North Vietnamese soldiers:

Today about the only reminder of what occurred is the landscape. Although foliage has covered some scars, the terrain is riddled with craters and holes. Many are from bombs and artillery shells. . . . As I stood on the former airstrip . . . a young man diligently working a metal-detector passed. Twenty-six years later the ground still yields an occasional artifact of war.

My life has taken many different turns in those years. . . . But I wondered—not with regret—how different my life might have been, how different it would be now, had not events here in some measure, at least, inspired me to enlist.

Deep thoughts for a dreary day. I gave a hand salute to those Marines who had fought here and who had died here. You are not forgotten, my brothers. (p. 2A)

Ross also told of a train trip in a dimly lighted berth with two North Vietnamese men, one of whom had served in the North Vietnamese army. He described how the ex-soldier took four cans of 333 brand beer from his suitcase and shared them with Ross and a younger Vietnamese man. Ross said:

This man, whom I once would've tried to kill on a field of battle, raised his beer in a toast: "To friends."

As the train pulled into Danang, Mr. Thong [the former soldier] pointedly asked me why I had made this trip by train. His implication was clear: I could have afforded the quicker and more comfortable plane.

"So I could meet people like you, my friend," I said. I meant it. "I'm glad I took the train." (p. 4A)

Unfortunately, many Vietnam veterans have not and will not find the peace that Don Ross seems to be finding. One who tried valiantly but who couldn't make it was Lewis Puller, Jr. Puller was the only son of legendary Marine General Lewis "Chesty" Puller. Puller, Jr. was a Marine lieutenant in Vietnam who lost his legs and parts of both hands after stepping on a booby trap howitzer round in 1968. He inspired fellow vets with his 1991 Pulitzer Prize–winning autobiography *Fortunate Son*, a chronicle of his recovery from depression and alcoholism stemming from his experience in Vietnam. But his depression recurred, as the physical and psychological pain of his losses kept coming back. Senator Bob Kerrey of Nebraska, who lost his right leg in Vietnam and who was close to Puller, said that in the end, Puller could not fight his way out of the deep, dark hole of personal terror (which also included a recent estrangement from his wife of twenty-six years). In May 1994, Puller shot and killed himself while at home alone. In commenting on his death, *People Weekly*, said in its May 30, 1994, issue:

Puller's sad end seemed to support the belief of many veterans' groups—though no hard statistics are available to back up the claim—that Vietnam vets are committing suicide in alarming numbers. "There are 58,000 names on the Wall in Washington," says Jan Scruggs, a founder of the Vietnam Veteran Memorial. "Probably more than twice as many veterans have committed suicide as were killed in the war." (p. 68)

The survivors of victims of domestic violence have their own unending struggle with grief. That is particularly true for those who do not know who killed their loved one or why. Tammy Zywicki's family struggles with that reality almost two years after her death. They are trying diligently to deal with their feelings. In the Arias' interview for *People Weekly*, her mother JoAnn said:

We don't shy away from talking about her. . . . We're also not big religious people. We just work things out. Hank [Tammy's father] and I have our times, but we don't give up. I've had some pretty bad nights, or sometimes I'll forget to make dinner. Hank will hold things in. And the boys [Tammy's three brothers], they seem to be handling it. (Arias, 1993)

For these survivors, who number in the millions, there is no Memorial Day or great commemorative reunion. There is individual pain and grief that can neither be eliminated nor easily avoided. It will help if these survivors can find ways to remember their loved ones and give their deaths more meaning—similar to Victoria Crompton's mighty battle against teen dating violence. But nothing can totally eliminate their sense of loss and grief.

War Dead

With grey arm twisted over a green face
The dust of passing trucks swirls over him,
Lying by the roadside in his proper place,
For he has crossed the ultimate far rim
That hides us from the valley of the dead.
He lies like used equipment thrown aside,
Of which our swift advance can take no heed,
Roses, triumphal cars—but this one died.
Once war memorials, pitiful attempt
In some vague way regretfully to atone
For those lost futures that the dead had dreamt,
Covered the land with their lamenting stone—
But in our hearts we bear a heavier load:
The bodies of the dead beside the road.

—Gavin Ewart

7

FREQUENT LIFESPAN LOSSES

Hearts live by being wounded.
—Oscar Wilde

All things must change
to something new, to something strange.
—Henry Wadsworth Longfellow

This chapter discusses the many kinds of losses that occur over the course of a normal lifespan. These losses wound us in ways similar to the loss of close relationships. Some of them are subtler than others. Aging, for example, sometimes creeps up on us, but its potency is undeniable. Serious illnesses such as cancer also can appear slyly but then become mighty in the losses they exact. When we lose our jobs or have to be relocated and lose regular contact with our friends, the feelings of loss may be great. These are the kinds of lifespan losses that I address in this chapter, which provides a set of snapshots of the most prominent of these types of losses. I call them "frequent lifespan losses" because they are so common for most of us who live long enough.

Selectivity is essential in discussing this topic. As Judith Viorst's book *Necessary Losses* (1986) persuasively contends, there are many kinds of losses that simply come with the normal passages of living. Everything from the loss of one's pets to the loss of one's virginity may be construed as falling within this large and diverse universe. The key, though, is the *psychological sense of loss* experienced by the individual. In many instances, these kinds of losses are just as daunting to the spirit as the loss of a close relationship through death or dissolution.

Each lifespan loss probably has its own constellation of dynamics, some of which are more straightforward than others. The loss associated with relocation, for example, is getting more attention as people live longer. There is increasing recognition that millions of us will end our lives living in nursing homes or convalescent centers. Giving up longtime homes can represent a huge loss, especially for people who value what they have created in their home and its ambience. Relocations that occur earlier in people's lives also represent loss.

People often move from city to city for professional reasons. Some do so because national and international companies require this type of movement. Military personnel do not usually expect to be at any one installation very long. The losses of support and friendship networks that result from these moves, not to mention the sheer fatigue of packing and unpacking, can be defeating and cumulative, leading to loneliness and alienation after many moves. Whenever we leave a home, city, or region in which we have experienced important events, we lose something that we value. We may gain a new home and "place of the heart," but nostalgia and feelings of regret are common in our thinking about past homes and places. So often the past is meaningful because it is associated with people and relationship- or work-related events that help define who we have been and are in our lives.

One of the principal features of lifespan losses is that they are normal. They may not seem that way. They may, in fact, seem quite particular in their inflictions and debilitations. Yet, by definition, they are experienced by many people at various points in their lives. All of us, for example, will experience aging. That is just the way it is, a lifespan progression that can traumatize, humble, and/or be faced with courage and grace but that takes a toll both of body and mind. Another feature is that many such losses are subtle: We may not recognize them as losses because their effects creep up on us.

Aging often is one of the subtlest and yet most devastating forms of losses each of us experiences, be it our own aging or aging of those we love. It can be terribly demoralizing to begin to turn gray or to learn that you cannot do physical tasks on which you previously had excelled. The actor and director Robert Redford said as much in an interview for the *Chicago Tribune* on May 15, 1994, when commenting on what it felt like to be fifty-six:

> *It's not much longer I'm going to be able to do things I've loved so much—skiing, horseback riding, all the physical things. I've just enjoyed having my body be able to pretty much do anything I wanted it to. But that time is being diminished. . . .*
>
> *[T]he best part about being fifty-six is] . . . the wisdom, the perspective you gain that allows you to be more compassionate, more forgiving about some of your hostilities and anger.* (Chicago Tribune, 1994, p. 4)

In the section on aging, I describe one woman's successful quest to end her life at almost the exact point that she desired—with her mind still facile and the wisdom and perspective Redford spoke of intact. Unfortunately, many of us go out with little left of our mental facilities. An even more devastating experience than watching our own bodies slowly give way to time is observing our parents begin to forget to whom they are talking or failing to recognize us. Such is the nature of becoming quite old and of common aging diseases such as Alzheimer's. While such processes are frequently a part of our experience if we live long enough, their impacts nonetheless accumulate and reverberate.

AGING AND THE LOSS OF HEALTH, HOPE, AND MEANING

The worst fear of people who are at risk for Huntington's disease is that they will eventually get the disease and life will become meaningless for them. . . . [The meaning of life] varies from day to day, even from hour to hour. The meaning of life constantly changes but never ceases to exist.
—Dennis H. Phillips

It isn't painful in the way cancer is, but even as you are watching yourself, your brain cells begin to die, you lose control of yourself, you lose control over your actions, and you become somebody else. . . . And I watched this over a period of six or eight years with my mother. And it got to the point where she would get up at 2 A.M. and put on two dresses and go down for breakfast. And then somebody would take her back to bed. And she'd be up an hour later and she'd do the same thing. . . . She knew what was happening to her and was humiliated because she knew she was a different person and she was ashamed.
—Senator Jay Rockefeller

The aging process certainly does not have to involve the loss of health, hope, and meaning. It often does, however, when an individual is contending also with a quickly deteriorating body, degenerative diseases such as Alzheimer's and Huntington's, relocation to a convalescent center, or the loss of a support network of friends and close others. People in these situations quickly become marginalized in our society.

As suggested in Chapter 8, part of the loss associated with aging involves the stereotyping of the aged. Both younger and older people often minimalize the value of the elderly: "Old people usually are childish and set in their ways." "Old people are disabled and have to be in nursing homes." "Old people are often depressed and noncommunicative. They do not think straight." Such comments may even have a self-fulfilling effect on the elderly. The loss that results from such sequences is grave for society. Not every person beyond, say, the age of eighty, exhibits the behavior associated with such stereotypes. Further, to manipulate people in that direction through casual commentary and other ill-conceived behavior means that we begin to lose them as functioning citizens. Finally, it is an enormous loss to the younger person to let him or her judge others in such simplistic ways. It results in a rigidity of thinking that in itself is a mental loss. It reflects an inability or unwillingness to look closely at the great diversity exhibited by older people, what they really are like, and what they really can do. It reflects a failure to let the evidence determine the type of person. The real senility here is in the judgment, not in the target!

In an August 21, 1994, article in *Parade Magazine*, Hugh Downs addressed the theories of Leonard Hayflick, a cell biologist and founding member of the Council of the National Institute on Aging. Hayflick contends that having a long life is no more important than having a life that toward its end does not involve considerable suffering and anguish. He says that we may imagine the perfect life to be long, full, and happy, ending when we die quickly without the loss of our faculties, but that such an image is a recent development. Life in the Middle Ages was a terrible ordeal, except for the rich and powerful. Most people then probably would not have wished to live twenty or thirty years longer, as they may now.

Unfortunately many senior citizens today spend their final years leading institutionalized lives that they find to be devoid of much meaning, ultimately leading to great anguish or depression. Consider these comments from persons contributing to Gubrium's provocative book *Speaking of Life* (1993) in which he interviewed people living in nursing homes:

> I have wanted to die ever since I went in that home. . . . I have thought of taking my life. I don't want to be in the shape I see these people [other residents of the home]. I just wish I could die today.—Roland Synder, age seventy-eight, three months before he died (p. 31)

> I lived with my daughter for a while when she decided, well . . . she met this gentleman she was going to marry. She decided I guess there wasn't room for mother. So from then on I got thrown out, lived here and there. . . . I tell you, life looks pretty empty. I feel really unwanted. I am trying to overcome that now. For some reason, the good Lord leaves me here. I have almost died from my breath. . . . Mainly, life's dull, just dull. I just sit there and think and wonder how it all come to this.—Mary Stern, age eighty, a heavy smoker and suffering from emphysema (pp. 61–67)

> Well, life looks to me like a big blob! . . . I've often wondered why the Lord lets me live on, because what good am I to anybody? I'm a burden, you see. . . . I'm a bump on a log. I'm absolutely useless. . . . Just sitting here and I have to be cared for. I'm not able to contribute to anything. I hope I don't live the

rest of the year out because there's no point in it. There would just be more worry and more trouble on my son and his wife. . . . Life don't mean anything now. There's nothing to look forward to. All you've got is your memories to look back on.—Myrtle Johnson, age ninety-four, suffering from Parkinson's disease (pp. 55–57)

The reader conversant with institutionalized older adults will find many of these comments to be right on the mark. How do we as a society reconstruct these institutions to help them to be more empowering? This question is daunting, particularly as we move the average lifespan ever closer to the hundred-year mark through new medical technology. What good will it do if we live our last fifteen years in a vegetative condition?

Both the individuals faced with this final stage of life and their children and caretakers experience despair. On May 6, 1994, Kim Painter of *USA Today* described how Ginger McCray, living near Chicago, took care of her mother, Dorothy Allen, who was suffering from Alzheimer's disease, until her death at age sixty-three in 1993. Alzheimer's disease is a degenerative brain disorder that causes memory loss and sometimes an inability to control emotions. Dorothy Allen's struggle with Alzheimer's disease lasted over five years, but Ginger viewed her opportunity to help her mother as a labor of love:

I had never prepared myself to take care of a parent. But I did it. And I was glad to do it. . . . There were a lot of times when my mother made it hard for me. She would reject me and she wouldn't let me hug or kiss her or anything like that. But I knew that wasn't my mom, that was the sickness. . . . I knew it was only because she didn't know who I was and she was protecting herself against a stranger. I would say, "It's me, Mom, I love you. It's me Ginger."

Sometimes when we were just sitting together, she would reach out and just start touching me. She would start feeling my face or just touch my hand or just start putting her hands in my hair. And I knew that she knew me, even if she didn't know what day it was. Those were the times when I was glad.

I still have my mother's spirit with me every day. Every day, my mother is with me. (Painter, 1994, p. 6A)

Many other conditions associated with the aging process are daunting to the spirit and reduce people's ability to find meaning in their lives. Some are individual, while others are societal. Many older people have very modest means and can be wiped out financially and emotionally when major health care problems develop. In 1994, the U.S. Congress tried to develop legislation to help more of the 30 million or so citizens, many in their midlife and beyond, who do not have health insurance. Whether much will be accomplished in 1995 is still quite uncertain.

Perhaps the most dispiriting aspect of life for many elderly is the disproportionate emphases in all areas of society on younger people and their activities and interests. We see clearly such an emphasis in the media, especially in advertising, and in TV and movie actors and news anchors. As a society, we could benefit greatly from more movies like *On Golden Pond* that showed the bridges that can and need to be built among people at different passages in their lives. Being old is such a relative matter in society. As a college teacher who has spent over twenty years around people who are in their late teens to early twenties, it still shocks me to hear students refer to people over thirty as old. At the same time, visitors to nursing homes regularly hear comments that reflect residents' more refined analysis of oldness. Old to them is a lot farther down the road than thirty!

At the individual level, many physical and psychological conditions seem to go with aging. Columnist Art Buchwald's autobiography, *Leaving Home* (1994), poignantly describes his long battle with depression. Buchwald, now sixty-eight, said that he came very close to committing suicide on two occasions, in 1962 and in 1987. He said that he decided not to kill himself one time because his wife Ann, who is now deceased, had very tactfully put up a photograph of his children to remind him that he was not alone—and in effect to quell his urge to kill himself. Buchwald finally got psychological help and feels that he has licked his severe case of depression.

Buchwald's discussion of his depression is a valuable contribution to the estimated 17 million or more Americans who suffer clinical depression. Many of these people are between sixty-five and ninety years of age—ages at which the suicide rate is the highest for any group in the United States. Clinical depression is depression that is deep and durable, not the moderate and occasional depression we all experience. It has been estimated by the National Institute of Aging that over 50 percent of clinically depressed people do not receive treatment.

The rest of this section provides examples of people living their final years with zest and in the way in which they want to. To end the discussion of nursing homes on an upbeat and amusing note, consider David Greenberger's book, *Duplex Planet* (1993), which has opened up a whole new way of viewing nursing home residents who are usually seen as having little left to offer and as suffering from old age dementia. Greenberger, who has created an industry of books, compact discs, and newsletters filled with the funny and wise sayings of the people who live in these institutions, perceptively discovered the too little recognized talent of nursing home residents to tell amusing tales while he worked as an activities director for the Duplex Nursing Home in the Boston area. He wanted to help residents create a collective memoir of their community, so he started asking them questions (often amusing questions such as "Do apes have picnics?") and writing down their answers (to the ape picnic question, Ernie Bookings replied, "I don't know, my dictionary's too small," p. 45). In discussing his interviewees, Greenberger said:

> [T]he names of their conditions of deterioration mattered little to me; what did matter was that this was someone still very much alive, very interested in conversing, in entertaining or being entertained, in connecting with someone else. (p. 7)

Examples of the gems reported to Greenberger (1993) include:

> I can't complain too much. I've been to California.—Ed Poindexter (p. 47)

> I got eighty-six hours of sleep since last Friday. Fifty-six hours of sleep is a good amount of sleep for a week and I had thirty extra hours of sleep. And I have another business: I'm starting to sell cigarettes to my friends.— Henry Turner (p. 80)

> Everybody's askin' who I was.—Charlie Johanson (p. 9)

> In answer to the question, "Can you tell me what a compact disc is?": Who the hell knows?! Write this down: Where do you get all these stupid questions? What's a compact disc?! Where do you think we went to school anyway? That's like asking why doesn't snow fall up instead of down. If you look at it long enough it does fall up.—Frank Kanslasky (p. 138)

Through his publications, Greenberger continues to report what residents in different nursing homes say in answer to his "stupid" questions. These publications have been praised and used by many people, including the comedian George Carlin, to show their appreciation of the wisdom often displayed by the elderly. The *New York Times* has likened these gems to modern-day versions of Chaucer's reports from the road to Canterbury.

Ernest Hemingway's *The Old Man and the Sea* embodies a spirit of finishing one's life with as much daring and self-reliance as a person can muster. This story of an old man's relentless pursuit of a fish symbolizes the quest of many elderly people to battle old age and death with valor and dignity until their final breath. That is the message that I hope readers will get for all aspects of loss discussed in this book. Keeping the faith and trying to conquer one more obstacle may be extraordinarily difficult as we age. As discussed in Chapter 11, there likely is a point at which each of us—if we have the choice—will need to let go of life. But until that point, the charge issued by many courageous people, some of whom are discussed in the following paragraphs, is that we should never quit.

Many older individuals are shining examples of "generativity," or giving back much to other generations (a topic that is expanded on in the final two chapters). For example, in 1990, Paul Reese, age seventy-three, ran from California to South Carolina and plunged into the Atlantic Ocean at Hilton Head with television cameras recording his historic moment. It took him five months to accomplish this feat with the help of his wife, who drove a van to accompany and assist him. His accomplishment was the equivalent of running a marathon for 124 consecutive days! In 1993, Reese published *Ten Million Steps*, a chronicle of his run. In describing what he felt about his accomplishment for an article that appeared in the *Chicago Tribune* July 31, 1994, Reese told Bard Lindeman:

> It was somewhat sad to see so many homes with older people, meaning 60 and upwards, sitting in a chair on the front porch or in the yard, just watching the world go by. Hey, this should be "their" day. To sit there, hour after hour, seems a waste of body and brain.
>
> I think how fortunate I am to be able to experience this run, especially at my age. Yes, fortunate to be able to handle it physically and financially [it cost him about $45 a day], fortunate to have the time and blessed to have Elaine's [his wife's] help. (Lindeman, 1994, p. 6F)

Reese, an ex-Marine, had suffered prostate cancer only three years prior to his run. He continued to train right through the period of his treatment. In the end, Reese ran to heighten the sense of possibilities of later life—a noble achievement that can give new meaning to many senior citizens who believe that they, too, can in some way reach possibilities that they otherwise might not have entertained.

In August 1994, Virginia Eddy, eighty-four, of Middlebury, Vermont, died. Why was her death so special that it was reported by the Associated Press and picked up by the *New York Times* and other newspapers? Because she, too, lived her life in an exemplary fashion. Her death was both planned and peaceful. This woman, who was described by her son David Eddy as the proverbial little old lady in sneakers, faced a number of health problems toward the end of her life, but she did not want to die in a nursing home, "declining with little more than a blank stare," as she told her son. Nor did Eddy want to die after a protracted period of grave illness, being cared for by others. She said:

> I've lived a wonderful life, but it has to end sometime. And this is the right time for me. I don't want to spoil the wonder of my life by dragging it out

in years of decay. I want to go now, while the good memories are still fresh.
(Lindeman, 1994, p. 8F)

So, after consulting with her family, Eddy celebrated her eighty-fifth birthday with a rousing party. Then she stopped eating and drinking. On the sixth day of fasting, with a relaxed, natural smile, she died. That's not all. She requested that her son tell others about her decision. He did in an issue of the *Journal of the American Medical Association*, and the story was then picked up on the wire services. Indeed, Eddy had lived a life of vigor and accomplishment that had involved traveling across Africa at age seventy and surviving a river rafting accident at age eighty-two. She offered this question to all of us who may face her situation in the end: "Is the quality of life defined by its duration? Or does life have a purpose so large that it doesn't have to be prolonged at any cost to preserve its meaning?"

LOSSES ASSOCIATED WITH ACCIDENTS AND DISEASE STARTING AT MIDLIFE OR EARLIER

I know a man who in his forties experienced a brain hemorrhage, rapid bleeding that resulted in loss of much of the functioning in his left cerebral hemisphere. This man, who had been a prominent scientist, does not know what decade he lives in. He knows that he has experienced a tremendous loss that also has exacted a huge toll on his wife, children, and family of origin, but he cannot precisely understand what he has lost either physically or psychologically. As his wife once suggested, he would not have wanted his life—maybe forty-plus more years—to slowly ebb away in this fashion, sitting in a nursing home wearing diapers since he cannot control his bowels. She has often said, "It would have been so much better if he had just died."

Yet, that was not to be, nor is it to be for millions of other brain-damaged individuals. As the neurologist and writer Oliver Sacks (*The Man Who Mistook His Wife for a Hat*, 1970) wrote, many people suffer brain injuries that transform their lives and the lives of their loved ones into something that is akin to constant sorrow. It is never the same as it was and will never be the same, even though the patient may look normal and be in otherwise fine health. The adjustment process for all people concerned in these situations can be very difficult, and divorce is common.

One of the most salutary developments in the area of treatment of brain injury is the growth of strong, active support groups for spouses and family members. More than anything else, such groups stand by their members, whom others may dismiss as being whiny about their loss. Outsiders may judge survivors' lingering grief as an obsession about something small in the scheme of major losses that can confront people: "So he got hit on the head and is different now. Why is that so life-shattering? How is that like getting cancer or something?" But a brain injury can change the whole interaction and emotional dynamics of a family. A person with a brain injury may not be capable of the type of affective expression that he or she showed prior to the injury. With automobile accidents resulting in major brain injury increasingly common, support groups and public activism must be better recognized in our country, particularly among professionals concerned with loss, grief, and adaptation.

There are many other types of injuries and diseases that can cripple the body, mind, and spirit at a relatively early point in life. Estimates indicate that each year as many as 10,000 Americans suffer serious brain or spinal cord injuries in accidents. Eighty percent are men, and most are between the ages of fifteen and thirty-five.

One of the most uplifting stories I have heard by a survivor of traumatic injury is Bob Wieland's story. Wieland was a medic in the Vietnam War. In 1969 he stepped on a booby-trapped shell that blew off both of his legs. His injury has not stopped Wieland from achieving a great deal in the last two decades, however. He has become a world-class weight lifter, benching over 500 pounds. He has worked as the Green Bay Packers strength and conditioning coach. He travels extensively and is a motivational speaker. Incredibly, he gained national attention starting in 1982 by walking on his hands, one yard at a time, from Los Angeles to Washington, D.C. It took him over four years, as he transcended deserts, mountains, horrible weather, and pain from the struggle. His journey raised more than $315,000 in pledges for disabled veterans. In a motivational talk to the Green Bay Packers football team before a game, he said:

> *I lifted myself 2 inches off the ground and moved ahead 3 feet. I did that 4,900,016 times. I know because I counted. . . . If you guys can't run up and down a football field for 60 minutes, you ought to be ashamed of yourselves.*
>
> *Players don't often look at things that way. They take their God-given ability for granted. . . .*
>
> *Wieland's message from his ardous trip was simple, "You're alive, so use your life to the fullest." (Didinger, 1990, p. 6C)*

LOSS OF EMPLOYMENT

> *I felt so low, I really didn't care what I did. Then I thought about how I had wanted to study law when I was younger, but I didn't because of finances. Well, I still had no money, but it didn't seem to matter. My situation couldn't get any worse. So I applied to law school and got in.*
>
> —A Forty-eight-year-old Former Executive

It is hanging over your head every minute of every day. I wake up in the middle of the night; there it is. No matter what I do, it is there.

—Nanette Bellefleur

The loss of employment can be just as devastating as any other kind of loss. In this section, I will focus on the experiences of people who are laid off from permanent jobs. Something vast is sweeping the world of work. A combination of automation, instant communication, globalization, standardization, and cheap means of transport is creating changes unseen since the Industrial Revolution. Everywhere, businesses are seeking the cheapest costs and lowest wages. Technology lets businesses find these without sacrificing quality. Jobs now can be moved all over the world at will, from suburban Chicago to Mexico to Sri Lanka. Yet people, especially those with families, do not move around the globe to keep their jobs or to find new employment. Seldom has there been any warning about many of the layoffs that have swept major corporations in this country—265,000 in 1994 alone. Usually only a terse statement is offered, while cuts in the thousands occur and careers and families are left in turmoil..

For many people, the loss of a high-paying salaried job signals the start of being unable to find work except for temporary $5-to-$6-an-hour jobs. As one Detroit worker said about her quest to find a job that pays a reasonable salary:

I've seen all the help wanted signs, but it's crazy to think that I'll work for minimum wage. How can I ever think about buying a house on those wages? I don't care what work I do, as long as I get what I deserve. (Smith, 1994, p. 6C)

U.S. Secretary of Labor Robert Reich has been said to have noted in 1994 that people must become accustomed to the fact that job security is a thing of the past. The tens of thousands of secure, high-paying manufacturing jobs of decades past are not going to return to the U.S. job scene.

It is not only blue-collar jobs that have been cut. People at all levels of employment have been the targets of cuts since the mid-1980s. Mid-level management has become a particularly prominent target for retrenchment in the 1990s as companies try to cut their expenses and make themselves more competitive. Hardly a week goes by when a big company does not engage in a major job reduction. For decades, the employees of large corporations, such as IBM and Sears, were employed throughout their careers and then retired with outstanding pension programs. While some still do in the 1990s, many others have been let go. Increasingly, companies are decreasing their supervisory levels and are looking to computers for monitoring performance. Many employees now work out of their automobiles, homes, or hotels using computers, phones, and FAX machines and not have offices per se. Such arrangements cut down on the overhead companies have to pay to conduct business.

For better or worse, many of us define ourselves and our value to a considerable degree in terms of our occupations: professor, nurse, writer. Such definitions are loaded with meaning about our experiences and the work that we have done and continue to do in our lives. They may connote something about our ego and our expectations for how others will respond to us. Practically, jobs feed and clothe us. Psychologically, jobs give us pride and add to the meaning of our lives. Thus, when our job is yanked or we are forced to retire, our senses of value and self-worth are on the line and may suffer for a long time. As one recently unemployed person said, "The hardest part is the mental aspect. I know I can't sell myself to anyone if my spirits are down" (Ehrlichman, 1993, p. 4).

In recent years, we have heard of people becoming violent after being fired. When fired, people reasonably ask questions such as: Was my work that bad even after years of success and pay raises? How do I start over at this late age? How do I tell my family and friends that I have lost my job? How can I assure my family that their needs will be taken care of now when I retire? How can I meet the bill for my children's college tuition and help them as they try to get started in their adult lives? Without answers, some people may become desperate and seek revenge.

A secondary problem associated with the massive cutbacks is the tendency for some workers to push themselves to the limit. They sometimes fear their company's impending downsizing and want to position themselves for survival. Eugene Griessman, a commentator on work tendencies, suggests that the rubber band is being stretched for many of these workaholics and that a price will be paid eventually. For the purposes of this analysis, even if they survive in the job, workaholics experience major latent loss and ultimate grief about missing much in life, for example, their children growing up. Beyond the issue of the number of hours one puts into a job is the problem of a slide in wages. Yearly increases are small, if at all, in some job areas, and health and other benefits have been cut. Overall, the accumulation of job-relevant uncertainties and hardships that face many individuals in our world may be associated with many problems in their domestic lives and with drug addiction and mental health difficulties as well.

U.S. Secretary of Labor Robert Reich once estimated that a young person entering the work force will change careers, not just jobs, two to three times and may change positions within a particular profession six to seven times. That is a lot of movement and potentially a lot of disappointment and dashed hopes and plans. Our understanding of the psychology of loss associated with job reductions is embryonic at best. Many magazines devote stories to this type of loss and what to do to get a new job. However, very little research has been done on the psychology of job loss. Leading textbooks in industrial psychology and organizational behavior seldom, if ever, discuss the loss to self-worth and the grief that often accompany job loss.

To illustrate what many workers fear in the 1990s, consider the following excerpts from a letter by George Kaforski, chairman of Ameritech Downsized Employees, to John McCarron, a business columnist for the *Chicago Tribune*:

> *We are composed primarily of former Ameritech employees who were "downsized" out of employment during the previous couple of years. . . . Until recent years, downsizings were done by corporations in financial trouble, and were needed as a matter of survival, to reduce huge overheads. However, during the past few years a very disturbing trend has been taking place. Many very solvent and prosperous companies have jumped on the downsizing bandwagon. The real goal is to rid these corporations of larger numbers of employees who have 15 to 30 years of service and replace them with employees who are better educated, younger and willing to work for a much lower salary. This is done to obtain huge amounts of cash that can be used to boost stock price, to expand or do whatever the corporation deems appropriate, including large bonuses and stock option plans for senior officers. . . . In a number of these downsizings, the real goal is to rid these major corporations of employees who have worked themselves up to good salaries, have obtained a number of good benefits and are close to good pensions.*
>
> *What is lost in all this rush for money is the social responsibility these companies should practice toward their employees and their communities. Instead they have chosen to turn their backs on a large number of middle-aged Americans who unfortunately believed what these companies told them when they were working. (McCarron, 1994, sect. 7, p. 2)*

As is true with so many lifespan losses, at any point in time any person, however wealthy or otherwise secure, may be only a bare margin away from economic disaster. As Jack Beatty, a senior editor at the *Atlantic Monthly*, noted in the *Chicago Tribune* on September 25, 1994, "most of us are only a restructuring, a re-engineering, a firing, a major illness, or a divorce away from joining [the ranks of the working poor]" (p. A1).

What do we do when we are fired? We need to take time to grieve. We also need to consider carefully our options. Many former salaried workers have created successful small businesses after being fired and finding no comparable job. I have paraphrased some steps toward recovery from the previously cited article by John Ehrlichman (1993):

1. Process what has happened as carefully as possible. Don't try to cover up anger about the firing. Be open to mourning and willing to talk to close others and professional counselors about your feelings and future plans.

2.   Assess yourself and try to identify your strengths that may facilitate your movement to another field or to the creation of your own business.

3.   Create a first-class résumé and write an effective cover letter when mailing out new job applications.

4.   Network with friends, colleagues, and acquaintances about your interests in certain types of jobs of which they may become aware.

5.   Market yourself. Remember that perseverance in finding new possibilities and then pursuing them with vigor often pay off.

THE IMPOVERISHED AND THE HOMELESS

In our world with its billions of people are millions of people who are significantly impoverished and malnourished. Some of them also are homeless. Poverty, malnutrition, and homelessness also represent lifespan losses. These states are not so frequent as to be normal, thus meeting one of the chief characteristics of loss noted in the introduction, but they are frequent enough to be close to normal. In fact, it is uncanny how many people describe events in their lives with the remark that "were it not for the grace of God, I, too, would be homeless [or destitute, or, in general, without many of the fine things of life]." In the United States, the Great Depression of the 1930s showed how quickly any human being, however wealthy, can lose every physical resource. In preparation for the Jewish High Holy Days in 1994, Rabbi Gordon Tucker of Temple Israel in White Plains, New York, commented on the frailty of all our lives and our constant vulnerability to loss: "There's a sense we increasingly have in this world of a very thin line that we're all up against that separates us from very different kinds of fate" (Berger, 1994, p. B8).

The social and behavioral science community has recently awakened somewhat to the need to study homelessness. In *Homelessness: A National Perspective* (1992), edited by Marjorie Robertson and Milton Greenblatt, a number of scholars have analyzed the many facets of homelessness in the United States and found that among the problems and needs of the homeless are the need for temporary shelter, the need for adequate food and nutrition, and the need for clothing. Among their problems are sexual victimization, especially among women and young people; criminal and legal problems, including police harassment; poverty and inadequate financial assistance; poor physical health and inadequate medical service; drinking problems and alcoholism; social isolation and absence of a supportive social network; absence of leisure, recreation opportunities; and mental health problems.

This list of needs and problems adds up to a staggering number of losses for the homeless. And, indeed, many of these people have ended up homeless because of their inability to cope with earlier catastrophic losses. An interesting aspect of this long and still partial list of problems faced by the homeless is that grief is not on the list! Such an exclusion probably means that the question has not been asked explicitly in research done with homeless respondents.

The sense of loss and grief clearly exists. Consider the following story of a young man, age fifteen, who was interviewed in a New York shelter and discussed by Petry and Avent (1992):

> [*After telling about a number of times running away from home and re-turning*] *What comes to mind is running from home, where I experienced a lot of abuse. Without asking any questions at all, my mother would beat me, either with her hands, her fists, a belt, belt buckle, stick, frying pan, or spatula.* . . . *She once came to school with a tree branch, took down my clothes in front of my whole class, and beat me.*
>
> *. . . My mother grew up in a home in which, if she did something wrong, she would get beaten by one of her parents.* . . . *My mother had a cousin who she never got along with. This cousin stole nail polish one day and said that my mother did it. My mother got stripped and tied to her bed and beaten by her father and grandfather. So when I was growing up my mother thought that that was the way a child should be raised.*
>
> *. . . When I visited my uncle, he would ask me if I would watch him masturbate* . . . *it was a regular thing.* . . . *The abuse also happened with my two male cousins.* . . .
>
> [*After a period in adolescence working as a prostitute and being virtually on the street, he returned home and tried to kill himself and then took to the road completely.*] *Yes, I do feel pushed out by the fact that my mother did not give me an opportunity to be a kid.* . . . *One time she told me to get out of the house and never come back. If I had said I'm not sure I want to date girls, or I want to talk to you about the abuse that I experienced while I was growing up, she would have said, "I'm tired of this, get out of here." (pp. 303–304)*

Of course, there probably are as many stories of loss experience among the homeless as there are homeless people in this country. *A Nation in Denial* (1993) is an extremely valuable book containing stories of homeless persons and an analysis of policy issues involved in homelessness by Alice Baum and Donald Burnes. Baum and Burnes contend that it was only in the late 1970s that this country began to recognize the problem of homelessness. They argue that only by overcoming this denial, especially as it pertains to our failure to see the roles of alcoholism, mental illness, and drug addiction as central to the homelessness problem, will this country be able to offer help and hope to the homeless. They suggest that huge class prejudice and stigma prevent the homeless from receiving the type of public empathy and aid that they need.

One final story about homelessness reinforces Baum and Burnes's denial argument. In December 1993, Yetta Adams, age forty-three, froze to death on a bench in a bus shelter across the street from the U.S. Department of Housing and Urban Development. This death coincided with a battle within the federal government over the annual budget for the homeless. HUD Secretary Henry Cisneros said:

> *You could describe me as a secretary who's shamelessly describing the death of this woman while talking about budget increases, but I'm told there were homeless people outside who knelt in prayer at this woman's body. So when I raise my voice in search of funds, I know I'm not alone.* (New York Times, *1993, p. A1)*

Adams was a single mother, who suffered from depression and had experienced a series of major losses prior to becoming a street person. It is estimated that at least a third of the homeless in this country suffer from serious mental health problems. Where Yetta Adams died is a fitting testimony about a gigantic social welfare system that has many holes in its safety net. *USA Today* writer Mimi Hall reported that Adams's stepmother Geraldine Adams said, "She [Yetta] would never lie down on a grate. She was too proud for that" (Hall, 1993, p. 8A).

LOSS OF HOME AND RESOURCES BECAUSE OF DISASTER AND WAR

> *"I wish I could get a book that tells you how to deal with something like this," said Michele Hanks. "Yeah, how about a 'how-to-reconstruct-your-life,' " said her husband Jim as they stared distantly at the blackened, smoke-stained remains of the building that had provided their livelihood that had just been destroyed by fire.*
> —Dallas Morning News, *December 26, 1993, p. 46A*

Many people lose their homes and places of work in natural and wartime disasters. For example, the nuclear power generator accident at Three Mile Island, Pennsylvania, and the land contamination by dioxin at Times Beach, Missouri, literally ran people out of town in the early 1980s.

Times Beach is a classic story of environmental pollution and the subsequent wipeout of a community. In the 1970s, dirt roads all over Times Beach were contaminated when a waste oil dealer sprayed them with dioxin-laced oil to keep down the dust. The toxicity of dioxin then was in doubt. But Times Beach residents began to suffer a wave of cancer deaths, immune system diseases, and miscarriages. Birds died at alarming rates, and household pets developed strange, fatal diseases. One resident indicated that every day something traumatic happened in this small river community. After widespread complaints by residents and accumulating evidence that dioxin was contaminating the soil, scientists recommended a government buyout of the town in 1982. Dioxin has a half-life of ten years, meaning it decomposes by half its strength every ten years. News reports indicate that practically every family who lived in this community now has health problems that were probably caused by the contamination. It is not just one family member who has health problems in most cases but every family member, including the children born in recent years. In Times Beach, the only thing with a longer half-life than dioxin in the 1990s is grief!

As the destruction and loss of life in the mid-1990s wars in Croatia and Bosnia have demonstrated, the wartime losses of homes and neighborhoods in places like Sarajevo, Bosnia, are astounding. When we suffer loss of home and place, we need to read the history books. There are immense lessons about such types of losses to be learned. Chapter 9 describes the destruction of Oradour-sur-Glane, France, and most of its people by the Nazis. The ruins have been left beside the new town to symbolize the cruelty that knew no bounds in this vicious act.

Many major European cities have been completely rebuilt since being bombed and burned to skeletons during World War II. Stalingrad, Russia, is perhaps the most historically notable and powerful example of loss of physical place and human life. Its World War II history, as well as that of the whole of Russia, reflects an immense sacrifice of life. In total, over 20 million Russians died during World War II. Russia's losses were greater than those of any other country, and a great number of those who died were civilians.

According to Hoyt (1993), Stalingrad, originally founded in 1589 and called Tsaritsyn, was renamed in the 1920s. Stalin wanted it to be a model Soviet factory city with all the amenities of which communist society would be proud. It was to be the Soviet city of the future. The wide Volga River dissected the city. This river was the lifeline of Central Russia. Single men and women lived in dormitories, but families had their own detached houses. Stalingrad's living accommodations were more modern and spread out than the accommodations found in most Soviet cities. The yards of the houses had flower and vegetable gardens. The Red Army was located on the edge of the square, and the newspaper *Pravda* was there, too. South of the city was a mining community, Kuporosnoye. North of the city lay the massive factory complex, the pride of the USSR planners, which included the Red October factory and a tractor factory. Each factory complex had its own schools, parks, housing, provision stations, and other amenities. West of the city lay large communal farms of the Don basin with tens of thousands of wheat fields and orchards. Thus, Stalingrad was a major industrial, mining, and agricultural center for all of Russia.

I have gone into this much detail about Stalingrad because its physical structures were almost totally destroyed in the siege by the German Army in late 1942 and early 1943. This battle alone probably did more to assure the ultimate downfall of the Nazis than did any other battle of World War II. If the Germans had prevailed at Stalingrad, it is believed that they could have encircled the entire Russian Army and gone on to conquer Russia—and what else? More than thirty divisions and over a thousand planes ceaselessly pounded away at the city and its wharves on the Volga. *Every* structure in Stalingrad except some stone buildings was reduced to rubble. Nazi tanks broke into the heart of the city and piled up thousands of Russian dead on the main square. Although the fighting went on day and night, house to house, the Germans could not overcome the incredible will to survive of the Russian Army and Stalingrad residents. Hundreds of courageous factory workers operated as snipers and saboteurs and killed thousands of German troops when they advanced on the factory complexes.

At the end, because of the Russians' tenacity and the Germans' tactical errors, especially in the use of their air force, the German armies were trapped on all sides and forced to surrender; 91,000 men, including 24 generals who had been key leaders during the Nazis' military successes throughout Europe became prisoners of war. More than 300,000 German soldiers died in the battle for the city (Shirer, 1960, p. 1217).

But at what price did this historic victory for Russia and the Western allies come? The sacrifice of ordinary citizens in this battle was extraordinary in the annals of wars and people's attempts to save their homes and cities against outside armies. Of the over one-half million residents of proud Stalingrad before the battle, only a little over one thousand survived!

What did the city look like at the end of the battle in February, 1943? Hoyt (1993) cites reports that for as far as the eye could see, there were lonely chimneys, buildings, and vehicles in rubble. One correspondent felt that Stalingrad looked somewhat like the Warsaw Ghetto did after the Nazis got through with it earlier in the war, although Stalingrad was much larger. Railroad carriages mixed with bent and broken rusted rails and smashed locomotives littered the area near the Volga, and the river itself was horribly polluted by destroyed barge and steamer debris and dead human and animal bodies. The ground was honeycombed with smashed trenches whose sides had fallen in and the wreckage of pillboxes and bunkers. Dugouts and shell holes pocked the whole countryside. Carcasses of horses lay twisted and frozen everywhere. Mamayev Hill, previously a lover's lane area but more recently the scene of the fiercest fighting in the city, was scattered with bones and frozen bodies. The whole earth looked as if it had been swept by fire, ravaged by an earthquake, and then finished off with a volcanic eruption. There was no relationship to the previous meticulous workmanship on display in the city. Hoyt notes that reports indicated:

> *The whole area was a wasteland. . . . This frozen desert was unrecognizable as the corpse of a working city. There was no visible line where the town ended and the countryside began. It was all rubble and ruin. (p. 287)*

In 1943, only the wildest dreams of the survivors could conceive how Stalingrad could be rebuilt. Yet it happened. Stalingrad, renamed Volgograd by Khrushchev in 1961, stands as a remarkable symbol of human sacrifice, courage and ability to overcome perhaps the greatest of losses of home and place that are imaginable. Overall, this section shows the diversity of significant types of losses that people sometimes experience. Wars, natural disasters, and events leading to people's becoming homeless involve many different elements. Yet there are common social psychological effects and means of coping with these effects.

FINDING WILL AND HOPE DESPITE LOSS

The lifespan losses described in this chapter often require great effort and willpower to transcend. There are good examples everywhere of people rising to the occasion to deal with loss and anguish with grace and courage. Perhaps if nothing else, this coverage suggests the value of taking a minute to reflect on the many different ways people lose and yet cope—taking a day at a time—as a part of life. Perhaps we would all be stronger if each day we took time to try to understand how someone else is dealing with life's stressors. Consider what Beverly Fine (1994) reported one woman and her husband discovered when they spontaneously decided to stop their trip to the beach to talk with a stranger, an elderly woman whom they observed waving from the front porch of a nursing home:

> *[The woman smiled and walked toward them when they stopped.] "I'm so glad you stopped. I prayed that you would have a few minutes to sit and chat. Many people pass by here, especially in the summer, and peer from their car windows and see nothing more than an old building that houses old people. But you saw me. . . . And you took time to stop. Some people believe that old people are senile; the truth is that we're just plain lonely. But we old folks do rattle on, don't we?"*
> *[After the woman had been taken away briefly for her medication, she returned and gave the travelers a small box with a letter attached:] "Dear Ones, These past few days have been the happiest ones in my life since*

Henry, my beloved husband, died two years ago. Once more, I have a family I love and who cares about me. Last night, the doctor seemed concerned about my heart problem. However, I feel wonderful. And while I am in this happy mood, I want to thank you for the joy both have brought into my life. . . . This gift for you [the woman] is the cameo brooch I wore the day we met. My husband gave it to me on our wedding day, June 30, 1939. . . . Enjoy wearing it, and I hope that someday it will belong to your children. With the brooch comes my everlasting love. Margaret"

Three days after our visit, Margaret died peacefully in her sleep.

As long as you see each new day as a chance for something different to happen, you can stay young.

—Sadie and Bessie Delaney

8

LOSSES THAT DISENFRANCHISE AND STIGMATIZE

J.J. Goedken found out in 1986 he was HIV positive [he and his brother were hemophiliacs who years earlier had been infected by a tainted blood transfusion]. But his five children might suffer if word leaked out, so he kept the information from them. In a nearby town, Connie [his daughter] said rocks were thrown through the windows of people with AIDS and crosses were burned on their yards.

—Val Swinton

STIGMATIZATION

As the above quotation suggests, major losses often are associated with discrimination and stigmatization directed at victims. Why? Because the victims are clearly viewed as tarnished and different, and the perceivers want to keep a distance from people with such differences. Perceivers may feel that their personal welfare is imperiled by the difficulty of the victim, or perceivers may not understand or want to understand the victim's problems—they may simply want the victim isolated or somewhere far away so that he or she will not remind them of the problems they have encountered. Victims violate perceivers' assumptions about the way the world works. These reasons may seem too harsh. Do not perceivers also show sympathy and even empathy with others who suffer? Of course, some do, and maybe we all do on some occasions. However, the extent to which victims regularly report feeling stigmatized, or disenfranchised, suggests that the phenomenon of stigmatization is widespread. We all need to try harder each day to imagine walking a mile in another person's shoes.

Unlike some of the other loss topics discussed in this book, stigmatization has generated a large literature. In 1984, Edward Jones, Amerigo Farina, Albert Hastorf, Hazel Markus, Dale Miller, and Robert Scott published *Social Stigma: The Psychology of Marked Relationships*, which is one of the most comprehensive analyses of social stigma yet produced. Jones et al. cast social stigma in terms of "marks": "*Mark* is thus our generic term for perceived or inferred conditions of deviation from a prototype or norm that *might* initiate the stigmatizing process" (p. 8). Hence, in the Goedkin family example, the whole family was "marked" by outsiders' perceptions that several of them had AIDS. Marking, or labeling, usually results in some type of ostracism from the outsiders' circle. As sociologist Erving Goffman (1963) eloquently argues, every human being may be marked—because of physical features, disease processes, behaviors, or mental illness or retardation. Over three centuries ago, women who were labeled witches were burned at the stake, a dreadful consequence of perceivers' ill-conceived assumptions about other human beings. Such dire consequences associated with stigmatization have happened repeatedly in human history.

Jones et al. (1984) provide the following story about the psychological hurt that many stigmatized people suffer:

> *November 26, 1981. A UPI report in the* Hartford Courant *is headlined "Teenager describes how it feels to be retarded." The article describes how the teacher of a trainable, mentally retarded 17 year old transcribed his thoughts in a brief book: "Sometimes it makes me want to cry inside because I am retarded, but sometimes other people may forget about me being retarded. I can't stand it if someone teases me, it makes me feel weird inside. I can't stand it! Nobody likes that. But when they realize that they are hurting my feelings sometimes they come over and apologize to me." (p. 2)*

Sometimes a loss that stigmatizes can serve as an explanation for a person's negative behavior. In 1994, Glenda Caldwell, who suffers from Huntington's disease and who had been in prison for nine years for killing her teenaged son, was finally given a new trial because of new knowledge about the behavior that sometimes accompanies the disease. Doctors said that she had suffered from this disease at the time of the killing, but that fact had been minimized in her trial. Her new trial should help draw attention to Huntington's disease, but it also may stigmatize other sufferers as potentially violent. Philip Cohen, a spokesman for the Huntington's Disease Foundation of America in New York said:

The sword is double-edged. Not every Huntington's person is violent. That would be a gross mischaracterization. . . . Being penalized for something you're not able to control seems to be inappropriate. (Cohen, 1994)

Ronnie Janoff-Bulman argues in *Shared Assumptions* (1992) that victims are threatening to nonvictims because they are manifestations of a malevolent universe rather than a benevolent one. Janoff-Bulman suggests that most of us hold a set of assumptions about life, such as the world is benign, bad things happen to other people, and people get what they deserve and deserve what they get in life. These assumptions do not help us when we suffer major losses and must deal with the reality that bad things can happen to us, too. However, until we have had that experience and have empathy for others who suffer, we may regard them as deviants marked by misfortune. Their victim status sets them apart from ordinary folk, we may implicitly conclude. Such a conclusion brands victims as somehow flawed or blemished. Janoff-Bulman contends that victims are stigmatized because they violate the expectations established by people's illusions.

ON TYPES OF STIGMATIZATION

Aging and the Elderly

Nowhere are stereotypes more widespread, entrenched, and ruinous than in the area of older adults. The negative ideas linked to later life cut a wide swath, minimizing every aspect of humanity: in health ("Older people are disabled" or "Typically, they are in nursing homes"); in thinking ("Their mind goes"); and in personality ("Older people are depressed, childish, set in their ways"). These stereotypes apply to the main transitions in later life, too—retirement and widowhood. Each event oozes with connotations of unmitigated loss.

—Janet Belsky

How very perceptive are Belsky's observations. Perhaps there is no group that is as regularly (almost as a matter of due course) stigmatized as the very old in our culture. Instead of honoring them, as some other cultures do, we relegate them to nursing homes. Too often, the elderly—especially those whose spouses and friends have died—are lonely and anxious, have low self-esteem and morale, and have little will to continue living. It is immensely difficult for them to construct new meanings for their lives, particularly if their bodies are wracked by disease and normal aging processes. Macdonald (1983) comments on this experience for elderly women:

The process of aging has been hidden from us all our lives. We are told with the help of modern medicine and technology old age isn't really necessary.

One can have an active life right up to the "end." You are as young as you
think you are. There are hair dyes to make your hair look its "natural
color," with creams to remove the wrinkles and brown spots, and with all
of these no woman should look as though she is "failing"—she should look
"well-preserved." (p. 99)

Lisel Mueller's poem "Face Lift" (1986) raises related questions about
aging. The first line sets in motion the question of how old someone really
is if she has been altered to appear younger. When spotted by a female acquaintance in the grocery store, the new appearance of the woman suggests a set of questions to her acquaintance, including: How many years
that had been indelibly sculpted on her face had been magically removed?
Where were the remnants of smiles, the looks of dread, the expressions of
sadness and grief? Now, her face "has retracted sleepless nights, / denies
any knowledge of pain" (p. 21) and no longer has the dark eyes left by
mourning someone she loved. The onlooker wonders how it feels to remember, "under the skin of a thirty-year-old, something that happened at
forty" (p. 21).

The French futurist Gerard Delteil has predicted that in 100 years, advances in cosmetic surgery will allow sixty-year-olds to look indistinguish-
able from teenagers. Would most of us want that fate? Is aging so stigmatic
that we want to wipe away the thousands of experiences that stand behind
the lines on our faces? As I suggest at the end of this chapter, there may be
something to be said for accepting the slings and arrows of living with
grace and recognizing that death is a natural experience—one like so many
others that deserves honor, not avoidance.

Violent Crime: Victims, Survivors, and Families

Survivors of violent crime are also stigmatized by their losses. Shelley Neiderbach, a trauma counselor, suggests that victims often are treated as
losers in society. She contends that victims already may feel guilt and little
trust for strangers and that even friends begin to show behavior that makes
the victims feel tainted. People may avoid crime victims to avoid thinking
of the possibility that crime could happen to them. Also, as noted in Chapter 6, the American public has become increasingly numb to violence and
deaths due to violence. We have grown accustomed to it and don't recognize the lifelong grief that ensues for the victim's family. Neiderbach says
that people listen patiently to their friends' and acquaintances' losses from
violence for about two weeks. After this point, they think the victims should
be progressing beyond the traumatic event. They do not understand the frequent long-term PTSD-like consequences of these losses. Beyond that, criminal cases that spend years in the justice system leave wounds open.

A November 26, 1993, article by Robert Davis in *USA Today* told of many people who require years of counseling to begin to come to grips with losses in their lives due to violence. One woman and her husband, whose daughter was stabbed to death in 1986, reported spending over $50,000 for psychological help for the posttraumatic stress they suffered. Part of their continuing grief has been caused by the fact that their daughter's murderer has not been caught. Jacque MacDonald, whose daughter was murdered by a slash to the throat in 1988, reported intense aging, high cholesterol, and regular abdominal pains. She said the knots in her belly come from clashing feelings of anger, helplessness, and sadness. This mother, like so many other relatives of persons who die at the hands of an unknown perpetrator, spends much of her time fighting to get publicity for her daughter's death. This continued struggle for answers about the crime often distances survivors even more from their associates who believe that they should be moving on with their lives and not obsessing about their loss and the whys and hows of the death. MacDonald and her husband left their home state and moved to the state in which their daughter was killed because of pressure from associates to drop their crusade to find their daughter's killer. Jacque MacDonald said that one reporter called her a squeaky wheel, but she did get heard. She said, "I'm a mother. As a mother, you do what you have to do" (Davis, 1993, p. 8A).

Davis's article told of one victim who was stigmatized in the criminal trial process. This person, who was shot during a motel robbery, said, "I was treated like a mere piece of evidence. I was ridiculed and made fun of on the stand by the defense" (p. 8A). This victim's experience in court is often faced by rape victims who are made to appear to be guilty because of their dress, behavior, or previous sexual conduct, however remote those matters may be from the perpetrator's act of raping them.

For major loss resulting from violence, early counseling is essential and can help a survivor avoid the pitfalls of long-term serious depression and drug addiction, which are common among survivors. Shelley Neiderbach argues that survivors' mental health should be checked regularly in the same way a physician might check the physical condition of someone who had had a near fatal heart condition.

Women's Bodies and Health

Delese Wear and Lois Nixon's *Literary Anatomies: Women's Bodies and Health in Literature* (1994) contains many examples of how women feel stigmatized by mastectomies, hysterectomies, and other induced and natural changes in their bodies. They contend that breast cancer is particularly dreaded because in this culture, women's breasts are a symbol of femininity and sexuality. Attention is given to breasts, clothed or unclothed, in the media and everywhere in our culture. Thus, upon the threat of breast amputation, the loss can seem insurmountable. Scherer says of this experience:

> *Breast amputation is mutilating. . . . Particularly significant is the fact that it affects a part of her body intimately associated with sexual fulfill- ment and child-bearing. Concern with appearance after surgery may be mitigated only partly by the use of prosthetic devices. The change in her body is one that the woman herself must learn to accept and cope with, re- gardless of what measures she may use to conceal the disfigurement from others. (1991, p. 703)*

Wear and Nixon say about the "ubiquitous hysterectomy":

> *So tied to women's reproductivity, the uterus becomes easy for others— physicians, husbands, lovers, children— to discount or trivialize, or liter- ally and figuratively throw away once childbearing is over. . . . Hysterectomy forces a quick burial with too little time to mourn and grieve, with no ritual passage like that afforded by menopause. (1994, p. 99)*

This attitude is echoed in Lynne Schwartz's account (1987) of her doctor's advice before surgery:

> *The decision is entirely up to you. However, I like to take the ovaries out whenever I can, as long as I'm in there. . . . There is really nothing you need ovaries for. You have had three children and don't intend to have any more. . . . (p. 43)*

Incest Survivors

> It hurts like hell . . . it's easier to stay sick, stay in denial, commit suicide, stay drunk, or perpetrate the crime onto another victim for relief [than to have to confront it].
>
> —Thirty-one-Year-Old Male Who Reported Being
> Repeatedly Raped by His Mother

There can be no greater stigma associated with the loss of trust in close re- lationships and the sense of a violated self than that experienced by incest survivors. My colleagues and I (see Harvey, Orbuch, Chwalisz, and Gar- wood, 1991, and Orbuch, Harvey, Davis, & Merbach, 1994) have studied the feelings of over 100 incest survivors in a series of questionnaires and inter- views conducted in Iowa, Illinois, Michigan, and Colorado. The survivors whom we interviewed were both women and men who had experienced years of sexual abuse by family members, including fathers, mothers, brothers, stepfathers, stepmothers, grandfathers, and uncles. In a few cases, the offending family member also invited outsiders to participate in the abuse. Our respondents were provided with complete anonymity. Their only reason for participating was to provide information that might be of use to other survivors, scholars, and counselors.

Since the late 1980s, a major controversy has developed over so-called false memories, i.e., the accuracy of the memories of persons who, years later, report having been sexually abused by members of their families. This controversy has pitted supporters of persons making these claims (see, for example, Bass and Davis, *The Courage to Heal* [1988]) against scholars, attorneys, and defendants contesting them. Psychologist Carol Tavris provided the lead review of the counterarguments in the January 3, 1993, *New York Times Book Review* and challenged therapists' claims of their clients' incest experiences based on the clients' sudden recall of events occurring many years earlier (and often after a controversial technique called regression is used). Tavris argued that there is strong reason to believe that people often make up stories (many times unintentionally) as they try to conjure up the past. She reviewed the ample evidence of distortion and false reconstruction in retrospective memory research. She also suggested that the profile of the "typical incest survivor" provided by therapists such as Bass and Davis could apply to almost anyone. In the 1990s, there has been at least one civil lawsuit settled on behalf of the defendant against his daughter and her therapist on the ground that the memories of incest were not real and were induced by the therapist.

I have gone into some detail about this controversy in part to distinguish the reports of stigmatization by incest survivors that follow from this contemporary debate. Our respondents' names were not known, and they were not involved in legal actions concerning their reports. They had to go to great lengths and summon considerable courage just to provide these anonymous reports. These facts lead us to believe the general details provided by the survivors, although we did not have the ability to verify the reports.

Incest survivors frequently feel stigmatized because the incest occurred when they were quite young and could not talk about it. If they attempted to talk about it with persons in their families, the person in whom they attempted to confide sometimes shut them out and told them that breathing a word to anyone would destroy the family. Thus, the victims went into a shell, sometimes for decades, before they found the courage—usually through therapy—to begin to discuss the incest and confront the perpetrators. One female survivor in her thirties said:

> *The first time I revealed the abuse [by her brother between the ages of 8 and 18] was to a state agency and my parents when I was 12. The agency concluded it was normal sibling curiosity. My parents reacted with anger towards me, yelling about my brother's reputation if it should get around*

town. Their reactions left me feeling totally isolated and lone. . . . [f]orcing
me to be victimized for another four years. . . . (Harvey et al., 1991, p. 526)

Dale Larson provides detailed discussion in *The Helper's Journey* (1993) of the long-term consequences of keeping dark secrets. He argues that people who avoid coming out for a long period after an event often show high negative self-images and use words such as *weak, frightened,* and *shameful* to describe their behavior and self-concept. Avoidance and denial are natural strategies that may be effective in the short run when the individual simply cannot bear to confront reality in any palpable way (see the following discussion of Holocaust survivors). Avoidance and denial may also occur without the person being aware of the process. Over the long run, however, avoidance and denial appear to be far less effective than openness and active working through. Even if it "hurts like hell . . . and [is] easier . . . to commit suicide," as suggested in the opening quote of this section, the only way to healing and a diminution of the pain is through opening up and confrontation in combination with caring support from others. Probably over time, the survivor tries to create meaning and develops a story in her or his mind. The critical step at this point, then, is talking about that story and confiding with others.

What came through in a profound way in the Harvey et al. incest study (1991) was the importance of caring empathy from the persons in whom a survivor confides. When the confiding occurs relatively soon after the event and is met with empathy, the survivor is able to begin the healing process and usually suffers far less psychologically in subsequent years. When there is little empathy, the burden of the secret and associated stigma cannot be confronted and, hence, continues to take its toll on the survivor. For example, a female survivor in her forties who had been sworn to secrecy said of her life after being raped by her father, stepfather, and uncles when she was between five and ten years of age:

I cannot have a close relationship with a man, only as a friend, because I
hate to be touched sometimes. And they think I'm having sex with another
man because I get this way. I try to explain about my past, but they say
that's over. It shouldn't bother me anymore. If only it was them instead of
me. . . . I often cannot sleep and when I do I have dreams [of the rape
events] and wake up in a cold sweat. (p. 527)

Orbuch, Harvey, Davis, and Merbach (1994) conducted a study of male survivors of incest that also revealed major psychological dysfunctions in survivors over an extended period. Shame and deep embarrassment are themes of these survivors. A thirty-one-year-old man who had been assaulted by his father and a family friend between the ages of three and seven said, "I suffer from depression constantly, and feel deep inside that I am damaged goods" (p. 260). A man, age thirty-seven, spoke of how damaging incest perpetrated by his father and mother had been to his ability to form close relationships.

> *It has affected every portion of my external and internal life. Close relationships? I don't have any, and never have had. . . . And I've been married for 25 years now! But it is not close, personal or intimate. If anything, it is abusive to me. I don't trust anyone. (p. 260)*

In Harvey et al. (1991), a woman spoke of abuse by her mother as leading to "shame and guilt that are deep and pervasive and a constant sadness and frequent anger" (p. 528). Thus, a current running through both of these investigations is the extensive damage associated with the survivors, when parents are the perpetrators, particularly the mother. It is the mother who usually is the chief caretaker and nurturer of her children. Thus, to have the trust in one's mother violated is to have one's trust in all humans violated, too. More generally, incest always has debilitating effects, and incest by parents has the greatest detrimental impact. To the survivor, incest means a loss of "safe harbor" and trust in persons who are inherently expected to provide nurture and support.

Holocaust Survivors

As discussed in Chapter 6, the Holocaust exemplifies loss at its penultimate. Countless examples of stigmatization and degradation of the human condition are associated with the Holocaust. While Chapter 6 related some of the survivors' stories of destruction and horror, this chapter will relate some of the stories of what it was like to be liberated. In truth, there has been no psychological liberation for many of these survivors. They have seen too much. Their minds cannot occlude their experiences as they try to get on with the rest of their lives. Thus, the hour of liberation was neither joyful nor lighthearted for many. It occurred against a background of destruction, slaughter, and suffering, the likes of which cannot be adequately described in words. Just as many of those liberated felt they were returning to their normal lives, they encountered the sorrow of dispersed or lost family; the universal suffering all around them in Europe at that time; their own exhaustion, which seemed past cure; and the problems of beginning a life, often alone, all over again amid the rubble. Leaving pain behind was possible for only a few fortunate beings or for only a few instants; almost always it coincided with a phase of anguish, severe depression, and a sliver of morale to continue living. Such conditions would be insurmountable for most of us. They were for quite a few of the Holocaust survivors, but some persevered. Still, those who did go on faced stigma and disenfranchised grief.

In Lawrence Langer's *Holocaust Testimonies* (1991) survivors described their feelings on being liberated:

> *You sort of don't feel at home in this world any more, because of this experience—you can live with it, it's like constant pain: you never forget, you never get rid of it, but you learn to live with it. And that sets you apart from other people. (p. 35)*

> *I feel my head is filled with garbage: all these images, you know, and sounds, and my nostrils are filled with the stench of burning flesh. And it's . . . you can't excise it, it's like—like there's another skin beneath this skin and that skin is called Auschwitz, and you cannot shed it. . . . And it's a constant accompaniment. And though a lot of the survivors will deny this, they too feel it the way I do, but they won't give expression to it . . . because we carry this. I am not like you. You have one vision of life and I have two. I—you know—I lived on two planets. After all, I was—it seems to me that Hitler chopped off part of the universe and created annihilation zones and torture and slaughter areas. You know, it's like the planet was chopped up into a normal [part]—so-called normal: our lives are not really normal— and this other planet, and we were herded onto that planet from this one, and herded back again. . . . And we had to relearn to live again. . . . And it's too much; it's very hard to get old with such . . . memories. (pp. 53–54)*

> *No, no, everything that happened destroyed part of me. I was dying slowly. Piece by piece . . . I am not what I would have been if I didn't go through these things. . . . Life was one big hell even after the war. So you make believe that you go on. This is not something that you put behind. And people think that they can get away from it, or you don't talk about it, or you forgot your fear when you lay in an attic and you know that the Gestapo is a minute away from you. And rifles always against your head. You can't be normal. As a matter of fact, I think that we are not normal because we are so normal. (pp. 140–141)*

> *Now I am talking here as if this were a normal thing. Inside my heart burns. My brain boils. (p. 141)*

WHAT CAN WE DO TO ADDRESS STIGMA?

Stigma is a lot like prejudice: It is difficult to eradicate when it lies deep in the hearts of people. However, we need to recognize that any so-called protection afforded by labeling the less fortunate is illusory. We too will be less fortunate on occasion. We too will need the support of our friends and colleagues. We too may be shunned. I believe that by honestly examining stigmatization after loss, as is done in the foregoing statements of persons who have experienced this type of pain, we can grow in tolerance, perspective, and recognition of the commonality of our bond in incurring losses. It will take a caring, thoughtful, and feeling person, however, to make this journey of empathy. Too many suffer, and many suffer silently. Recognizing the extent of loss and people's feelings of being stigmatized (everyone from the disabled person to the mentally ill person to the person with AIDS or cancer to the elderly to those perceived to be ugly or fat) requires grand vision and countenance of the condition of our fellow humans. We can, however, acquire a bit of this vision each day by recognizing our ambivalence toward different peoples. We can become more cognizant of the existence of the suffering that goes along with being marked.

We can also address stigmatization through the minds of the persons who feel stigmatized. They, too, need to face the issue head on and recognize what being shunned does to them. Most probably, trying to conceal one's condition will not help one's self-esteem over the long run. Instead, being assertive about the right to make public one's condition and to be respected as a person nonetheless seems essential to healthy coping and accomplishment. Jones et al. (1984) reinforce this point in arguing that confronting others who try to mark us may be an effective strategy for maintaining self-esteem and neutralizing others' degrading observations. The following excerpt from Carole Shaw's *Come Out, Come Out, Wherever You Are* (1982), addressed to people perceived to be overweight, is an example of positive assertiveness:

> *Stand up straight, throw your shoulders back and look the world straight in the eye. Don't be afraid to take up space. You have a perfect right to it.*
> *Nobody!—not your doctor, your lawyer, your spouse, your in-laws—REPEAT, REPEAT—Nobody is entitled to demean you.*

As the many support/activist groups in our society have discovered, the key to rebuffing being marked is to nourish a strong self-concept and to look to others with similar situations for social support. We have countless types of support groups to facilitate people's effective dealing with their special kinds of losses and difficulties in living. These groups say it is OK to have encountered these losses. It is OK to be expressive about them. They do not warrant exile or derision.

DISENFRANCHISED GRIEF

Disenfranchised grief, which is closely related to stigmatization, can be defined as the grief that persons experience when they incur a loss that is not or cannot be openly acknowledged, publicly mourned, or given much social support (Doka, 1989). The Goedken family, suffering from huge losses due to AIDS, must have experienced great disenfranchised grief. In fact, this disenfranchized grief is one of the reasons that three years after the final AIDS death in their family, the daughters of J.J. Goedken told the story of their losses to their friends, college classmates, and the media. They were telling how difficult it had been to bear both the loss of their loved ones and the stigma surrounding the reason for their deaths. J.J.'s daughters were acting as advocates for other victims and victims' families who experience similar stigmatization by their communities. When a high-grief death is treated by people in society as if it were not a significant loss, the process of adjustment is made more difficult for survivors.

As an illustration of disenfranchised grief, a widow wrote to Dear Abby in 1994 about her friends who seemed to be ignoring her loss of her twenty-three-year-old husband nine months earlier. She said that some of her friends avoided her to the point of ducking in the supermarket aisles and then acting as if nothing had happened when they did encounter her. This woman did not understand the tendency of many people to be threatened by death, especially early death. She said that all she wanted was to have her loss acknowledged—just a simple "I'm so sorry." She also pointed out that only other widowed people understood how she felt and took her feelings seriously. She concluded that the best thing anybody (who did not know her husband personally) said to her was, "I was so sorry to read about your husband's death. Would you like to talk about it?"

This woman learned a lot about humans the hard way. Humans frequently are fickle in their friendship when they feel threatened, and nothing is more threatening than death. Support groups serve an invaluable role in providing a forum for others who have experienced similar losses and know what it is like to have friends avoid you in your time of need.

In *A Grief Observed* (1961), C.S. Lewis said about the embarrassment he seemed to cause others because he was "now alone because of death":

> *To some, I'm worse than an embarrassment. I am a death's head. Whenever I meet a happily married pair I can feel them thinking. "One or the other of us must some day be as he is now." (Lewis, 1963, p. 11)*

The avoidance or shunning of associates who have a fatal or disabling illness both stigmatizes them and prevents them from grieving their loss, or possible loss, openly. Like the survivors of persons who die, these individuals sometimes become pariahs. In an article for the *Washington Post*, on May 24, 1990, Victor Cohn discussed what pariahs sometimes experience and how they feel in our society:

> *Those of us who lose a loved one begin to feel as though we have some loathsome, contagious disease. After the Emily Post proprieties—and the*

*flowers, cakes and fruit baskets of the official mourning period—the friends
disappear. . . . Whether we've lost a mother on whose guidance we de-
pended or a lifelong spouse . . . or a child's suicide, the ultimate rejection,
we feel lonely or abandoned. (p. 6B)*

In the article Cohn noted that avoidance by our friends is hardly what we
need when we experience such losses. He suggested that many simply need
the reassurance of continuity with the nongrieving world (although, as I argued at the outset of this book, I think experience will teach us that there is
no nongrieving world!).

Cohn went on to describe a professor of medicine at Vanderbilt University, David Rabin, who in 1980 was dying of Lou Gehrig's disease but
wanted to attend one more European meeting in his field before he died.
His condition was quite serious, but he was able to make the trip. He noted
how people walked past him with eyes averted or called hurried hellos. He
said that nonverbal messages clearly indicated what others thought of him:
that what Susan Sontag has called "the passport of the healthy" had been
revoked. Rabin later wrote an article for a medical journal about his experience of being shunned at the meeting. He received hundreds of letters from
physicians and other people who had had similar experiences. He said that
this flood of support helped him to feel that he was not somehow to blame
for inflicting the sight of his condition on his colleagues. Cohn concluded
his piece with the admonition that all of us should learn how to take responsibility for looking at, talking to, and showing simple acts of support to
colleagues who are suffering the loss of their loved ones or their own grave
conditions. Saying "I didn't know what to say" is easy, but it is a cop-out on
friendship and responsibility—much less on the decency we hope others
will afford us when we are in a similar situation.

TOWARD GREATER RECOGNITION OF THE NECESSITY AND HONORABLENESS OF GRIEVING

Dennis Ryan (1992) wrote a poignant article about underestimated grief:
after his first son's death. In the article, he says that he pulled back at the
time of his son's death and was overwhelmed by his wife's great grief and
his own guilt. He indicates that his wife received an outpouring of support
from mourners. He did not, but he wishes he had. He thinks that the way in
which he was raised by his father, to be a model of strength, undercut his
ability to express his pain. His guilt was due to the fact that his son had been
born at a time when he and his wife were young and struggling financially.
They did not need another mouth to feed. Thus, thinking back to the time of

his son's death, he felt the pang of resenting his son's birth during those struggling years. Furthermore, he felt guilty because he had dismissed his wife's initial concerns about the health of their son. He put her off a day before agreeing to seek medical help. Thus, after the death, Ryan slowly began to recognize the complexity of his feelings of enormous guilt and grief. He concludes his article with the following recommendation of what is needed in educating all of us about death and grief:

> We need to teach people how to be in touch with their feelings of grief and how to express these to others in words. Also, we need to teach them how they can express their grief by acting it out. This area is not only the most creative area but also the one most easily understood. For the acts are often irrational, if not in their design then in the intensity with which they are executed. However, it is the nature of grief to be irrational. This fact needs to be repeated until everyone accepts it and allows it in themselves and others.
>
> If we do this, if we educate people and free them from false judgments about values in relationships, if we empower them to express their grief and to help others to express theirs, then there may no longer be a need to deal with disenfranchised grief. Our goal, then, is a society where all grief may be openly acknowledged and socially supported. (p. 133)

I believe that Ryan's message is well conceived. The main theme of this book has been that each of us will experience many types of losses and grief in the course of our lives. Loss and grief are normal and need not be hidden. As has been argued in the literature on grief work (e.g., Worden, 1982; Parkes and Weiss, 1983; Stroebe and Stroebe, 1987), we need to encourage people through classes, books, support groups, and media presentations to be willing to embark on a number of difficult steps at the time of a major loss, such as the death of a loved one:

1. *Try to accept the reality of the loss and search for meaning by creating an account of the loss and its implications for those who grieve.*
2. *Try to achieve an emotional acceptance of the loss and experience the pain of grief, which will probably require confiding in close others about the deepest feelings of hurt associated with the loss.*
3. *Try to adjust to an environment in which the deceased is missing and regain mastery over one's life. This step may be the hardest because, in many instances, the loss involves one's anchor and closest support. Thus, accommodation to the loss and discovery of a self that is new and capable of making a new life may take time and a lot of sharing with others who have traveled the same road.*
4. *Try to withdraw emotional energy and reinvest it in new relationships. This step goes hand-in-hand with number 3 because it may in-*

volve getting ready to date again and seeking close relationships at an age and time in life when such behavior may seem silly or inappropriate. Even so, it is essential for living fully in the present.

These steps can be taken even while reserving a special memorial place in the mind for the lost loved one and the events and special moments of the relationship. (I address more fully this balancing of living in the now while remembering the past and its meanings in Chapter 12.) As Ryan suggests, steps such as those just outlined can help the bereaved deal with the sense of disenfranchisement as well as stigma—in effect, making grief and movement through the grief an "honorable franchisement of loss, pain, and loving memories."

> *And that is our duty, those of us who must never forget. It is our duty to intervene, always, every time we see a dehumanized human being, no matter what the cause said to justify the cruelty. It is our duty to step up, speak out, stop it, whenever we see it, wherever we find it.*
>
> —Senator John Danforth

9

LOSSES THAT HAUNT

*The war veterans who come to see us will be very moved
and they will have many fine stories to tell you. . . . Those
grandfathers carry in their heart an adventure that haunts
them and which is much greater than that of comic heroes.
They are brave men, and there are not many of those
around.*

—Lower Normandy Regional Council

They are never gone unless you forget them.
—Seventy-four-year-old Widow

Why Jackie's was the face that haunted America
—Headline of Joan Beck's Column
in the *Chicago Tribune*, July 11, 1994

On some occasion, most of us will experience daunting, haunting memories
associated with major losses in our lives. These memories represent a psychological and emotional continuity among humans alive and dead, a continuity
that spans different times and places. Our experience of memories reflects the
power of human bonding and represents a positive memorializing of the lost
other. When these memories began to occur regularly and are not under our
control, however, they may reflect a type of intrusive, haunting bondage to the
deceased that impedes the progress of the bereaved in getting on with life.

To "haunt" means to cause distress or anxiety that occurs or lingers for
some period of time. Most of us have something in our memory that haunts
us. The great literature of every culture always contains some stories of
love-related regret that haunts people. For example, in Hemingway's "The
Snows of Kilimanjaro," the dying man Harry lashes out at his wife, blaming

her for his failure to write the literature he now cannot write. He regrets former wives, their quarrels, and not writing about both. Regret is a common human experience (Landman, 1993), but the topic of this chapter is the haunting regret that a loved one or loved ones died. It is a regret that a loved one could not have lived longer. It is often the regret that critical matters of relating were not settled before the loved one died. As discussed in Chapter 4, parents whose children have died, especially at a young age, often spend a lifetime of dealing with "what might have been" in the lives of their children. The following quotes, taken from Davis's *Empty Cradle, Broken Heart* (1991), are from parents who lost their children early:

> *We think mostly about what he'd look like and what he'd be doing now. Every year when school starts and at Christmas time I think about how old he is, and I've thought that I'll be thinking about that when he would have graduated from high school, that he would have gotten married, maybe gone to college.—Martina (p. 108)*

> *I'll always grieve the "firsts." What would have been the first step, the first word, the first day of school?—Cathryn (p. 108)*

WHAT IS HAUNTING BY MEMORY OF A DECEASED LOVED ONE?

I define haunting after a major loss as memories of a loss that occur unintentionally. These memories may include images of the person who was lost, remembrances of how the death occurred, and thoughts of what it meant or means to the survivor. This haunting occurs intermittently over an extended period and has a significant impact on a person's life. What I am referring to as haunting by one's memory also has been referred to as unintended, involuntary, unconscious, or spontaneous memory (Salaman, 1970; Uleman and Bargh, 1989). At the core of this type of memory is the *individual's sense of little personal control over its occurrence*.

STORIES OF HAUNTING MEMORIES

Shuchter (1986) has reported several instances of people who cannot find reprieve from haunting memories of their loved ones:

> *Harold was haunted by his memories and his sense of Rose's presence. Many times he would think to himself, "Honey, turn me loose." He repeatedly experienced the image where he would be waving goodbye to*

someone who is walking away very slowly. Eventually they get over the horizon but it takes much time. Perhaps they never get over the horizon.

Annette found herself feeling that Frank was looking down at her from a cloud in a place like heaven, observing her behavior on earth. This would happen particularly when she felt that she had been somewhat promiscuous sexually, reflecting her sense of guilt.

Joe considered selling his house but couldn't. He believed that Loretta was still in the house and that he would be abandoning her if he sold it. (p. 124)

In the excerpt that follows, the memories experienced by the individuals were even more haunting because the survivors could recall the suffering the spouse had experienced in dying:

After two years Harold felt continually tortured by memories of Rose. In his unhappiness he would remember how much she enjoyed life and then rue his fate: "It's been months since I've heard laughter or saw anyone enjoy life." . . .

After nineteen months Earl continued to have vivid memories of Rita's suffering, accompanied by his own anguish. "I can't stamp this picture out of my mind—how she suffered. I felt helpless while she was dying. The hardest part is to see an active person deteriorate." All he could do at these times was to look through their picture albums to remember the good times they had together. (Schuchter, 1986, pp. 151–155)

For some survivors haunting memories are derived from the fact that in one fell swoop, reality has been turned upside down: what they love most in life is gone. Consider the behavior and intense grief shown by this young widow, as reported by Serge Kovaleski for the *Washington Post*, March 20, 1994:

In one agonizing ritual after another, Joie White has been trying to hold on to the trappings of a life that was savagely torn apart [in December 1993], when a man who had been confronted by her husband, policeman Jason White, on the steps of a Capitol Hill row house, pumped four bullets into his face. . . . "I wear his clothes more than mine. . . . [Her husband's gold wedding band dangles on her ring finger; she also wears a small reproduction of his badge on another finger.] I will never take any of these off for as long as I live. . . . What I am afraid of is forgetting, forgetting all the wonderful things about Jason." (Kovaleski, 1994, p. B1)

In time, White may put aside this behavioral pattern. Indeed, she may stop trying to create her living environment in such a way that she is always reminded of him. At the time the article was written, however, her clinging to cues of him probably represented an important step for her healing. It may have eased the pain of having to disconnect lives that had been so happily intertwined.

Another type of haunting memory often occurs early in bereavement. It is the "seeing" of, or searching for, the deceased loved one in various situations in which that person might have been seen while alive. Six months after the death of her six-year-old son in a tornado, one woman said:

> *It seems like everywhere I'd go, all I could see was Luke. We went to the beach one day and I could still see him playing in the sand the way he did the last time we were there. (*Dallas Morning News, *1985, p. 57A)*

Shuchter (1986) provides these examples of searchlike behavior:

> *Earl: "A lot of time, if I'm watching the crowds at a football or baseball game, a person looks like her and the crowd is just passing by pretty swiftly, but I know it isn't her . . . it's just a person who looks like her."*
>
> *Beth never saw Barry's remains after the plane crash and had trouble accepting the fact that he was really dead. Six months later she still could not move his things and continued to search for him, anticipating his coming home. "I'd hear the back gate open and I'd think, 'Oh, there he is.' Then I'd catch myself and realize." (p. 119)*

As Schucter notes, haunting memories often occur in dreams and on anniversaries:

> *Over the years since Jeff's death, Agnes recalled dreaming about him every year. Her most recent dream occurred after she had had a fight with her new husband. In it, "Jeff was smiling at me getting out of a car. I was so happy to see him." (p. 161)*

> *The first anniversary of Barry's death was made more painful for Beth because of the media coverage of the plane crash, with vivid pictures on television and daily newspaper articles [depicting] the event. Beth's anniversary reaction started about one month before and built up to the date of the crash. "I had vivid memories of how things were, the last things we did. My feelings were very intense. I couldn't get rid of them." (p. 147)*

In an example of positive recurring memories and the effect of anniversaries on survivors, the January 24, 1993, *Chicago Tribune* ran a story entitled "Timeless Love," reported by Daphne Simpkins. In it, Thelma, a woman interviewed by Simpkins, tells of the love she and her husband Bill felt and of his death sixteen years earlier:

> *If Bill were still alive, we would have just celebrated our 50th wedding anniversary. We were married at Christmastime while he had a short leave [from his service in World War II]. . . . Bill was always surprising me with something. He might forget my birthday, but he would have shown me he loved me a hundred different ways throughout the year. I have only happy memories. . . .*
>
> *A year after Bill died I was in bed sound asleep one night when the silence of my house woke me up. . . . I have a pendulum clock. It would sound on the hour. . . . I got out of bed and when I felt the key, it was tight. The clock just stopped five minutes shy of 1 A.M.— the exact time he had died. I can't explain it. . . . It was July 18th, the anniversary of his death. To the minute."* (Simpkins, 1993, p. 8)

Simpkins goes on to say that it was as if in her sleep, Thelma was waiting for the silence of time to sound the anniversary that meant more to her than anything else in the world and that, in a way that surpasses logic, Thelma and Bill's marriage continues with every anniversary that Thelma tells the story of the night the clock stood still. Simpkins notes that the clock has never been fixed and its hands continue to mark a point in time that Thelma will not forget.

THE QUESTION OF GOOD ADJUSTMENT

There is an ongoing controversy in grief literature concerning the need to break ties between the bereaved and the dead to achieve a good adjustment. For example, Stroebe, Gergen, Gergen, and Stroebe (1992) have interpreted Bowlby's (1979) theory of affectional bonds to suggest that the individual's future well-being depends on the breaking of affective bonds with the deceased spouse or lover. Stroebe et al. note that Bowlby's position is that a short-lived continuation of this bond is appropriate to healthy mourning, but long-term continuation is probably pathological. Peskin (1993) argues that Stroebe et al. misrepresent Bowlby in contending that Bowlby believed ties with the deceased need to be severed after a brief period of mourning. Peskin suggests that Bowlby believed such ties could continue indefinitely without necessarily being problematic for the survivor. Peskin also claims the Stroebe et al. position epitomizes Western mythology, which holds that goal direction, efficiency, and self-reliance require the rupture of emotional attachments with the deceased.

I believe that some presence of the lost loved one will always exist in the survivor's memory, usually at a subconscious level, regardless of how diligently the survivor tries to break the bond. An effective grieving process does not need to eliminate thoughts and feelings of the lost lover. Rather, healing is likely to involve the development of a respect for this presence.

In all probability, each human being has a potential set of circumstances that will trigger at least a trace of haunting memory. Consider the scenario in which two young people have been involved for a few years and are progressing steadily toward marriage. They have made many commitments and plans for the future. They have anticipated much. They have laughed and cried together. They already have learned to overcome adversity together. They have discussed in detail the nature of their future family. Each has relied on the other as a primary anchor for emotional support and principal confidant. Without warning, one of the young people is struck dead. What does the other do to cope? How does the other continue to live?

This scenario has happened many times, and it happened to one of the participants in a study reported by Harvey, Banner, Carlson, and Haig (1995). There can, of course, be variations on this scenario. Suppose, for example, one of the partners leaves the other just before marriage. What will happen to the person who has been left? It would take great psychological strength not to be crushed by either of these events. It also would take an unusual person not to be bound for some long period to the chain of grieving and wondering what might have been. I once knew a woman who wore a large engagement ring, but she had not been engaged for five years. What had happened? She had been jilted at the altar by someone whom she really loved and with whom she expected to spend her life. The ring on her finger was a sign of her psychological state in maintaining an unrequited love; her frequent mention of this long-departed other was a further indication that her "ball and chain" was of immense symbolic weight.

Being haunted by memories of a lost loved one may affect a survivor's daily life as well as his or her perception of personal relationships in the past, present, and future. It may be simply too painful for an individual to immediately acknowledge and accept the death of a close partner. The example of the young police officer's wife reported earlier in the chapter serves to illustrate how some survivors cling to memories of their lost loved one. In this case, the bereaved person maintains a phantom relationship with the deceased, at least for the short term. This behavior, which sometimes includes monologues with the deceased loved one, is a natural part of the healing process. Based on a study of widows and widowers, however, Bowlby (1980) contended that for some bereaved individuals, this type of grieving may go on indefinitely and may be helpful to recovery. He said:

> *In many cases, it seems, the dead spouse is experienced as a companion who accompanies the bereaved everywhere. . . . There is no reason to regard any of these experiences as either unusual or unfavourable, rather the contrary. . . . it seems likely that for many widows and widowers it is precisely because they are willing for their feelings of attachment to the dead spouse to persist that their sense of identity is preserved and they become able to recognize their lives along lines they find meaningful. (pp. 96–100)*

Why do some people seem to be frozen in their grief and unable to adopt a new identity after a major loss? Perhaps one explanation is found in analysis of what relationship resources have been lost to the grieving party. Duck (1994) has indicated that couples need to find and construct meaning in their relationships through daily talks. Wrenching away such talks and the other's presence, nonverbal support, and sharing from a person's life leaves a tremendous void. If there was great closeness and intimacy, there simply is no ready substitute for the grieving person. The character of that grief may be intrusive and pervasive. When grief is of this profound nature, the individual may feel that to try consciously to move beyond the past identity would be tantamount to giving up on his or her personal life.

A derivative of this discussion is that the grieving individual must also release future plans and hopes for interaction with the lost other. Relationships by their very nature are future oriented, and individuals are consistently engaging in exchanges that build toward, or at the very least will affect, the future. In discussing parents' grief when miscarriages occur, Savage (1989) argues that a factor in grief that endures and impairs is the loss of expected future interaction and the memories that would derive from such interaction.

WHEN IS AN INDIVIDUAL MOST VULNERABLE TO HAUNTING?

The idea of haunting memories of a lost loved one implies that the memories have remained immovable over time. The memorial focus often is fixated on the positive qualities of the lost other, the "what ifs" and "what might have beens," and other aspects of our relationships with them. An interesting idea proposed by San Francisco poet Thom Gunn is that just as our relationships with our living colleagues change over time, so do our relationships with loved ones who are dead. Perhaps, though, such change is a marker that the individual does have control over the possible negative haunting character of the memory; in effect, the individual may *choose to effect the changes in his or her mind.* Gunn says:

> *The surprising thing about one's dead is that your relationship with them can change over time. Even after they've been dead for years, you still find*

your feelings about them changing, or growing. And that makes them seem to alter, too. . . . The longer people are dead, the more your relationship with them changes. (Lesser, 1994, p. 39)

Gunn has found that his relationship with his mother, who committed suicide when he was fifteen, has changed over time. Gunn and his brother found her body in the parlor of their home. In recent years, as the result of an accumulation of changes within himself, Gunn has used his poetry to write about her. A 1992 poem entitled "The Gas-Poker" begins as follows and captures a bit of the catharsis he has undergone:

Forty-eight years ago
—Can it be forty-eight
Since then?—They found the
door
Which she had barricaded
With a full bureau's weight
Lest anyone find, as they did,
What she had blocked it for. (p. 39)

Another example of transforming a haunting loss into one that is under the individual's control is found in Krzysztof Kieslowski's movie, *Blue*. Set in France, the plot revolves around a young widow's intense mourning over the deaths of her husband and son in an automobile accident. Her sorrow is so great that she sells all of her possessions and tries to escape to another city where she will be unknown. She lives for a long time with no meaning until, by accident, she discovers that her husband had been having an affair for many years during their marriage. The discovery jolts her out of the shackles of only revering her husband in her memory, and she returns to her former life with purpose and a quest to start over with a new love and new goals.

Thus, one condition for haunting is a significant loss that cannot be transformed in memory into a relationship that changes over time—thus, the memory controls the bereaved person.

Another condition for haunting involves the sudden, unexpected loss of a very close other. When death is expected, the opportunity to *plan to mourn* and to begin the processes of account-making and confiding may mitigate extended, unpleasant, memorial intrusion. Planning to mourn, or anticipatory grief (Rosenblatt, 1983), may be just as important as the actual mourning since it, too, probably conveys a sense of some control over how one deals with his or her impending loss.

Haunting by memory may also be influenced by the environment that the grieving person structures for him or herself. We often hear of survivors who pack up and leave a residence or locale to try to avoid being reminded of their lost loved one. The bereaved person who leaves the lost loved one's room as it was when the loved one died is maintaining reminders of the deceased other. This appears particularly true of parents who leave intact the rooms of their children who have died unexpectedly.

> *Lisbon, Maine—Not much has changed in Jeff Izer's room. Football trophies glisten. Glow-in-the-dark stars cover the ceiling. Scribbled on notebooks are teen-age drawings of hearts with "Angie" written inside. . . .*
>
> *"Jeff was saving up to buy a ring for Angie," said Steve Izer. . . . "I wish we had known her better."*
>
> *Jeff and his girlfriend, Angie Dubuc, both 16, and two of their friends were killed [in October, 1993]. A trucker apparently dozed at the wheel and his 80,000-pound-rig smashed Jeff's disabled Ford. . . .*
>
> *Photos of the dead teens cover walls and the coffee table at the Izer house, where parents and friends of the victims gathered recently with lawmakers for one of the first meetings of PATT—Parents Against Tired Truckers. PATT is determined to get the message out that professional truckers must be held responsible for accidents caused when they nod off behind the wheel because they failed to take required breaks. . . .*
>
> *"This is the way to honor our kids if we can make some changes here," said Jeff's mother Daphne Izer.* (Tulsa World, June 20, 1994, p. 5A)

The crusade against truckers who take risks is the basis for the cues Jeff Izer's parents have chosen to keep salient in their home (in the form of posters and campaign material). Such cues and their campaign may help them fight the haunting reality of the loss of their son.

As I discuss in a later section, unintended negative memories occur quite naturally for some people who have witnessed horrors of great magnitude. Holocaust survivors, war veterans, and survivors of devastating natural disasters represent categories of people who often report that their experiences were so gruesome that they could only try for years to avoid thinking about and discussing them. These survivors pay a price in their minds and bodies for the inability to confide their traumatic experiences to others.

WHY'S OF HAUNTING

> *Grief fills the room up of my absent child,*
> *Lies in his bed, walks up and down with me,*
> *Puts on his pretty looks, repeats his words,*
> *Remembers me of all his gracious parts,*
> *Stuffs out his vacant garments with his form.*
> *—William Shakespeare*

Shakespeare's words poignantly speak to a parent's sense of void and unending grief when his or her child dies. I believe that closeness or the interdependence of the people's lives may affect the nature and magnitude of memory intrusions that continue after a death. I would suggest a very close bonding leads to a high degree of imprinting and a slow fading away of memories. In a study by Harvey et al. (1995), some grieving persons said that practically everything they encountered every day reminded them of their deceased loved ones.

There is also the dynamic (often involving psychoanalytic theory) of why haunting continues over time. Survivors of combat action in war often have wondered, and felt guilt pangs, about why they survived while many of their colleagues were killed. Specific scenes and acts haunt survivors. The research on Normandy veterans' long-term grief, described in Chapter 6, recorded many instances of haunting memories. One World War II veteran admitted he was haunted by the memory of how he had whirled to confront and kill a Japanese soldier who unexpectedly came up behind him. The veteran discovered after killing the Japanese soldier that the soldier was unarmed and carrying a picture of his family—a family very much like the veteran's family. Fifty years later, the veteran said, "That's the sonofabitch that keeps bothering me."

Freud argued that a repetition-compulsion existed for veterans who had been shell-shocked in World War I. He believed that people who are thus traumatized continue to return to the recollections that haunt them, mainly to try to master the memories or to find something in them that absolves them of their pain or guilt. If they cannot, they are rendered a helpless object by the memories.

WHO IS HAUNTED?

We are all haunted to some degree; that is a corollary of the thesis in Chapter 1 that we all grieve. Again, however, some feel the oppression of haunting more than others. What categories of people are most susceptible to haunting memories of their lost loved ones? In a grief study by Harvey et al. (1995), a fifty-eight-year-old woman made this remark about her husband who had died suddenly five years before the interview took place:

> *I have felt extremely vulnerable and alone—even when surrounded by family and friends. On these occasions, the silence has been deafening. I have kept anticipating that he [her late husband] would return. I have often found myself saving things to share with him.*

She indicated an unusual number of instances of continued episodic memories of her husband who had been dead five years.

This woman represents a group of people who appear to be highly vulnerable to being haunted by memories of their lost other and thus hindered from making significant changes in their lives. In their study of bereavement during the first year, Glick, Weiss, and Parkes (1974) report that widows and widowers in their midlife (forties and fifties) who lose their significant others unexpectedly, exhibit a greater degree of anxiety, self-reproach, and depression than other groups of mourners who are older and who had time to prepare for the loss of their significant others.

Glick, Weiss, and Parkes also report that parents who lose adult children in sudden traumatic ways, such as traffic fatalities, have significantly more problems than parents who lose children to chronic illnesses, such as cancer. Whether or not death comes suddenly, however, the loss of a child is a high-grief type of loss. It usually has many long-term impacts on parents, including depression and bouts of anger and self-blame. Writers appear to be particularly susceptible to long-term haunting memories, which, to some degree, they may seek to lessen through their writing. David Morrell's *Fireflies* (1988) and David Ray's *Sam's Book* (1968) tell stories of their children's battles against terminal illnesses and how the loss of their children still affects them *daily* after many years of grieving. In part, these writers offer their accounts as a way of achieving further healing. Morrell indicated that for seven years after his son's death, one of his first thoughts on awakening each morning was about his deceased son. He has said that he believes these thoughts indicate that he has a deep emotional void in his life that will not soon be filled or easily accepted.

Whether the death of the child occurs quickly or is more drawn out, a parent's capacity for working on the meaning of what has happened and confiding to close others may be reduced by the sheer emotional burden of the loss or impending loss. David Morrell (1988) notes that the start of his recovery, which involved account-making and confiding to others through his book, *Fireflies*, did not commence until about a year after his son's death.

It is likely that parents who lose children encounter some of the most regular and haunting unexpected memories of their deceased children. Many of us assume that we will bear and raise children. We expect that we will die before they die. A child's death always is out of season for parents. It leaves a void that cannot readily be filled by anything, even by other children.

I have a friend who, now in her eighties, has written to me for almost twenty years every Christmas about her son who was killed while in graduate school. She always comments that her fine young son would be such and such age now and writes about what he *might* have accomplished in his life and career. It is a lonely vigil for a parent whose child has died because the deceased person's friends and acquaintances may only infrequently remember him or her. It is, however, a vigil that the parent may choose to carry on and that is perceived by others to be honorable and dignified. Reminding others of the positive nature and accomplishments of the deceased person is a continuing tribute to that person. Such reminders also may be motivated by a desire to persuade others that some deaths do not have to occur (e.g., as in the case of a person killed by a drunken driver).

Research and clinical case work suggests that young children are most vulnerable to haunting memories. Based on a review of the grief literature and their own clinical work, Volkan and Zintl (1993) argue that until a child has completed adolescence, a parent's death is, by definition, full of unfinished business. During adolescence, the individual often reviews his or her childhood relationships with parents and family and frequently rebels against or relaxes emotional investment in them. This rebellion or curtailing of investment is a natural breaking away and beginning of the formation of allegiance with the larger world. An early adolescent or young child who loses a parent or parents probably will not have completed this separation and thus may be particularly affected by the death. These young persons may be so paralyzed by the loss that they do not actively pursue account-making and confiding for many years—perhaps until midlife when people often try to go back and finish the business of their relations with their parents that is impeding their fulfillment.

Another group of people whom I believe are highly vulnerable to haunting are those who have had a series of major losses in a short time and have not recovered from one or more of the losses when a powerful new loss occurs. The maxim, "When it rains, it pours" applies well to the emotional erosion experienced by people who are hit by multiple losses. In the recent study of grief by Harvey et al. (1995), one respondent had a twenty-four-year-old brother die unexpectedly, a close romantic relationship terminate, and a business partnership dissolve within six-months. She withdrew from all people in what she described as the lowest point of her life; she began to recover many months later when she suddenly realized that there were reasons to continue living and that she still had a support system.

The person who has suffered multiple losses may have made some progress in dealing with one loss when along comes another and dashes that progress. This pileup of loss may destroy storytelling and confiding activities, or even the will to engage in them, and leaves the individual in a psychologically and physically bleak emotional desert for a substantial period. How one finally crawls out of this desert is a question for both researchers and counselors.

Finally, because of the horror of their losses, avoidance may be the only way some people feel they can cope with the losses. It has been suggested that some Holocaust survivors have been unable to use storytelling, emotional venting, and confiding for many, many years because of the horror and enormity of their losses. Langer (1991) provides telling examples of this type of reaction by survivors. For some, avoidance appears to be effective, at least in the short run, since the magnitude of work needed to mourn their losses effectively is beyond comprehension for most people.

There are many stories of haunted memory by survivors of war. Perhaps none surpasses that of the few survivors of Oradour-sur-Glane, France. In 1944, Nazi SS soldiers rounded up the 652 men, women, and children who made up the population of this village and killed 642 of them. They were killed apparently in revenge for D day and the fact that the French Resistance operated in this general region of southwest France, about three hours from Paris. The killings were systematic and brutal. The villagers were led to believe that they were being held temporarily while the Nazis searched the town for weapons. The men were driven into barns and shot. The women and children were herded into the town church, which was then set on fire. Persons trying to escape were shot down with machine guns. Only ten in the village managed to escape. The Nazis also destroyed most of the dwellings of the village.

For years after the war, the survivors and their children did not discuss the massacre. Their haunting memories have been preserved by the ruins of the town, which have been left alone since 1944. According to the mayor of the town, which has been rebuilt adjacent to the old village, these ruins have been kept as a living reminder of how savage and brutal humans can be toward one another.

CONTENTS OF UNINTENDED MEMORIES

There is little evidence about the contents of recurring, unexpected memories. Emily Dee (1990) interviewed emergency medical personnel who dealt with injured and dead persons after the crash of a United Airlines jet in Sioux City, Iowa, in 1989 that killed 111 of 296 people on board. Almost one year after his experience, a young medic provided this commentary for Dee on the memories that had stuck in his mind:

> *What I can remember is people's eyes, and what I saw in their eyes. There was so much fear. There was so much pain. When I connected with their eyes, it was awful. That's the thing that just rips my soul out now, their eyes. . . . Oh my God I keep seeing those eyes looking at me. The people keep looking pleadingly to the rescue workers because we were their only hope at that point. (pp. 102–103)*

A doctor had memories of parts of bodies:

> *I can see parts of bodies everywhere. . . . There is a lady, still strapped into her seat, with her arm on the armrest and her hand hanging down at the*

end. Her fingernails were manicured and her watch was still on her arm.
. . . I continue to imagine her as having a beautiful face and hair fixed just
right before she got on the plane. (p. 114)

Based on our study and informal reports, we suggest that the content of
survivors' memories may lean heavily toward images of the deceased person's face and his or her expressions. Smiles, tones of voice, how it felt to
be touched by the deceased other, and particular verbal expressions may
also be prominent. People who have experienced the dissolution of close relationships report memories of entire episodes such as their first sexual experience, their wedding, a major event such as the birth of a child, warm
feelings associated with celebrations and travels, and major fights, separa-
tions, or breakups (Harvey, Flanary, and Morgan, 1986).

CAN WE TRANSCEND MEMORIES
THAT HAUNT?

We can never completely "get over" a major loss in the sense that all its
effects are negated, that is "forgotten." Our losses become part of who
we are, as precious to us as other aspects of ourselves, and so does the
transcendence of those losses.
—Patricia Weenolsen

A major loss may change us irrevocably and then, if transcended, become an
event that serves as a positive turning point because we learn to confront the
loss cognitively and emotionally and to talk about it. It may make us more
able to cope with other major losses that will come our way. It may humble
us, and that is a critical condition for much human accomplishment. It may
make us stronger and able to give back to others who suffer similar plights
(similar to what Erikson [1963] referred to as "generativity," giving to other
future generations based on one's own experience).

I believe that the approach that involves survivors' moving to the point
at which they can confront a loss directly and not avoid it or distract themselves from coming to grips with it is the best way of coping. We can transcend haunting memories through the development of stories about the
events and confiding parts of our stories to close others. As has been shown
in related work, confrontation helps people move through a sequence of
healing steps, while long-term avoidance or distraction does not help them
(Pennebaker, 1990). The point at which survivors are ready to confront a
loss probably is highly idiosyncratic to each bereaved person, and there
probably is no linear path to map it.

I now present excerpts from the accounts of two survivors who were interviewed in a recent study (see Harvey et al., 1995) of how people cope

with major loss due to the death of close others. The individuals described to interviewers how they had tried to adjust to their losses. Each reported a period of significant intrusion of thoughts and feelings about their lost other and how they found peace with the memories or were beginning to arrive at a point at which the memories no longer exacted a significant toll on their lives. Each individual was trying diligently to find meaning in the loss and, thereby, to transcend it. Each also was engaged in the act of confiding during the interview. The comments of these survivors also help us to understand why thought suppression (through concentration on something else) may be a common approach to dealing with intrusion. Wegner and Schneider (1989) believe that, in the long run, thought suppression is not effective in dealing with memory intrusion after major loss. They advocate that people "stop stopping" their thinking about their loss until completion or resolution and emotional venting have occurred.

[From a woman, age sixty-three, who lost her husband to an unexpected heart attack, while on vacation, four years previous to the interview] I was *absolutely devastated by his death. We had been married 42 years and were very close to one another. I couldn't eat or sleep or function normally for a long time. I dwelt on him and what it meant to lose him. . . . I finally de-cided that* I had to help myself. . . . *I went to a very good grief recovery support group and later became an outreach volunteer working with the newly widowed. . . . You have your precious memories but you have to talk, talk, talk about it and do things for yourself like changing the bedroom around. . . . I talk openly about our former life with my children, friends, and new husband. I often go to the cemetery. I highly recommend getting into a grief support group. You have to work through your grief, and you learn a lot by listening to others. . . . Life goes on. You're here such a short time.* Live and enjoy family and friends.

[From a twenty-one-year-old junior in college who three months previously had lost her boyfriend of five years, a nationally recognized college basketball player, in a traffic accident in which the young woman also was involved] I think about him every minute of every day. I ask myself what he would want me to do. He would want me to be strong. He hated it when I was a "wimp." We had been best friends since high school. We did everything together. . . . I'm getting a little bit better . . . because I have kept busy doing my school work [having reduced the term load from seventeen to nine hours] and my work in the sports information office. . . . His team-mates and coaches have been great to me. They talk to me and give me pic-tures and momentos of him. I have his pictures up all over my room. Before, I didn't have any pictures of him on my walls. I often listen to tapes I made for him and watch a video a friend made of the newscasts of the ac-

cident and media interviews with me. This video helps bring me back to re-
ality because I still haven't accepted that he is gone. . . . He went on bas-
ketball trips all the time and in the summers and I got used to waiting on
him to return. . . . But now I'm trying to accept that he won't return. . . .
Some of my close friends have disappointed me. They should be able to see
that I want to talk about him and how I feel. . . . They seem afraid to lis-
ten. . . . For that reason, I like to be with his family because they are strug-
gling too and show their emotions frequently. . . . I'm trying to get on with
my life. . . . But around here all of his friends and even the whole state
thought they knew him, it is hard to move on. . . . It is as if I should always
be grieving. . . . I've talked to men who have indicated that they would find
it difficult to be in a relationship with me because I was his girlfriend and
am having such a hard time. . . . I look forward to going away to work this
summer because people there will know me as myself and not mainly as his
girlfriend, with all those stares and whispers. . . . I've thought a lot about
what I lost when he died—it was our plans. *We planned to marry next*
year and immediately begin a family. I can't believe that so short a time ago
I was planning to start a family soon. I lost everything because we were
not married. . . . If we had been married, at least I could have said that I
was his wife. . . . I've learned that I can be strong when I have to be and to
try to give time to my friends and family because you never know how
long you'll have with them. . . . (Harvey et al., 1995)

This young woman was interviewed again almost six months after the
initial interview to see how she was coming in her grief. She had become a
senior in college and was twenty-two at the time of the second interview:

It's harder now than in the spring because it has sunk in. Before my friends
tried to keep me busy. Now, they are gone. I cry a lot and am depressed. I often
cannot sleep until early in the morning. I call people just to have someone to
talk to about nothing. . . . I've not been going to classes regularly and have fallen
behind in some of them. . . . This summer I wrote letters to him [her late
boyfriend] about my experiences in my new job back East. At my job this sum-
mer, I met someone and began to date him. I told him about my story on our
first date, and he was real understanding. He fell "head over heels" for me. It
was a high. When I got back to school, we planned to visit regularly. I went back
last week and I didn't feel anything. It's too soon to have those feelings again.
There is no rush. I don't want to get upset by discovering that there is no one
like him [her late boyfriend]. . . . I just want to be friends with men now. . . . I
have an acting class and for an assignment, I acted the part of myself speaking
to him at his grave. The class was in tears, but I wasn't moved. I talk to him [her
late boyfriend] more now when I am by myself, but I can't bring myself to go
to the cemetery. . . . I considered lots of options about two weeks ago, when I was

particularly depressed. I even considered suicide, but he would not want me to join him like that. He wants me to be strong. I feel like he is always there with me in the decisions I make. . . . This time last year, I knew exactly what I'd be doing in the future. Now, I don't know. I would like to leave here [the state where she now lives] when I graduate. I want to be away from here—I have so many memories. . . . I have to go on with life, and try to find happiness. Our sixth anniversary is coming up as is Thanksgiving and Christmas. I am not looking forward to them. It's going to be tough. . . . If I had any advice to give others based on my experiences, it would be to be a lot more open to others' feelings. Try hard not to forget people who may need you to be there for them. You can lose those whom you love so quickly. (Harvey et al., 1995)

A final commentary comes in the form of a poem from a close friend of the graduate student whose mother continues to write to me of her grief over his untimely death. The poem was written soon after his death and reflects the friend's images of the young man. This poem helped both the writer and the young man's mother in their grief:

With love to David to light forever
Hair flowing free
Red to rust
Gentle face, smiles I'll miss
Reaching for the Sun
Swimming in the Wind
A speck like we younger
Green, Brown and Blue of the World
Seeing, clearer, touching, sensing . . .
Knocking on Doors opened painfully
We see bright skies and streams
Cascading from above
Interlocking into his eyes
Looking into a gentle Son
Our Brother, Us, You, We die too
on to Peace.

—Written for Ms. Venita Kelley, mother
of David, by one of David's close friends

These excerpts suggest the difficulty of accomplishing any complete liberation from unintended memories of a lost other. They reveal in people's own words the importance of developing a story that attributes meaning to what happened and having someone to whom the story can be confided on a regular basis. They also reveal the tenacity of spirit that is necessary to properly memorialize our departed loved ones, while at the same time live our current and future lives to the fullest. These survivors help us understand how we owe it to our departed loved ones to go on with life and have other close relationships that we cherish and nourish. As the older respondents in our grief study suggested, it is crucial that new companions be willing to recognize and accord significance to the past losses that each has experienced. A type of graciousness in dealing with loss seems required. New companions or lovers should be able to tell their stories of lost love freely, and in so doing, become better able to nurture and understand one another. A final point of this chapter is that after great loss, peace will not be found without a struggle of the mind and heart. But with such a struggle, we can revise the phrase "haunted by their memories" to "embracing gently their memories."

10

LOSSES RESULTING FROM NATURAL DISASTER: A STUDY OF STORYTELLING*

What people need to realize is that these losses are very similar to the death of a close family member.
—Director of a Family Resource Center

This chapter is unlike others in the book in that it represents a study of account narratives provided by people in the midst of major loss. The chapter provides further evidence of the value of a theoretical and methodological approach to how people deal with significant stressors that emphasize stories. The stories to be told are of not only pain, devastation, despair but also hope, resiliency, and growth.

In the early summer of 1993, the entire midwestern region of the United States received an unprecedented amount of rain over a period of approximately eight to ten weeks. The frequency and amount of rain resulted in the flooding of the Mississippi River, especially in Illinois, Iowa, and Missouri, and the flooding of tributaries of the Mississippi River, including major rivers such as the Iowa, Des Moines, and Cedar. Several large reservoirs could not contain the influx of water, and U.S. Army Corps of Engineers officials had to release water on downstream locations, creating further significant flooding. The losses associated with this flooding were on the order of sixty deaths and billions of dollars of property. Losses of homes and pos-

---

*This chapter was co-authored by Shelley K. Stein of Ball State University and Nils Olsen of the University of North Carolina at Chapel Hill.

sessions including automobiles, outside buildings, crops, pets, and farm animals, were common in the regions most affected by the floods.

This tally of losses does not begin to summarize all that flood victims lost. Less quantifiable losses include plans for the summer; holidays that were used to fight floods and clean up; health (including nonfatal heart attacks and strokes), especially in older persons who exerted great physical and psychological effort worrying about and fighting the flood waters; travel throughout the region, which also affected commerce; and an unknown amount of tourism.

Our research focused on the psychological effects associated with major losses due to the floods. We operationally defined *major loss* as that which involved property loss of at least $10,000, although all of the forty-five people who provided narratives experienced far greater financial loss than this figure. Our theoretical approach in studying survivors' coping responses was guided by Harvey, Orbuch, and Weber's (1990) model of the roles of account-making and confiding in response to severe stressors. As described in Chapter 2, this model suggests that people who encounter major stressors, such as the death of a close other, experience a number of early reactions such as psychic numbing, outcry, and denial but then may begin to adapt by developing a story or account of their loss, why they think it happened, what it means to them, and communicating parts of that story to close others in acts of confiding. The model proposes that account-making and confiding facilitate recovery, whereas the failure to engage in such activities may eventually lead to various negative physical and psychological consequences. While there are many other models of how people deal with major stressors, the account-making and confiding model is one of the few that explicitly emphasizes the narrative activity of the survivor. The research literature on trauma contains very little information in the form of direct narrative accounts by survivors. While in the area of interpersonal relations, Berscheid (1994) has addressed the promise of research on narrative accounts, she has also noted the relative scarcity of research in which actual narratives are collected.

The most extensive literature on flooding and its psychological effects stems from investigations of the 1972 Buffalo Creek, West Virginia, flood disaster. This flood was caused by the creation of a slag dam from coal waste deposited in the Buffalo Creek by a local coal company. The water broke through the dam after several days of rain, inundating the valley area below and creating instant chaotic destruction in several mining hamlets in the valley. One hundred twenty-five people were killed, and 5,000 were left homeless within a few hours. This disaster was particularly traumatic for survivors because it was so devastating, occurred so quickly, and involved survivors' observing people and animals (both alive and dead) among the debris being swept down the valley by the floodwater.

Titchener and Kapp (1976) and Gleser, Green, and Winget (1981) reported high levels of symptomatology and impairment, including anxiety, depression, confused-disorganized thinking, and difficulty in controlling emotions, in the survivors of the Buffalo Creek flood. Grief over the loss of relatives, friends, possessions, and momentos such as family Bibles was widespread. Further, for a period after the disaster, many survivors showed heightened vigilance, anger, isolation, hopelessness, inability to concentrate and work effectively, and survivor guilt—classic PTSD symptoms. In a follow-up investigation, Green et al. (1990) found that relative to a group of comparison people living on a nearby river that was also flooded, Buffalo Creek survivors continued to show major depression, generalized anxiety disorder, and PTSD symptoms.

Highly related to our focus on people's storytelling and confiding is Lifton and Olson's (1976) analysis of the narrative themes emerging from reports by Buffalo Creek survivors. Lifton and Olson embraced a psychodynamic perspective in analyzing survivors' narratives. They found a strong "death imprint" and ongoing fear of rain in survivors' reactions soon after the flood. One family reported this fear two years later: "When it rained hard last week it was like the past came out again. I took the family down to the cellar and I just know the whole flood is going to come back" (p. 2).

Fear of crowds (which was associated with disaster images and thoughts of who will or will not survive), terrifying dreams, death guilt (i.e., guilt that they survived while many around them died), psychic numbing, anger toward mining officials involved in the buildup of the dam, and lasting despair also were found by Lifton and Olson. The following account illustrates some of the despair they noted:

> There's the life you lived before and the life you live after. Before the disaster it seemed like you go up and you looked forward: there was something I was going ahead to—to garden, the horses, the job. The garden is gone; there are trailers where the horses were; there are no jobs left. (p. 13)

Unlike the present work, investigators of the Buffalo Creek disaster neither provided evidence about how these flood survivors ultimately coped with their losses nor emphasized family functioning during the crisis. A further difference is that all of the published work about Buffalo Creek of which we are aware involved survivor-respondents who also were litigants in a class action suit against the coal company whose negligence led to the dam and eventual flood.

There is a great deal of evidence available in trauma and disaster literature that is relevant to the present study of PTSD-type symptoms associated with various types of natural disasters. For example, Nolen-Hoeksema and Morrow (1991) reported that college students suffered elevated depression reactions and other stress symptoms for some time after the 1989 Loma Prieta earthquake in California. Freedy et al. (1994) found similar distress reactions in the survivors of the 1991 Sierra Madre earthquake in Los Angeles county.

For this extensive literature on the psychological effects of natural disasters, the present study is unique. In terms of the nature of the event and magnitude of losses, the 1993 Midwest floods appear to be comparable to the Buffalo Creek flooding disaster, which we refer to in the discussion of our results.

Our working hypothesis was that narratives of people who had adapted well to the flooding situation would emphasize the roles of private reflection or account-making, talk and confiding with close others, and the social support of families and communities as factors in adjustment. By "adapted well," we meant that the narratives of these survivors would indicate that they had accepted their losses and were beginning to take constructive steps toward restoring parts of their lives that were affected. As we discovered during the study, "adapted well" also meant that survivors had bonded with close others in their families and communities and gained greater respect for one another as a consequence of the experience. We also were interested in whether the narratives from this sample would report the severe trauma found by Lifton and Olson in the narratives of the Buffalo Creek survivors. Because of the extensive loss of property, it seemed possible that they would be similar to some degree.

METHOD

Between one and four months after the peak flooding, we contacted by phone residents in areas that were hard hit by flooding, asking them to participate in a study of their reactions to the flooding. Media reports and information provided by persons involved in the flood relief in each community were used to select those who were contacted. In the phone contact, respondents indicated their willingness to provide written summaries of the events they experienced, family interactions during those times of stress, the consequences of the flooding for them and their families, and how they thought and felt about the flooding then and now. Respondents were solicited from Illinois, Iowa, and Missouri and were paid $25 for participating.

An attempt was made to sample across socioeconomic groupings, age, and gender. The average age for participants was 47.5 years. The average education was fourteen years. Occupations included farmers, small business owners and workers, homemakers, and manufacturing and retail employees.

The sample included forty-five people (thirty women and fifteen men) all of whom had experienced major loss (beyond $10,000). Respondents were screened to make sure that they met the criterion of serious loss, and many had experienced losses (e.g., homes, crops, possessions, work) far beyond this level. All respondents who provided narratives filled out an open-ended questionnaire addressing these points. They were invited to write as much as possible about how the flooding affected them and their loved ones and how they reacted to it. All questionnaires were handled by mail.

RESULTS

Two members of the research team served as coders and developed theme categories for the narrative reports. Three major theme categories are included in this report: (I) general reactions reflecting how severely people's lives were affected, with emphasis on loss of control, despair, and helplessness; (II) reactions reflecting loss and negative coping; and (III) reactions reflecting resiliency and positive coping, including direct statements about reflection, story development, and account-making activity and about confiding and supportive social activities in families and communities. Within each of these theme categories, subcategories pertaining to extent of loss, personal reactions (e.g., reflection and prayer), and family and community interaction (e.g., confiding, physical labor in cleaning up after the flood) are identified. Table 10-1 provides the excerpted narrative accounts.

In terms of number of respondents emphasizing certain coping reactions in their narratives, twenty-five emphasized a loss and pessimism pattern. These narratives sometimes mirror the reports of survivors in the Buffalo Creek studies. Twenty of the respondents emphasized strength and optimism. These strength-oriented narratives reveal the value of personal reflection, confiding, and social support from family, friends, and community organizations of volunteers.

One major point that is highlighted in these narratives is that many people who felt their marriages/close relationships had major problems before the flooding reported that the stress of the flooding had caused even more problems in their marriages. In contrast, several people who felt that their marriages/close relationships were in good shape before the flooding reported that they had been strengthened as a consequence of the flooding. These latter couples reported that they worked well together to face the adversity of the flooding and the resultant losses. The tangible implementation of friendship or its betrayal in time of need also occupies center stage in the respondents' commentaries. One of the most remarkable commentaries is by respondent C, section III (Table 10-1). She indicated that, despite her

TABLE 10-1   Excerpts from Narrative Reports

Account Themes

I. General Reactions

A. Man, age fifty-three, farmer and small businessperson, married with two children; home destroyed

On Sense of Helplessness: "I think a very important emotion many of us felt was that there was nothing you could do to stop this destruction. This was very hard to deal with. All of us have lived here most of our lives, always worked and made a living. But this flooding left us powerless."

B. Man, age thirty-nine, small businessperson, married; lost crops, money, and possessions

On Loss of Control: "I felt like the mouse in a glass cage with a snake. I know the snake is there and I know he will get me. I had no direct control over what happened to my life and that of my family."

C. Woman, age forty, homemaker, married with three children; lost home and many possessions

On the Loss of Pride in Not Being in Control of Her Life: "All of our lives, my husband and I have paid our bills and taken care of ourselves. I guess a loss of pride is what hurt us the most. We felt so needy. People I work with gave us money, clothing, everything we have now. People we don't even know gave us money. To be homeless! We didn't have a place to live. We now live in a [FEMA] trailer because we had no place to go and no money. But all this did make us realize that if we can live together homeless, then we can make it through anything."

D. Woman, age forty-five, works at convenience store, married with three children, lost most of home furnishings

On Psychological Difficulties Faced by Families: "I blame myself for not being able to protect my family. . . . My husband and I both experienced periods of blaming someone [the government] and feeling thankful that we are alive. We went through the range of emotions every time the flooding started. It was hard to sit and watch my family. At times, my husband was very depressed and angry because he couldn't stop it from coming back again and again. We just went through the motions all summer. You work night and day to clean up the mess and our house starts to dry out . Then here it comes again. It's awful to watch your life's work just float away."

II. Reactions Emphasizing Loss

A. Woman, age twenty-five, homemaker, married with five children

On Losses: "At times, we were imprisoned in our own home when the water began to rise. We had damage to my home, yard, and possessions. We had water standing around 2½ feet around my home up to the foundation for several months [flooding over three to four months with constant standing water during that time]. . . . We lived in our home for four months without plumbing or drinking water and sometimes without electricity. All of the Christmas things and children's toys were damaged and had to be destroyed."

Continued

TABLE 10-1 *(continued)*

On Personal Relationship Disappointments and Family Effects: "I am 5'9" and weighed 125 pounds before the flood. During and after the flood, I lost 9 pounds. I had to seek medical treatment from my doctor for stress. . . . I had problems with vomiting, loss of appetite, headaches, sleeping, and anxiety—something I've never experienced before.

"I lost faith in my husband and family members. My husband is a long-distance truck driver. He was never home during the floods. I was always left alone with the five children. I had to carry the kids on my back through the floodwater to safety. I had no help from my family—ten brothers and sisters (eight of them living close by). I would call for them to help me move our belongings, pets, and vehicles and with the kids. No one would help. My husband would come home from the road. He would go over everything that was not done right. . . . . I was to blame because the water got into the house.

"My husband is not an understanding person. I can't really share what I feel with him. . . . He always makes me feel weak when we discuss things that have to do with the floods. . . . [Now] I don't expect anything from anyone but myself. *People don't realize what the flood has done to people emotionally* [emphasis added]. . . . I know now not to waste time on the telephone looking for help. My children [all less than twelve years of age] and I did everything on our own. My children are my first priorities. . . . The experience made them mature a lot faster.

"I blame and have less feeling for my husband who could have been there and chose not to be. I blame my family members who could have been supportive and who didn't seem to care."

B. Man, age fifty-four, works at large company as a spray painter, married, with one son

On Losses: "We lost everything—home, all appliances, carpets, furnace, water heater, three beds, three dressers, three night stands, truck, mowers, tools and shop. . . . Everything in the house was ruined by four feet of standing water. . . . It would be easier to list what we saved.

"I took a three-month leave of absence from my employer and lost approximately $15,000 in wages. Before I took a leave, I had arguments at work. My left arm went numb. I had blood pressure of 170/96 and felt terrible. I went into the hospital for one day. I also farm 32 acres and never even got into the field in 1993."

On Personal and Relationship Effects: "I blame myself. I never thought the water would get so high. I feel helpless. I had planned on retiring in a couple of years. Now that's impossible. We fought the flood for four months—until the day we moved out in a boat. . . . *I felt like the mouse in a glass cage with a snake. I know he is there and I know he will get me* [emphasis added]. I now drink nearly every day. I don't even go into my garage and tool area [that was damaged seriously] unless I have to. . . . At first, my wife and I were closer, but now we're not. She says I block her out. I don't mean to. I talk with a friend [who had experienced floods before] which helps, but I can't talk to her about it and am becoming more distant."

C. Potpourri of narrative comments emphasizing letdowns by friends, family members, and significant others.

Woman, age sixty-four, unemployed, unmarried, lost major possessions due to the floods: "I drink nearly every day. I don't even go into my garage [where her car and

TABLE 10-1 *(continued)*

various possessions were destroyed by the water] unless I have to. I felt total help-lessness. It's hard to sit and watch all that you have worked for ruined almost overnight."

Man, age thirty-five, married: "It has changed my relationship with my spouse. We are constantly fighting and thinking of separating. Some of my relatives and friends who were hit hard also have gotten divorces."

Woman, age fifty-three, married, homemaker: "Friends who you have loved and trusted turn out to be selfish and self-serving. I'm very insecure. John and I have grown apart. All we do is yell at each other and show little affection."

Woman, age thirty-eight, married, farmer: "I sorted my friends about as fast as I had to sort my things in the flooding. Those you thought were friends didn't want to hear about our troubles. I now have no time for superficial friendships. When one refused to look at our pictures of destruction or go down and see what our base-ment had become, I realized what a shallow friend he was and vowed never to speak to him again. I feel really emotional about everyone who hurts and cry often. My life is so much less than what it used to be."

Woman, age thirty-six, sign language interpreter, has cohabitating male lover, in-curred major health problems (serious increase in blood pressure, both she and housemate experienced rash and allergic reactions to standing water in home): "Richard was temporarily insane—cussing God for the flooding. Later, he changed to cussing the Corps of Engineers. We were living in a friend's trailer that should have been destroyed in the 1940s. *I thought about killing him* [Richard, emphasis added]. He was totally stressed and in denial. We are constantly fighting. The floods caused dangerous tensions in our house and undue stress. . . . I turned to friends for support, and you definitely found out who was a friend and who wasn't."

Woman, age thirty-nine, domestic labor, divorced, one son: "I lost my home and the flooding caused such stress between my boyfriend and me that we separated. We now live separately. *It hurts that I lost so much and makes me mad because I couldn't stop it from happening. I can't get it back either"* [emphasis added].

Woman, age sixty-four, retired, married, oldest son age twenty-eight at home: "My security and love of living are gone. I never have drunk and smoked as much as I do now. Our son didn't do anything to help us save our things or clean up. He sat and watched TV. I can't understand why. It hurt me a lot. My husband didn't do much more. I feel I can't rely on them if this ever happens again."

III. Reactions Emphasizing Resiliency

A. Woman, age forty-seven, two children, married, farmer, emphasizes diary work and prayer

On Losses: "Because of the flood, we lost 85 percent of our crops and had to liqui-date our entire hog operation. We lost our security for the future."

On Personal Journal and Prayer Activity and Family Support: "We had to move out of our home for three months and live with my husband's parents. It caused some strain, especially for my teenagers. But after several weeks, we all learned how to get along. While I have lost faith in our government (that said they would help but never did), I have gained faith in God, my family, and my friends. Our friends came

Continued

TABLE 10-1 *(continued)*

and helped whenever we needed it. *They were wonderful! I coped by praying a lot and starting a journal during the flooding* [emphasis added]. I also tried to find some time alone to unwind and think. I have thought a lot about the flood situation and what it has meant to our family. My husband and I talked and shared all the time. Also my parents, although 100 miles away, have been very supportive."

B. Man, age sixty-one, married, in sales, owns small business, emphasizes confiding, faith, and support of good friends

On Losses: "Could not operate business during summer. Thousands of dollars in income. Lost some of home property. Couldn't travel in town because of the water that covered roads and prevented access to businesses."

On Personal Account-Making and Family/Community Support: "I thought a lot, talked a lot to close friends to 'get it off my chest,' and looked to the future with optimism. It's great to have good listeners! Our faith in people was strengthened. Friends, relatives, church friends all pitched in to help. I have so much thankfulness toward so many other people. I tried to show appreciation by taking many out to dinner and to encourage them in helping others."

C. Woman, age forty-seven, farmer and insurance agent, married, indicated strong close relationships and community support

On Losses: "Home was completely destroyed, as were 600 acres of crops. . . . ½ foot of water in business office for weeks. . . . Mother was having health problems before the flood, but fighting back. When it continued to flood, she had to go to a nursing home and gave up. She could no longer stand by herself."

On Talking and Relationship Bonding: "Always had a strong relationship with husband that got stronger. We talked a lot. I have made new friends by meeting many wonderful volunteers who have come to help. *We have coped also by helping others less fortunate than we are* [emphasis added]."

D. Woman, age forty-three, homemaker and small businessperson

On Changed Priorities Based on Help From and Bonding of Community Members: "When you have men and women go down in a slimy, muddy, smelly, mosquito-infested basement and carry out the slimy mess and look happy while they are doing it, you realize you have been missing something in your life. Yes, my priorities and values have changed. Material things mean a lot less now."

E. Potpourri of narrative comments on personal coping, family, and community experiences emphasizing strengths in these areas

Woman, age seventy-six, married, farmer: "When we sent a supply truck to Georgia [to help with the flooding occurring there in the summer of 1994], that was the point when I realized I could finally move on. . . . I know how the people in Georgia feel and realize how much we appreciated it when volunteers and outsiders came here to help. Now, we *can* help them."

TABLE 10-1 *(continued)*

Man, age sixty, married, cloth cutter: "We [he and his wife] still love one another very much, and our real friends are standing by us. I think I have learned not to take everything for granted anymore."

Man, age eighty-two, married, retired: "The flood renewed my faith in mankind [by meeting so many volunteer helpers]. Despite our losses [which included their home], we are healthy and happy. We are almost finished rebuilding—life is beautiful!"

family's serious losses, she and her husband coped with the help of regular confiding, the assistance of friends and volunteers, and helping other people less fortunate than themselves.

THE SPECIAL CASE OF HULL, ILLINOIS

Surprisingly, all of the respondents from one community in our sample indicated in their narratives that the town had bonded together and citizens had helped one another during the period of major flooding. Seventeen adult female and male survivors from Hull, Illinois (a small town of about 500 people bordering the Mississippi River and across from Hannibal, Missouri), showed considerable optimism in most of their narrative accounts. To gain more perspective on why respondents in Hull showed such strength, we interviewed seven of the seventeen original respondents on the phone and in person during a visit to Hull, Illinois.

Without exception, these interviewees reinforced the narrative responses sent from the community. Families, many of whom are interrelated by marriage and birth, and the community as a whole pulled together to assist one another to a very high degree during the flooding that destroyed many homes, possessions, and the town's churches. Flooding in this low-lying town was up to the roofs of most of the homes and businesses for over three weeks. The well-organized support efforts of Hull's citizens were supplemented by the work of Mennonite and Amish church relief volunteers from as far away as Pennsylvania. Forty-eight of these out-of-town volunteers moved into the town and began the process of working with the townspeople to clean up buildings, renovate, and rebuild. Many of these volunteers were still there finishing up their work twelve months later.

While Mennonite/Amish relief efforts occurred throughout the region, the relief efforts in Hull were amplified greatly by the traditions of the town (including those of organizations such as the town's three churches). These traditions emphasized sharing both at the practical tangible level and at the psychological level. A crucial contribution involved the establishment of a soup kitchen by a couple of the town's key leaders. At this kitchen, survivors gathered regularly for noon meals and to plan ways to keep the river levee from breaking up completely. After it broke, they planned relief, cleanup, and restoration work (including how to keep the town's school and churches functioning). They also met to share their stories, losses, and emotional support. The excerpt from the narrative of the final respondent in Table 10-1 illustrates well the collective spirit that was reported by Hull respondents and is an excellent example of what we heard in the interviews with Hull's citizens.

DISCUSSION

In general, the narrative reports were consistent with our model, which emphasizes the coping value of private reflection and confiding and sharing of stories with close others in times of major loss and adversity. Persons who reported highly positive adaptation indicated that they had strong social support from family, friends, and community. Some people who did not report such positive adaptation indicated that they had also worked on their account of what happened and had engaged in other personal activities such as prayer. It was rare, however, for those people to indicate that they engaged in the personal strengthening activity and received strong social support from their families and communities. Thus, from our perspective, it seems likely that the combination of personal and interpersonal factors may be most helpful to survivors in adapting to their losses and moving on with their lives.

We found only partial indications in our narratives of the type of trauma that characterized Buffalo Creek survivors or of the type reported for other kinds of recent disasters such as the California earthquakes. As can be seen in the narrative excerpts, there are indications of PTSD-like symptoms (e.g., serious depression, drinking behavior). For our sampling, which occurred relatively early after the worst part of the flooding, there was little of the intrusive imagery, dreaming, and other traumatic experiences reported by Lifton and Olson (1976) approximately two years after the event. Consider, for example, this person's dream recorded in Lifton and Olson's study:

> *I dreamt about the baby I found with half its face torn off and the truck full of bodies. Sometimes in those dreams you're running, or trying to get hold of someone to help them out of the mud. (p. 313)*

Or this person's:

> *I've never been to funerals except the ones right after the flood. . . . In the dream there is a big crowd at the funeral. . . . I'm being buried. I'm scared*

to death. I'm trying to tell them I'm alive, but they pay no attention. (p. 310)

Compared to the Buffalo Creek disaster, the impact of the 1993 flood was subtler and more dispersed (suggesting possibly that measurement at long-term intervals might be more revealing) and thus may have led to less trauma. Survivors did not go to funerals of people who died as a result of the flooding. They did not typically report vivid memories of gruesome events connected to the flooding. Further, although the protracted nature of the flooding was very stressful, after the first round in the mid-summer of 1993, there was time for many people to get ready practically and psychologically for the next rounds of flooding. There was a lot of early support from government leaders, with President Clinton and then Secretary of Agriculture Espy visiting, comforting survivors, and offering financial aid for the affected states. (At the same time, there was widespread blaming of the Federal Emergency Management Agency and the Army Corps of Engineers for delays in aiding survivors and for red tape and hassles in general.)

For the Midwest flood survivors, the psychological imagery was horrifying. Survivors watched their barns, homes, and possessions quickly destroyed by water or even floating down a river. By and large, however, not everyone who sustained major damage experienced intrusive imagery. In contrast, many Buffalo Creek survivors and some major earthquake survivors who witnessed the loss and destruction of human life in gruesome detail have experienced intrusive imagery. The scenes of destruction they saw have had a profoundly enduring effect.

We believe that this study suggests the importance of the context of people's lives as they deal with major stressors. It is suggested in the narratives that if a person or family is having major relationship or economic problems when a disaster occurs or if a person's or family's friendship circle is unclear or untested, the disaster may seriously impair their ability to recover. The same may be true if the individual has not yet learned the value of such coping activities as confronting a loss through confiding.

In commenting about the economic impact of the flooding, one older farm woman said that the flooding was but a story within a story for some struggling Midwest farmers. She meant that farming has become such a difficult way for some to make a living that they were on the brink of going out of business *prior to* the flooding. Many of these farmers likely will get out of farming altogether.

One question that shows up in field research like ours is the possibility that the self-selected nature of the sample undercuts any generalizations that may be made. Our small sample clearly was selective in terms of focusing on only a small fraction of the tens of thousands of persons affected severely by the floods. Many respondents indicated that they were participating with the hope of contributing to knowlege about such natural disasters ("so that others will learn from them") and because of the modest financial incentives. We could also suggest that some who participated did so, in part, because, as one survivor said, "just writing about my losses helped me work through them." It is interesting how many people in the more optimistic narratives emphasized the positive relational and communal results of the flooding for them. While some survivors may have coped very well by various means other than those identified here, the restorative power of the community and family and the individual relational acts of storytelling and confiding ring clearly through all the reports. As one volunteer helper in Hull said, "The thing that really stands out is the invisible thread that runs through these people—to see how they depend on each other, and the little things they do for each other."

11

EXPERIENCING DYING

Burning to death on a mountainside is dying at least three times. . . . First, considerably ahead of the fire, you reach the verge of death in your boots and your legs; next, as you fail, you sink back in the region of strange gases and red and blue darts where there is no oxygen and here you die in your lungs; then you sink in prayer into the main fire that consumes, and if you are a Catholic, about all that remains of you is your cross.

—Norman MacLean

This is the true joy in life, the being used for a purpose recognized by yourself as a mighty one; the being thoroughly worn out before you are thrown on the scrap heap. . . .

—George Bernard Shaw

VARIATIONS

How can anyone address the topic of how we experience dying since each and every one of us may experience this process in a different way? Some may die gradually after a long illness. Some may die quickly without warning. Some may die with great pain accompanying them each step of their final days. Some may die without pain at all. Some may die feeling that their life's work and tasks are completed. Some may die feeling that much is incomplete. Some may die with no survivors and alone, while others may die closely linked to and in the presence of many kin and friends. So, the idea of representing this topic in generalities is daunting. Even so, a discussion of the dying process is vital to this book. It provides the one chapter that deals with the dying loved one's impending loss (of life), grief, and possible storytelling. While most of this book has been about survivors' experiences of loss and grief, our treatment would be incomplete if it did not consider the very process that leads to such experiences.

In his book, *How to Live Between Office Visits* (1994), Bernie Siegel said that he started to believe such a book was necessary in 1977 when he sat down next to one of his cancer patients who said, "You know what I need to know? I need to know how to live between office visits" (p. 1). Essentially, that is one of the main ideas of this chapter. Many of us will reach the point at which we know that our death is imminent. We may have a terminal illness. We may be quite old and frail. We may be embarking on some expedition similar to the Normandy invasion in which we know that our probability of survival is low. We may be sacrificing our lives for others, as did Sydney Carton in Dickens's *Tale of Two Cities*, which is set in the time of the French Revolution, when he gave his life to save Charles Darnay at the end of the story. Carton said as he was led to the gallows, "It is a far, far better thing that I do, than I have ever done; it is a far, far better rest that I go to than I have ever known" (p. 367).

The vast variability of the dying experience can be illustrated by comparing Carton's positive conclusion to the interminably grim, deathlike reality painted by Elie Wiesel's *Night* (1960), an autobiographical statement of his experience as a teenager in Nazi death camps:

> *I awoke on January 29 at dawn. In my father's place lay another invalid. They must have taken him away before dawn and carried him to the crematory. He may still have been breathing.*
>
> *There were no prayers at his grave. No candles were lit to his memory. His last word was my name. A summons, to which I did not respond.*
>
> *I did not weep, and it pained me that I could not weep. But I had no more tears. And, in the depths of my being, in the recesses of my weakened conscience, could I have searched it, I might perhaps have found something like—free at last. (p. 106)*

For Weisel, does "free at last" mean to be free from the anxiety of death or the death of a loved one? Does he imply that seeing death so regularly, with little display of guilt or shame or any other emotion by either victims or murderers gives one an immunity to death's power? Does he suggest that given all that he and other survivors have seen, it simply does not matter? Probably not. After all, *Night* is the result of all that he has seen. It has affected and will continue to affect many people and, in so doing, has led some readers to intense emotional experiences.

Let it not be thought that Weisel's message in *Night* is dated. In 1994, as the bloody civil war in Rwanda continued, *every hour*, 10,000 poor, and in many cases dying, refugees fled from the country into Zaire. Over 500,000 refugees arrived in Zaire in a three-day period. Perhaps as many as 500,000 already had died. These refugees, carrying few possessions—maybe only the rag of clothing on their bodies—had limped along on weak, malnourished legs and blistered feet for hundreds of miles. They had little food or water, few suitable camps for resting, and the great possibility that epidemic disease would break out among them. The situation could only be described by observers as "worse than catastrophic." It is highly unlikely that any nonhungry, nonweary, unafraid, nonterrorized observer can begin to fathom the desperation felt by the dying refugees.

Knowing that death is at hand entails a sense of loss and grief for many. Do we passively wait on death? Or, as the quote from George Bernard Shaw suggests, do we confront life as fully and strategically as we can each precious moment that we live? I would naturally advocate the latter answer. I believe that each of us has that opportunity—however weak, discouraging, or hopeless our physical situation may be deemed by others. As long as our minds are alive with our spirit and values, we are empowered to construct our own meanings of the circumstances of our lives and to defy the odds and obstacles stacked against us. Only when we psychologically give up are we indeed hopeless, and usually our bodies then begin the process of terminating functions. I said at the outset of this book that this chapter was partly about dying with dignity. In truth, it is more about living with dignity to the final moment.

What is such dignity? Just before the 1994 High Holy Days, *New York Times* writer Joseph Berger interviewed Rabbi Gordon Tucker on the meaning of the holidays. Rabbi Tucker spoke of his quest to give his congregation a greater sense of hope that in their lives they can capture a certain amount of immortality and timelessness:

> *To use a photographic metaphor, you're looking through the lens, and you've got to merge the focus and get those two together, to see yourself not as confronting things but to see yourself as part of a world that has a beauty and eternality all its own. . . .*
>
> *[He then told of performing a recent funeral for a congregant whom he had never met but wished he had] you instinctively feel it was a loss to you that you did not know them. Everyone who knew him said he had achieved a certain kind of acceptance and peacefulness, not only through life but even [through] a painful death from cancer. He wasn't looking for the universe next door. (Berger, 1994, B8)*

THANATOLOGIC REALIZATION AND WHEN ARE WE READY TO DIE?

Weisman (1986) defines "thanatologic realization" as the time when the realization that death is imminent becomes foremost in a person's mind. Is this realization necessarily grim and demoralizing? Weisman suggests that it need not be. He argues that there is triumph in death after a full life, especially when we stop thinking of death as an evil force. Weisman contends that while we seldom have a choice about how, when, and where we die, death with dignity is possible, provided we do not ask that it necessarily be propitious, heroic, or ideal. It is what it is. Weisman points out that to achieve what we view as an appropriate death, we must rid ourselves of the notion that death is *never* appropriate. By holding this notion, we shut ourselves off from creating the conditions we want to exist when we die (e.g., work at reconciling differences with people with whom we were very close at one time but from whom we now are alienated). Appropriateness also may include protecting ourselves from needless, dehumanizing, and demeaning medical procedures (e.g., through the creation of a living will indicating that no artificial means to sustain life will be made in the event of brain death).

Weisman (1986) argues that the aged have an advantage in facing death because the contrast between living and dying, so pronounced in earlier years, has been smoothed out and cooled down. Discontinuity and separation can be dealt with. Weisman's logic may be true for many people late in their lives, but it also may be a bit unfair. Why should they not have every right to expect to live many more years, just as young people typically have such an expectation?

The readiness for death varies greatly across people, depending, in large measure, on when they consider their life's business to be complete. Most of us are ready when we have let go of life, which occurs when we no longer have a meaning that is so strong that it will not permit us to let go. Chapter 6 noted that many veterans of Gettysburg died on their return from the fiftieth anniversary of that battle. Apparently, they had had the will to make the reunion. That gave them meaning.

Siegel (1994) reports that this phenomenon is well known in the medical community and is referred to as "postponement of death until symbolically meaningful occasions have occurred." He notes that in every culture, many people die just after birthdays and holidays. When we have a major occasion to look forward to, we often hang on until that occasion occurs; we have a will to live. For example, Siegel notes he has heard people say, "I'm going to die at two o'clock when the kids arrive from California," and, indeed, that is what happens.

WHAT DOES IT MEAN TO DIE?

As I argued early in this book, from the beginning of our lives, we are almost always implicitly grieving, and we are always actually in the process of dying. That is nature, part of the order of our world. In exploring the death experience in psychological terms, however, the anticipation of death involves imagining our grief over the loss of our close personal relationships, our pleasures in living, our hopes and plans. Recall the young woman's words in Chapter 9, who noted that what mattered most about the death of her boyfriend was the loss of their plans for marriage and a family. Very likely her boyfriend also would have grieved for that incomplete aspect of his life, had he known when he would die.

An important extension of the foregoing discussion is that we die psychologically—a powerful form of death—when we lose hope and the will to be responsible and mentally in charge of our actions. As suggested in Chapter 7, progressive mental deterioration because of terminal illness (i.e., when a person is not lucid or capable of social interaction) may represent the most difficult type of loss. It may occur as part of severe Alzheimer's or as a part of other diseases. It often lingers, has huge practical costs, and demoralizes a person's caretakers and loved ones.

Many intriguing questions surround the way in which people interpret death. One question concerns the relation of the body and mind. Another, if we believe there is a spirit, concerns the relation of the body and the mind to the spirit. People often say that the grieving process begins when survivors view the body of their deceased loved one. Recently, a twenty-one-year-old college student and athlete died in a boating accident in the city where I live. His fiancé, family members, and friends waited on the banks of the river where he drowned until his body was found. Although these people experienced powerful grief when his body was discovered, they later reported that seeing that his body was not badly decomposed helped them to remember him as a vital, alive being. Thus, to many of us, the body is integrally related to who we are.

Others, however, believe strongly that the body is only a secondary part of who we are; they believe that the spirit is the primary part. Others may say it is the mind or the unique self or the personality. To these people, seeing the body may be of less consequence than remembering the person's special psychological and social qualities. For these people, the question is, Does the spirit or mind or self or personality die when the body dies? Many people believe that the spirit takes on another form and goes to heaven or some other place at the time of death.

Another interesting possibility is suggested in Chapter 9: People do not die until the memories we have of them die. This logic may seem specious, but it is as cogent as many positions that embrace spiritual existence beyond death. Whether alive or dead, who we are and what we have done in our lives are what reside in the minds and memories of many people, especially close others.

As the continuing outpouring of grief at the Vietnam Veterans Memorial clearly shows, many people have held onto the images of those who died in that war. In that sense, the dead live on through us just as they did in part while they were alive. Their death, then, occurs only when we die and they no longer are remembered in special ways. One may argue that such a continuing existence is marginal compared to life. That may be true. But not all of the days of our lives equally matter: We sometimes do more to celebrate life than at other times; we sometimes love with more vigor and impact than at other times; we sometimes lend a hand to help others more than at other times.

It is these *acts*, then, that are the essentials of our existence, personal history, and imagery in the minds of others who have observed and encountered them. *Our acts, in effect, define us.* These acts may continue to reverberate through time well after we have died. Imagine a time a thousand or more years from now, a time at which your progeny and their progeny have all disappeared from the earth. That point could be construed to be the point of ultimate loss. What will the fact of your having lived mean then? Even then, I contend, we exist in terms of the principles and values that we implemented in the course of our lives.

AMBIGUITY IN THE DYING EXPERIENCE

Death for some comes in a halting, uncertain manner. It simply is not clear whether death will occur soon or at some more distant point. This situation is fraught with anxiety. This is true for individuals who have begun the lengthy appeals process after being convicted and sentenced to execution. This is true for individuals who have life-threatening diseases but who recognize that there is a reasonable probability that they will survive. It is at this point that the bargaining process described by Kübler-Ross in her classic, *On Death and Dying* (1969), is most likely to occur. "If only I can have a few more good years" may be the refrain of the person.

Shortly before her death, comedienne Gilda Radner expressed this type of uncertainty in her memoir, *It's Always Something* (1989). At the end of her book, Radner speaks of a complicated reality that surrounds dying, even as it surrounds most of our moments on earth:

> *I had wanted to wrap this book up in a neat little package about a girl who is a comedienne from Detroit, becomes famous in New York, with all the world coming her way, gets this horrible disease of cancer, is brave and fights it, learning all the skills she needs to get through it, and then, miraculously, things are neatly tied up and she gets well. I wanted to be able to write on the book jacket: "Her triumph over cancer" or "She wins the cancer war." I wanted a perfect ending, so I sat down to write the book with the ending in place before there was an ending. Now, I've learned, the hard way, that some poems don't rhyme, and some stories don't have a clear beginning, middle and end. Like my life, this book has ambiguity. Like my*

life, this book is about not knowing, having to change, taking the moment and making the best of it. . . . Delicious ambiguity. (p. 268)

The ambiguity of the dying experience can also be quite difficult for families to deal with. In the July 17, 1994, edition of the *Chicago Tribune*, Barbara Brotman wrote of a family facing this situation. She told the story of the family of Kenneth Sampson, age sixty, a jazz drummer who had been diagnosed with lung cancer in 1991. By the time of Brotman's story cancer had invaded his heart muscle as well. Michael, Kenneth's six-year-old son asks, "When Daddy dies, will we still be a family?" It is a question that is difficult for Kenneth's wife, Susan, to hear. She notes:

For the last two and a half years, we've lived with imminent death. What do you tell your child? He knows his father is dying. He figured it out. He's seen his father in the hospital. He's seen his father when he was gray and down to 87 pounds. [It was especially hard on Michael.] It's not like they're pals, but Michael's almost his confidant. (Brotman, 1994)

Michael's mother went on to say that the family was having a difficult time making a living since neither she nor Kenneth works. She reported that Michael was showing a lack of concentration and frustration in school and had admitted to a counselor that he feared that his father was going to die.

I told him [Susan says] that when people die, as long as there's somebody to remember them, they live in your heart. . . . We do a lot of family things. We can't wait till next summer to go camping. We don't know if there will be a next summer. . . . We don't watch TV much. TV steals too much time. . . .

You know how you tell your child, "Mommy will never ever leave you?" Well, that's not true. What have you done to your children if you've told them it won't happen, and it will?

If he died in a car accident, you could say, "Daddy went to heaven," or whatever your religious beliefs are. . . . It would be over. (section 6, pp. 1 and 9)

Of all the situations involving the dying experience, the one faced by the Sampsons is most difficult to endure. It is one in which the person who faces death is weak and afraid. The family in waiting also is afraid and paralyzed in planning their future. Unfortunately, this situation is quite common because modern technology keeps many people alive with little quality of life and very poor prognoses.

Kübler-Ross (1969) speaks of the turmoil families often endure when the death of their loved one is less ambiguous yet there still is no certainty about when it will occur. She remarks:

> *This is the time when the relatives walk up and down the hospital hall-*
> *ways, tormented by waiting, not knowing if they should leave to attend the*
> *living or stay to be around for the moment of death. This is the time when*
> *it is too late for words, and yet the time when the relatives cry the loudest*
> *for help—with or without words. It is too late for medical interventions*
> *. . . but it is also too early for a final separation from the dying. It is the*
> *hardest time for the next of kin as he either wishes to take off, to get it over*
> *with; or he desperately clings to something that he is in the process of los-*
> *ing forever. It is the time for the therapy of silence with the patient and*
> *availability for the relatives. (p. 246)*

Kübler-Ross notes that it is important for the medical staff to help the family decide who will stay with the patient and who will go home and not feel
shame or guilt when the patient dies. Perhaps this is always more easily
said than done.

DEATH ANXIETY

At some point in our lives, each of us is anxious about our own death. When
will it occur? Will it be painful and drawn out, or will it come suddenly and
without warning? Will my life's work be accomplished? Will my loved ones
be provided for adequately? These are questions that each of us entertains,
perhaps more so as we become older. Some writers such as Becker (1973) believe that all people are preoccupied with death anxiety and persistently defend against it with strategies such as denial, religious faith in immortality,
exaggerated expectations about medicine's ability to cure diseases, and acting
out the "nothing can terminate me" fantasy. In their revealing book, *The Sea-*
sons of a Man's Life (1978), Daniel Levinson and his colleagues provide evidence, gathered from a group of men whom they were studying, that midlife
is a common point at which contemplation of death becomes more common:

> *At mid-life, the growing recognition of mortality collides with the power-*
> *ful wish for immortality and the many illusions that help to maintain it. A*
> *man's fear that he is not immortal is expressed in his preoccupation with*
> *bodily decline and his fantasies of imminent death. At the most elemental*
> *level, he feels that he is fighting for survival. He is terrified at the thought*
> *of being dead, of no longer existing as this particular person. (p. 215)*

Existential psychotherapist Irvin Yalom (1985) argues that we often try
to avoid confronting the reality of our mortality and that we do so in two
major ways. First, we involve ourselves in what Yalom calls "immortality
projects." We throw ourselves into various worthy activities with the idea
that as long as we are doing them, and doing them well, we are somehow

insulated from death. For some, this involves work; for others raising children; for still others doing major charitable activities. Doctors are famous for losing themselves in the myth of the immortality project. They, too, often worry about everyone else's health and neglect their own.

The second way that Yalom claims we sidestep the issue of our own mortality is to conjure up "the rescuer," some powerful person who provides insulation against the danger of dying. Doctors love to play this role, and we readily accord it to them. However, doctors may not want to admit the medical profession's limitations, and we would just as soon not hear them do so. Of course, there are limitations; the most significant limitation of all is the simple fact that we all die. Medical knowledge, even as it increases, may postpone the inevitable, but that is all it can do.

In *Fear and Trembling and the Sickness unto Death*, the philosopher Kierkegaard describes the price paid for avoiding confrontation with one's own death: despair. A person in despair, according to Kierkegaard, lives life as though it differed little from death, with no vibrancy, no important choices, no risks. Such a person avoids the importance of the moment of his or her demise. By implication, Kierkegaard suggests that vitality comes from acknowledging the fragility of our own being and the preciousness of time as an antidote to existential despair.

When your doctor notices a lump in your breast or orders important tests and asks you to come back soon for the results, it suddenly seems that you have left the world where everything is just fine and entered that gray zone of ambiguity about life. Suddenly, nothing else matters as much. "Depend on it, sir, when a man knows he is going to be hanged in a fortnight, it concentrates his mind wonderfully," said Samuel Johnson. There is a kind of freedom that comes with a recognition that your time is limited. Long-term consequences seem less important. A certain kind of fearless authenticity often comes from a confrontation with one's mortality.

GRACE AND PASSION IN LIVING WITH THE KNOWLEDGE THAT DEATH IS IMMINENT

Death be not proud . . .
—John Donne

Today I consider myself the luckiest man on the face of the earth.
—Lou Gehrig

Most of us hope to have the opportunity to face death with grace and passion. Such a goal may help us to overcome our dread of death or denial of its reality. We can do this by examining the way we live our lives as we age and by recognizing that death may come at any moment. Reaching that point requires a lot of work along the way to tie together in our minds the threads of our lives, to reach a point at which we believe we can conclude our life's story and feel satisfied with it.

There are many examples of people who have displayed a "grace under pressure," an expression Ernest Hemingway used to define courage. In April 1994, Bette Harrison of the *Atlanta Journal* interviewed several people who were facing imminent death. One was Joan Simon, age sixty-two, who was a fifteen-year survivor of breast cancer when the interview occurred. Ms. Simon had been a dancer, model, Las Vegas showgirl, social worker, and chef in her life. She also had raised three children. Now, weak, frail, and drifting in and out of consciousness, she was close to death at a relatively young age. How, she was asked, did she relate to this experience?

> *I never felt sorry for myself. After my mastectomy, I thought, "It's tempo-rary. I'll be dressed and out of here in no time." It took three weeks out of my life. I felt depressed for a while and then I got back to living.*
>
> *[After battling cancer repeatedly from 1979 to the present] I wish peo-ple would stop treating me like I'm helpless. They cradle me like a baby. They bring juice to my lips. I'm not helpless. . . .*
>
> *She wrote her own obituary, which began: "Ms. Simon battled cancer for 15 years which taught her the meaning of the word survivor and gave hope, help and encouragement to many others." (Harrison, 1994, p. C1)*

Many others likewise "do not go gentle into that good night" (to quote Dylan Thomas's famous line). Many of them are people with AIDS. As writer and AIDS activist Larry Kramer, who is battling AIDS himself, told David Patrick Stearns of *USA Today* in a March 15, 1994, piece, "Making the Dying Light the Brightest":

> *There is nothing like impending death to get the juices flowing—fast! [In speaking of his positive feeling on accomplishing a new creative project] . . . such liberation lasts about 10 seconds. And then you realize nothing has changed, the plague is still raging unabated, and you have to go out and write another version of it. . . . I still get pretty angry. But if I didn't have writing as an outlet, I might've shot somebody by now. (p. 2D)*

Many artists have accomplished major successes in the years prior to their deaths from AIDS. As his own condition has worsened, Kramer, fifty-eight, has finished his screenplay for a forthcoming Barbra Streisand AIDS film, *The Normal Heart*, and has completed over 1,000 pages of a novel. Bill T. Jones, forty-two, a choreographer, finished a dance/theater work entitled "Still/Here," drawn from interviews with people who are terminally ill. Singer Michael Callen, age thirty-eight, who sang "Mr. Sandman" in the film *Philadelphia*, recorded approximately forty-five songs in the months before his death. For many of these artists, the goal of *giving back to others, or "generativity,"* is high on their lists of daily priorities. As Kramer said:

> *I'm interested in creating change. The one thing that gives me energy is that I've never seen anything so wrong in my entire life as the set of circumstances that has allowed this illness to develop into a plague. I almost feel that I have a moral obligation to tell what I know. (Stearns, 1994, p. 2D)*

The phrase commonly used by Holocaust survivors "to bear witness" is similar to Kramer's "moral obligation to tell what I know." The knowledge or experience needs to be testified to because otherwise it terrorizes the human spirit and psyche and deadens the will to live.

Paul Monette's *Last Watch of the Night* (1994) is a vigil for himself and his friends who are living and dying with AIDS. Monette writes as if he were sentinel, witness, and guard on the graveyard shift. He says of the first year of the deaths of his friends and lovers:

> *I spent the first annihilating year of grief dragging myself out of bed. . . writing so I wouldn't have to think. I can't count the times when I'd crawl under one of the tables where Puck [his dog] lay sleeping, to hold him so I could cry. (p. 15)*

Monette's work covers the period from 1982–1994 when tens of thousands died of AIDS. He says that he has received "poster child credit" as a spokesperson of hope for those afflicted with AIDS and for managing to give lectures around the country without keeling over. Monette's commentary is filled with the passion of living, even as his own health continues to deteriorate, and pride about the advancing tide of gay and lesbian enfranchisement.

Cancer activist Jimmy Teyechea died at age forty-four in March 1994. He used his cancer, which was discovered in 1989, to focus the country's attention on Nogales, Arizona, a city on the Mexican border, and the health hazards faced by many of its residents. When Teyechea developed multiple myeloma, a cancer that attacks the bone, he began documenting other cancers and diseases in his community. His research led him to conclude that pollution and waste from U.S.-owned factories south of the border were strongly implicated in many of the deaths that had occurred in Nogales. Battling pain and fatigue and working until his final days, Teyechea spurred Arizona's governor and legislature to consider legislation to help the sick in Nogales with medical bills and to do a thorough study of the waste hazards facing its residents. Before dying, Teyechea said: "I think all of us were sent to this Earth to accomplish one thing" (Price, 1994, p. 2A). His mother said: "I guess he just ran out of life. But God bless him, he made every hour of it count" (Price, 1994, p. 2A).

Humor and vigor characterize still another prominent example of courage in the face of death, that of author, successful cardiologist, and avid runner and athlete George Sheehan. Sheehan was a pacesetter in the fitness movement for more than twenty-five years. In the mid-1980s, while in his sixties and fighting life-threatening cancer, Sheehan was a legendary figure in senior running races across the country. He would be wheezing and moaning but would shout as he approached the finish line, "Look out, here comes George." He died of cancer in 1993 at age seventy-five, ten days after finishing his last book and writing the last of his columns that appeared for over two decades in papers around the country. Sheehan even decreased his cancer medications because he felt they were interfering with his quality of life—which emphasized running! Near the time of his death, he said:

> *Cancer has focused me to a finality. Suddenly I'm thinking about issues and personal situations that had been on the back burner. . . . Ninety-five percent of us are observers. The best way I know to get involved is to write. Then you explore. . . . I'm an experiential writer and my available experience now is dying. Unfortunately, I've been feeling better lately so it's been harder to work on this book. I used to say it took three hours of running to produce a page of writing. Now it's three hours of dying. I suppose I shouldn't be so flip. . . . I'm going to take death and elevate it. (Patrick, 1993)*

> *Finding meaning in what one is doing is the critical ingredient in all of these examples of facing death with grace.* Stories are the focus of this book, and I believe that in the face of death, storytelling may help us to find meaning in what we are doing. Some medical doctors now recognize how talk and confiding behavior with friends and close others can help those who are facing death live with more quality (Spiegel, 1993). I end this section on grace and passion in facing death with excerpts from Herbert and Kay Kramer's *Conversations at Midnight* (1993). This book was begun by the Kramers during Herbert Kramer's final years of life after a long battle with cancer. The book presents touching dialogues between the two authors about dying and aspects of their lives together. It is an illustration of courage and insight by both the person soon to die and the person closest to him in life. The following tells of how they decided to write the book and the impact that writing it had on Herbert Kramer.

> *When the storm had passed [they were hiking in Switzerland], we walked to a nearby rest station, with the unlikely name of Mary's Cafe. It was*

there that we began to talk about writing a book together and there where he scribbled that first outline on a dinner napkin.

It was Herb's idea to write a book about my work [as a counselor] and his experience thinking about death. At this point he seemed to have little emotional connection with the idea of his own death, even though it was always with us. . . . I was angry that Herb had metastatic disease that I thought would kill him. That that terrible event was the motivation for our writing a book made talking about my work suddenly annoying. Yet, there he was, with his usual enthusiasm, contemplating a new assignment with the usual eagerness. . . .

That was the summer of 1990. There were still many months ahead of vigor and seeming health and very little perception on Herb's part that he was ill. When the disease signaled its growing presence in the spring of 1991, he began to write.

For him, it was the book he had always wanted to write but had been unable to do. . . . It's ironic that he would find his voice in the event of his death. Once found, however, he reveled in it and felt that he did some of his best writing. A well had opened within him, and he continued to write beautiful poetry and prose until a few days before his death. . . .

Writing this book not only opened Herb's voice for him, it opened up the process of thinking and struggling that resulted in his coming to terms with a much feared death that had been the source of panic attacks about dying throughout his life. He thought seriously, really seriously, for the first time about trusting some of his subjective experiences, found a framework in which to understand them, and discovered a whole new dimension of spirituality that he had longed for but never known before. As our friend Larry Leamer, who spoke at Herb's memorial service, said: "As the light died, he looked at the shadows, at the flickering remnants of the light, and he put down on pages what it was like.'" (pp. 229–231)

SACRIFICING ONE'S OWN LIFE FOR OTHERS

There are those rare occasions (perhaps not as rare as we sometimes think) when people defy death to save others' lives. Certainly we can say these people face death courageously. This topic may not seem to be relevant to the idea of how we usually experience death and related feelings of loss and grief. After all, how often does any average person have the opportunity to make a decision to put her or his life on the line for another person? Not often, it is true. And it is likely that in emergency situations, such decisions are made instantaneously with little deliberation. Nonetheless, this topic is fascinating for the present discussion because the people who act to help others are often acting in defiance of self-preservation.

One of the notable accounts of sacrifice that emerged from our interviews with the veterans of D day was provided by Harold Baumgarten (see Chapter 6). He described being wounded on the beach and encountering a soldier-medic who was ministering to the wounded without fear for his own safety:

> *I saw a fellow walking down the beach like he's taking a stroll, looking at all the bodies, pulling people onto dry sand. As he got closer, I could see he had a red cross on him. His name was Sgt. Cecil Breedan, and he was fearless. When he got to me and saw my face, he put sulfa powder on the wound and made me swallow 12 tablets. While he was doing it, mortar shells were coming in all over the place. I reached up with my right hand to pull him down by his shirt to protect him, but he smashed my hand away and said, "When I get hurt, you can take care of me." (Harvey and Davidson, 1994)*

Breeden's actions epitomize those of people who act when they see others in peril. These helpers often report that they did what they did because they had the opportunity and that they would expect others to help them in a like situation. Similarly fearless were the rescuers of passengers who landed in the Potomac River in Washington, D.C., in January 1992, when Air Florida Flight 90 crashed. Seventy-eight people died in the crash. The plane skimmed the tops of cars caught in a traffic jam on a bridge over the Potomac.

Rescuers included two people who observed the plane get over the bridge and then break up as it hit the Potomac. One was Roger Olian, who swam for twenty minutes in the icy river trying to reach survivors struggling in the water. He never reached them and almost drowned himself, but survivors said the encouragement he yelled to them helped them to hang on until they got help. Another rescuer, Lonnie Skutnick, had been caught in the traffic jam. He raced to the river's bank, jumped in, and pulled out a woman who was going under. A third rescuer is unknown but is believed to be passenger Arland Williams, a bank examiner from Atlanta. He had been holding onto a line from a helicopter but passed it on to a flight attendant who was close to drowning. By the time the helicopter got back to him, he had drowned. Olian and Skutnik each said they acted on the spur of the moment because people needed help. Arland Williams's memory, too, lives on in the minds of many who observed or heard about his gallantry, which involved an act so rare as to fulfill the definition of Greater love hath no man than this, that a man lay down his life for his friends.

The sinking of the RMS Titanic after it hit an iceberg in the Atlantic Ocean in April 1912, provided the context for many acts of heroism in the face of certain death. A September 8, 1994, set of interviews in the *Dallas Morning News* with survivors and descendants of survivors touches on some of the acts that led to hundreds of people being rescued. Most of the ship's crew knew that the vessel would soon sink, but they stayed at their stations to help women and children get into lifeboats and escape. Allen Pusey, the interviewer, discovered that 320 of the ship's engineers stayed at their positions and helped maintain the ship's lights so that panic would be averted. The ship's orchestra played while the passengers were debarking. All of the orchestra's members perished. So did all the bellboys, many as young as twelve years of age. They had calmly guided women and children to lifeboats and then had gone down with the ship.

One survivor told of Mr. and Mrs. Isidor Straus. First, the ship's crew had tried to get Mrs. Straus to leave her husband and get on a lifeboat. She had said, "I will not be separated from my husband; as we have lived, so will we die together." Moments later, because of his ill health, her elderly husband was offered lifeboat seats for both of them. They had declined. He had said, "I do not wish any distinction in my favor which is not granted to others." No stories were sadder than those of wives, children, and husbands taking leave of one another for the last time, as the wives and children were helped into lifeboats. Survivors reported that to lessen the fear of their loved ones, husbands turned their backs as the boats were lowered. The husbands then went on to the task of helping others escape before meeting their own deaths (Pusey, 1995).

Ordinariness, morality, and a sense of duty seem to characterize people who help others in crisis situations. These qualities were also found by Oliner and Oliner (1988) in their important study of rescuers of Jewish persons threatened by the Nazis. Over 700 persons, including rescuers, nonrescuers, and survivors who had lived in Nazi-occupied Europe were the respondents in the Oliners's study, which focused on the characteristics of those who helped. Oliner and Oliner characterized those who helped as

> "ordinary" people. They were farmers and teachers, entrepreneurs and factory workers, rich and poor, parents and single people, Protestants and Catholics. Most had done nothing extraordinary before the war nor have they done much that is extraordinary since. Most were marked neither by exceptional leadership qualities nor by unconventional behavior. They were not heroes cast in larger-than-life molds. What most distinguished them were their connections with others in relationships of commitment and care. It is out of such relationships that they became aware of what was occurring around them and mustered their human and material resources to relieve the pain. Their involvements with Jews grew

out of the ways in which they ordinarily related to other people—their characteristic ways of feeling; their perceptions of who should be obeyed; the rules and examples of conduct they learned from parents, friends, and religious and political associates; and their routine ways of deciding what was wrong and right. They inform us that it is out of the quality of such routine human activities that the human spirit evolves and moral courage is born. They remind us that such courage is not only the province of the independent and the intellectually superior thinkers but that it is available to all through the virtues of connectedness, commitment, and the quality of relationships developed in ordinary human interactions. (p. 260)

OBFUSCATION OF THE DYING PROCESS

In many ways, we prefer to obfuscate the dying process. By that, I mean we do not want to look at death in a point-blank way as an event that will happen to us and that is as common as conception in nature—it is too frightening. We often employ euphemisms about death. "Passed away" is a favorite euphemism, connoting the possibility that one has left but that the departure is simply a journey to another port—whether heaven or elsewhere. Kubler-Ross (1969) was one of the first scholars and practitioners to emphasize the value of recognizing death as a natural experience and, therefore, appreciating the importance of living life fully each day. She suggested that we have created many cultural scripts that help us deny death. At the same time, however, these scripts contribute to empty, meaningless approaches to existence.

More psychologically debilitating than our own day-to-day avoidance of death is the avoidance of this issue by some in the medical establishment who deal with patients who have life-threatening illnesses. A surgeon, Sherwin Nuland, wrote a book entitled *How We Die* (1994), that discusses in graphic detail the ways in which people die (whether as part of aging, accidents, or whatever). He also tells stories of dying that make clear the choices that can be made to allow each of us to have more control over our own dying process. One story involves a woman, age ninety-two, who had heart disease and was treated by Nuland for an acute digestive tract disorder that was causing an ulcer that probably would lead to internal bleeding and certain death. Nuland talked the patient into an operation for the digestive disorder, even though she argued that she had lived long enough and did not want any further intrusions into her body. Nuland was following a system of logic—the medical code—which he could defend by citing medical ethics and use in analyzing the case with his physician colleagues. He was not following the patient's system of logic, which was to use this sudden illness as a gracious way to die.

Nuland's story does not have a happy ending. The patient survived the operation but was very reproachful because of the pain, tubes, and multiple procedures that often are part of the postoperative period with elderly patients. She said that Nuland had let her down by not allowing her to die in due course without the pain and complications she was experiencing. Two weeks after the operation, she died of a stroke. Nuland notes that the woman's anger and reproach represented a major learning experience for him about death and dying and the role of medicine in these processes:

> *Hope lies not only in an expectation of cure or even of the remission of present distress. For dying patients, the hope of cure will always be shown to be ultimately false, and even the hope of relief too often turns to ashes. When my time comes, I will seek hope in the knowledge that insofar as possible I will not be allowed to suffer or be subjected to needless attempts to maintain life; I will seek it in the certainty that I will not be abandoned to die alone; I am seeking it now, in the way I try to live my life, so that those who value what I am will have profited by my time on earth and be left with comforting recollections of what we have meant to one another.*
>
> *There are those who will find hope in faith and their belief in an afterlife; some will look forward to the moment a milestone is reached or a deed is accomplished; there are even some whose hope is centered on maintaining the kind of control that will permit them the means to decide the moment of their death, or actually to make their own quietus unhindered. Whatever form it may take, each of us must find hope in his or her own way. (p. 257)*

Nuland's conclusion is cogent to me. It moves the question of dying and the "how" of it back to personal decision making until the end. It also focuses us on the living experience and the value of embracing it as where the greatest meaning lies. It reminds me of Erik Erikson's (1969) analysis of Mahatma Gandhi and why and how he became a great crusader for the Indian people in the early part of the twentieth century. After many diverse experiences with oppression, Gandhi developed his approach to nonviolent protest, which emphasized fasting. Truthful action for Gandhi was governed by the readiness to get hurt and even die but not to hurt others in the process. Erikson said about this stage in Gandhi's maturity:

> *A mature man of middle age has not only made up his mind as to what, in the various compartments of life, he does and does not care for, he is also*

firm in his vision of what he will *and* can take care of. *He takes as his baseline what he irreducibly* is *and reaches out for what only he can, and therefore*, must do. *(p. 255)*

ISSUES IN DYING AS THE TWENTY-FIRST CENTURY EMERGES

The twenty-first century promises to be a time of intense dialogue about how we die. The beginnings of this dialogue have been stimulated by Dr. Jack Kevorkian's stand in favor of the individual's right to commit suicide when suffering from a painful, terminal illness. Kevorkian, who has been criticized by many, including the American Medical Association, advocates and has practiced physician-assisted suicide. He has even been put on trial for assisting patients who have decided to commit suicide. At the same time, however, Kevorkian has many supporters who believe that they should have the right and means to take their own lives when they decide that their lives no longer are worth living.

Other organizations, such as Compassion in Dying, also advocate the individual's right to commit suicide when suffering from terminal illness. Compassion in Dying has developed elaborate rules for selecting those who will be assisted in committing suicide and the members of the organization who will attend the assisted death. Compassion members offer advice on lethal doses of drugs (often barbiturates), counsel bereaved family members, work with wary family doctors regarding what is ethically right, and hold the hand of those in the act of taking their own lives. According to the *New York Times Magazine* (November 14, 1993), a prototypical candidate for assisted suicide will say, "I'm tired. I'm in constant pain. I'm getting weaker by the day. I want to do this at home, before my body's here and my brain isn't."

According to Shervert Frazier's *Psychotrends* (1994), this debate will become even more intense than the current debate about abortion in this country. As the population ages, Frazier predicts that the majority of the population will support suicide to end acute pain associated with terminal illness or incurable disease. Frazier also predicts that a majority may someday support a spouse's decision to kill his or her mate in the event that the mate is experiencing great pain due to terminal illness.

As a final thought, lest we forget, thousands of people die every year without any recognition of their end—much less their existence, contributions, and loss and grief. They are the homeless, and their bodies inhabit the many potter's fields of our world. They often have no known family or money for funeral arrangements. They pass in and out of a land of plenty like shadows. Many of them have struggled so long just for a meal each day that the countless existential questions about death and dying raised in books such as this one are meaningless. Survival is what counted. Death for many of them was lonely and unspectacular. Only the Salvation Army and similar organizations pay any heed to their deaths and try to arrange a few small, dignifying details to mark their passing.

Millions of refugees, including thousands of children, throughout the world die each year without the knowledge of what a full life is about, much less the option of living one. May this discussion represent a challenge to all of us to recognize the grieving and dying processes of these people as every bit as sacred as the griefs and deaths of people of greater means.

All My Sad Pilots

Pilots always knew
man is matter, felt the secret
ooze past our hips
each take-off,
set our blood like concrete
in each loop,
each diving desperation risked
to cram for combat, that looming
snap-roll of the bone.

We know, and we do not approve,
do not resign,
No clear decision
makes us fly—(wings
do not sustain us,
Icarus our patron saint)—
some sad communion
with the wind, stunned into
silence by a throttled flame.

—Walter McDonald (1976)

The Departure

They say I have to go away soon
On the long trip to nowhere.
Put things in order, they say.
But I've always been disorderly
So why start now?
Not much time, they say.

What to do with it?
Not much different, I think,
Than what I've been doing.
My best friends have always been
The ones in books.
Read a few pages here, a few there.
No complaints, few regrets.
Thanks to everybody.

—James Laughlin (1993)

12

LOSSES THAT HEAL
AND ARE GENERATIVE

Many are strong at the broken places.
  —Ernest Hemingway

*The greatest use of a life is to spend it on something that
will outlast it.*
                                              —William James

*There is no problem in the world that cannot be solved
with a story.*
                                              —Anonymous

I begin this chapter with the idea that in a particular sense, *loss becomes gain*
as we heal and particularly as we use our losses and what we learn from
them to contribute to others who also suffer. In fact, that is the capstone idea
of this whole book. What is important is how we deal with loss. What is important is how we see our lives and our losses as inextricably related to
those of others, past, present, and future, and how we choose to make use
of what transpires in our lives for the benefit of humanity as a whole. As
Erikson (1963) defined it, such use of our lives is "generative" in its contribution to future generations. That is the message that the stories of this
chapter will tell.

Why do some losses heal and become generative? My answer, which I
illustrate with stories in this chapter, is that a crucial set of steps needs to
occur. The general social psychological model, which I refer to as the story-
action model, involves the following sequence of events: Major loss → development of a story or understanding of the loss → storytelling or

confiding to caring others about the loss → identify change → action that addresses the loss in some constructive way.

I have already discussed in Chapter 2 parts of this model such as story development and confiding. In this chapter, I describe the idea of action. Essentially, I define an "action" as behavior that reflects the beliefs and values that are reflected in a person's story of loss and grief. Identity change refers to the idea that who we think we are in the most fundamental sense changes drastically at the time of major loss. As noted in Chapter 3, when we lose a spouse, we have to discontinue thinking of ourselves as a member of a couple. Similarly, when we lose our job, we have to reorient our self-image as someone employed by a certain employer with certain perquisites associated with that employment.

Some researchers have argued that on occasion, major loss does not necessarily require a person to take action in order to heal but that time alone is sufficient to healing (see Berscheid, 1994). In fact, we often tell survivors, "You just need time." Logically, however, there is every reason to believe that it is *what people do* during the time after major loss that matters most. Simply not thinking or even avoiding thinking about one's loss appears not to be a viable way of dealing with the loss—however long a person does not think about it or actively avoids it.

I believe that the story-action model illustrates the elements of healing and generative behavior that give our own and our lost loved ones' lives more meaning. Sometimes, these elements may occur in an order that is different from what I have suggested. For example, after loss, confiding and story development sometimes occur simultaneously. Also, as Neeld (1990) and other articulate analysts of their own grieving have suggested, story-development, confiding, and identity change probably go on simultaneously, as well as cycling in one direction and then the next. Even so, I believe that each of the elements identified in this model is a necessary condition for full healing.

Each element is composed of several subparts. Story development and storytelling, for example, involve the release of emotions that build up after a loss. This release is necessary for the survivor to recover. In their stories of loss, grief, and healing, many people have provided powerful examples of transforming even the most crushing forms of loss into rays of hope and meaning for themselves and others.

In the following sections, I discuss the literature on clinical views of severe grief, mourning, trauma, and intervention approaches and relate them to the present social psychological approach. I believe that the healing concepts outlined here devolve to the elements of forming a story, confiding, and acting. The first section, Pathologic Grief and Complicated Mourning, is related to the ideas discussed in Chapters 4 and 5 on the loss of close relationships through death or dissolution and in Chapter 9 on losses that haunt the survivor. The second section, Psychological Trauma and Its Complications, discusses the issues of grief resulting from war and violence that were described in Chapter 6. Stress and Coping, the third section, is also related to this chapter and to Chapter 7. Even the loss of employment or one's home, as discussed in that chapter, may instigate such reactions.

Winer (1994) has argued that the best therapy is mourning. Mourning makes it possible, to use Loewald's (1960) phrase, "to turn ghosts into ancestors." If this is true, each of the following therapeutic approaches may help people develop their stories of grief, express them to caring others, and make ancestors out of the ghosts that have haunted them.

PATHOLOGIC GRIEF AND COMPLICATED MOURNING

While all people will suffer losses and grieve, pathologic grief has a particular meaning among therapists in this area. Jacobs, in *Pathologic Grief* (1993), defines this type of grief as a state that occurs when a bereaved individual experiences chronic, intense depression and/or separation distress, which involves yearning or pining for the lost loved one. Jacobs indicates that this type of grief occurs in 20 percent of acutely bereaved individuals (which is a huge number considering that most people will be acutely bereaved on multiple occasions in their lives). Jacobs also notes that this type of grief is most often associated with the haunting memories—intrusive thoughts, images, and flashbacks—that were discussed in Chapter 9. When chronic grief occurs after major traumas, such as war or natural disasters, in which fear is a central emotion, Jacobs indicates that the survivor may engage in dissociative behavior (showing multiple personalities or separation from one's normal personality). When chronic grief occurs in the context of personal loss, such as the death of a loved one, Jacobs indicates that the survivor is more likely to show disbelief and numbness. Unexpected death is the type of personal loss most often associated with pathologic grief. Almost 30 percent of the individuals who experience such a loss have reported PTSD-type symptoms such as depression.

Jacobs discusses a clinical case of pathologic grief that has some similarity to stories reported in this book. Mr. D was a businessman, age forty-five, whose daughter was assaulted and murdered by a stranger high on drugs. Mr. D then experienced severe bereavement for over a year before seeking counseling. His grief was compounded by anger at the failure of the judicial system to bring the alleged murderer to justice promptly. He was tortured with images of his daughter's death, which left him feeling helpless, violated, and revengeful. He also experienced severe depression, thoughts of suicide, and thoughts of taking violent action against the alleged murderer. Mr. D was the key player in his family's work to bring the alleged murderer to trial and was very frustrated by defense actions that led to delays in the trial.

Fortunately, Mr. D did seek and receive therapy. That step and his constructive action to prod the judicial system to act more efficiently led to a reduction in his intense grief. He could see "light at the end of the tunnel" in gaining some justice for his daughter. Jacobs notes that therapists have often effectively treated pathologic grief such as Mr. D's with antidepressant drugs and psychotherapy. From the point of view of the story-action model, Mr. D's case supports the roles of the development of a story, confiding in the therapist, and action directed at the judicial system as key factors in his improvement.

Elizabeth Neeld's (1990) ideas about grief were developed after her husband's sudden death. Neeld provides a convincing argument that people in deep mourning face a series of choices that can facilitate their successful recovery. She outlines the following seven choices in this process:

1. *The impact of the event and the choice whether to experience and express grief fully.*
2. *The choice whether to suffer or to endure.*
3. *The choice whether to look honestly at oneself and one's life.*
4. *The turning-point choice whether to make an assertion with one's life.*
5. *The reconstruction choice of whether to take action.*
6. *The working-through choice of whether to engage in the inevitable conflicts that come after major loss.*
7. *The integrative choice to continue to make choices—that is the nature of life—and to feel freedom from the domination of grief.*

Neeld's map of the grieving process is quite idealized. Do people engaged in powerful mourning have to go through this whole process? Will failures to choose at some interim point preclude the ultimate freedom from the domination of grief? Neeld's analysis helps us understand the consequences of loss because she outlines how each of these choices was involved in her own recovery. People do not make these choices in a vacuum. Neeld suggests that survivors can best deal with their choices when they have strong support from family and friends, when they have already dealt with past major losses, and when their social, economic, and personal circumstances afford them the time and opportunity to grieve fully. This latter factor is too often neglected in scholarly analyses of grieving: Do people have so little energy left from trying to scrounge out a living that giving time to grieving becomes an impossible luxury? Neeld notes persuasively that the behavior of family and friends is critical in the grieving process. For example, she argues that if these close others are uncomfortable with mourning, if they act as if the grieving person should already be done with grieving, then grieving may be extended indefinitely.

Neeld's approach to healing bears considerable similarity to the position of Therese Rando's *Treatment of Complicated Mourning* (1993), which was discussed in Chapter 4. Rando provides a thorough analysis of different aspects of mourning and recovery. She devotes considerable attention to the concept of "complicated mourning." This concept is quite similar to Jacobs's (1993) notion of pathologic grief: mourning that exceeds what is considered to be the norm and that defies modest attempts at intervention. In some ways, Rando's concept flies in the face of some of the discussion in this book, which argues that all mourning is complicated. However, it is true that some people reach peace and move on with their lives more readily than others. It is also true, however, that some people desire to move on but cannot readily do so. For them, the mourning process is most definitively complex in nature. Rando lists a set of risk factors that predispose any individual to complicated mourning: sudden, unexpected death (especially involving trauma, randomness, or violence); death from an overly lengthy illness; loss of a child; the mourner's perception of the death as preventable; a pre-death relationship with the deceased that involved high degrees of anger, dependence, or ambivalence; other losses that the mourner still is grieving; and the mourner's perceived lack of social support.

Rando believes that the mourner experiences six major mourning processes: (1) recognizing and acknowledging that the loss has occurred; (2) reacting to the separation by being willing to experience the pain—to feel, identify, and accept; (3) recollecting and reexperiencing the deceased and the relationship, which involves an attempt to plan times to review and remember realistically; (4) relinquishing attachments to the deceased and to ways of viewing the world that were idiosyncratic to the lost relationship; (5) readjusting to the new world without forgetting the old; and (6) reinvesting in new relationships and acts of meaning. These six correspond closely to the steps in the story-action model. Rando makes the following specific recommendations to the caregiver about working with a mourner in his or her act of confiding:

> *Help the mourner understand that it is precisely those emotions that go unexpressed that prompt loss of control and that there is great value in expressing a little emotion at a time in order to avoid an accumulation that will explode later on. . . .*
>
> *Encourage expression of feelings with those people and in those places that are comfortable and without threat. If none exist, work to establish them (e.g., enlist the aid of an appropriate family member or provide referral to a support group). Given that social support is critical in the mourning process, it is inadvisable for the mourner to remain isolated. (pp. 402–403)*

The importance of the confidant's role in a survivor's recovery also is emphasized by Meichenbaum and Fitzpatrick (1992), who suggest that the confidant (who may be a therapist) needs to "establish a nurturant, compassionate, nonjudgmental set of conditions" (p. 37) that permits survivors to tell their story at their own pace. Meichenbaum and colleagues have done considerable work with people suffering from various types of stress reactions and refer to stress inoculation training as a form of narrative reconstruction (Meichenbaum, 1985).

PSYCHOLOGICAL TRAUMA AND ITS COMPLICATIONS

Trauma may occur in a variety of circumstances. The sudden loss of a loved one may be traumatic to the survivor in much the same way that combat veterans' experiences of the death of friends and their own close calls may traumatize them. As an initial question, then, are certain types of personalities more resistant to the consequences of trauma?

One interesting study of Holocaust survivors and the lives they made in America after liberation was conducted by William Helmreich and reported in his book, *Against All Odds* (1992). Helmreich reviewed available data on the 140,000 Jewish Holocaust survivors who came to the United States and conducted over six years of interviews with them. His study points to the incredible resilience of the survivors under the worst possible conditions. He argues that the following ten traits or qualities characterized those survivors who were able to lead positive, useful lives in the United States: flexibility, assertiveness, tenacity, optimism, intelligence, distancing ability, group consciousness, assimilating the knowledge that they survived, finding meaning in their lives, and courage. Helmreich notes that not all of these qualities were present in each individual and that not all people who succeeded possessed most of these attributes. However, at least some of these qualities were present in the majority of those survivors who did well in their postwar work and personal lives. Further, the greater the number of these traits present within an individual, the greater the likelihood of successful adjustment.

A well-written analysis of psychological trauma appears in Judith Herman's (1992) *Trauma and Recovery*. Herman suggests that a number of types of survivors, including combat veterans, concentration camp survivors, crime victims, battered and abused children and spouses, and prisoners of war, frequently are traumatized by their experiences and sometimes to an extreme degree (i.e., "complicated trauma"). Complicated trauma involves behaviors such as denial, withdrawal, and aggression, as well as shame, hopelessness, and helplessness. Herman argues that the first principle of all recovery is empowerment of the survivor. She believes that there are three major phases involved in helping people deal with such trauma. The first is helping the survivor feel safe. This step is a prelude to effective healing. It involves creating an environment in which the survivor feels safe in confiding details of an event that may have greatly violated and degraded him or her. It also involves helping the survivor reestablish a sense of personal control such that he or she can begin to work on the meanings of the trauma.

The second phase involves facilitating a survivor's remembrance of the traumatic event and mourning the loss involved. This is the most difficult and potentially lengthy phase in the healing process. It involves story development and storytelling about the event. In this phase, the survivor actually reconstructs the event so that it can be integrated into her or his life story. Part of the difficulty in a survivor's work in the story phase is that the trauma may lead to emotionless, stereotyped reporting of what happened. Thus, it is important to help the survivor to achieve a comfort level wherein she or he can express emotions, including images and bodily feelings, as part of the interpretive, communicative act.

This act of confiding, or telling about one's loss and pain, may fill the survivor with anxiety (as well as the person to whom the confidence is directed). A person who had experienced incest made the following comment about what it felt like to confide in her family:

> *Initially I felt a sense of completion. . . . Then, I began to feel very sad, deep grief. It was painful and I had no words for what I was feeling. . . . This was just raw feeling. Loss, grief, mourning. . . . I knew there was nothing unspoken on my part. . . . I had said everything I wanted to say in the way I wanted to say it. I felt very complete about it and was very grateful for the lengthy planning, rehearsals. . . . Since then I have felt free. . . . I feel HOPE! (Herman, 1992, p. 201)*

It should be noted that Herman argues, and I strongly agree, that we never achieve total completion in our grieving and interpretive reconstruction. New reflections about loss will recur at various points in our lives, particularly at new turning points. Our regrets and horrors, as well as our joys, never completely leave our minds and sometimes recur in our thoughts and emotions when we least expect them. We nonetheless may achieve a high degree of completion and in so doing free ourselves to take on new challenges.

The third and final phase in Herman's model of recovery from trauma involves helping the survivor reconnect with the world and create a new future. It may involve reeducation about what is typical, what to expect, and what is possible. The survivor needs to reestablish personal control over how he or she continues to work on the trauma. For example, Herman presents the following quote from an incest survivor who was arriving at this point in her recovery:

> *I decided, "Okay, I've had enough of walking around like I'd like to brutalize everyone who looks at me wrong. I don't have to feel like that any more. . . ."*
>
> *I thought, "How would I like to feel?" I wanted to feel safe in the world. I wanted to feel powerful. And so I focused on what was working in my life, on the ways I was taking power in real-life situations. (p. 197)*

Herman suggests that reconnection involves a conscious decision to be willing to face danger in the future. It also involves an emerging tenacity, a learning how to fight in the face of vulnerabilities. It may involve some concrete act such as learning self-defense. I personally believe that another approach to dealing with past loss and continued feelings of vulnerability involves focusing on helping others in need.

Herman argues that the simple statement "I know I have myself" could stand as the emblem of a survivor's recovery and reconnection with the world. Reconciling with oneself probably will require creativity and energy, as does reconciling with close others in one's environment. There is a new focus on identity and intimacy in these reconciliations. Survivors often form close bonds with other survivors and plan futures together. A person introduced to an incest survivor's group commented on the affirmative nature of the group acceptance:

> *I will look to this group experience as a turning point in my life, and remember the shock of recognition when I realized that the strength I so readily saw in the other women who have survived this . . . violation was also within me. (Herman, 1992, p. 216)*

As suggested in the story-action model, Herman believes that an important aspect of reconnection is finding a survivor mission. This step involves using one's experience and renewed capacity for action to work with others facing personal difficulties. Common to various types of social action is a dedication to raising public awareness about issues and problems facing various types of survivors. A Vietnam veteran told Herman about the value of his work with homeless veterans:

> *This is about being an American, this is about what you learn in a fourth-grade civics class, this is about taking care of our own, this is about my brother. This feels personal to me. That feeling of isolation, it's gone. I'm so connected into it, it's therapeutic to me. (p. 209)*

STRESS AND COPING

Donald Meichenbaum, a cognitive behavioral theorist and therapist, has developed what he calls Stress Inoculation Training (SIT) to help people cope with severe stresses in their lives. At the heart of this approach is the individual's telling of his or her narrative about the stressful event.

As described by Meichenbaum (1985) and Meichenbaum and Fitzpatrick (1992), SIT involves (1) a (re)conceptualization phase, (2) a coping skills acquisition and rehearsal phase, and (3) an application and follow-through phase. Initially, it is critical for the therapist or trainer to establish a nurturant, compassionate, nonjudgmental set of conditions in which distressed individuals can tell their story at their own pace. The therapist may use reflective listening, Socratic dialogue, sensitive probes, imagery reconstruction, and other techniques to help the individual explain what has happened and why from his or her perspective. The exchanges between the therapist and client help the client make sense of the difficult experiences and give meaning to the experiences in his or her life. The therapist may ask, "Has anything positive come out of this experience for you?" Because meaning can determine the extent to which a given circumstance is a stressor and because meaning varies among people and with time, those in the same circumstances may be coping with qualitatively different stressors. It is important to understand this meaning so that it can be confronted and its implications considered.

In the second phase, the therapist begins a type of narrative repair. The therapist tries to help the client normalize his or her reactions to the stressor. The therapist helps the client appreciate that his or her reactions to the stressor are not abnormal, that these reactions reflect one of a set of normal ways of perceiving and reacting to a difficult situation. The therapist may help the client reframe the stressful symptoms as part of a normal, spontaneous, reconstructive process and not as a sign of weakness. Thus, emotional numbing and denial are characterized as ways individuals who have experienced trauma pace themselves because they can deal with only a limited amount of stress at a given time.

A later aspect of SIT involves appraisal of the distress process. The therapist helps the client develop a more differentiated and integrated view of the stress by helping the client break complex distressing reactions into specific, concrete, behaviorally prescriptive components. This may help the client to recognize the difference between changeable and unchangeable aspects of stressful situations. The therapist may also help clients rescript what they say to themselves. Clients also are taught to practice these coping skills so that they can review the results of their efforts. Consistent with my view of the power of storytelling and story-reframing, what matters most about this type of narrative reconstruction is not its historical truthfulness but its narrative truthfulness—the coherence of the story for the individual's life, goals, and new plans for action.

THE SPECIAL ROLE OF WRITING IN HEALING

The next thing most like living one's life over again seems to be a recollection of that life, and to make that recollection as durable as possible by putting it down in writing.
—Benjamin Franklin

Writing appears to have a restorative power. The work of social psychologist James Pennebaker (1990), which has been mentioned in connection with the importance of confiding behavior, sheds light on the value of writing. He and his colleagues have conducted several experimental studies over the past decade that have shown that people who write about their traumatic experiences (including sexual abuse and suicide attempts) visit medical doctors for health problems much less often after writing about their experiences than they did before writing; they also visit doctors less often than people who wrote not about their traumas but about trivial events in their lives. Pennebaker and colleagues have argued that writing reduces the physical and mental stress involved in inhibiting thoughts (i.e., thoughts designed to avoid or distract oneself from thinking about personal traumas) by helping the survivor face the chaotic thoughts and gain a sense of control in dealing with them.

In fact, in the last two decades there has appeared a plethora of books by people grappling with traumatic experiences. These works conform closely to the story-action model: Writer experiences a trauma that devastates him or her for some lengthy period. Writer begins to come to grips with the event, develops a story, becomes aware of comfort instead of uncontrollable anxiety and helplessness. Writer starts to change in major ways who he or she is as a consequence of the event. Writer starts to talk about the event to close others and then to the public at large in the form of speeches and a book. Writer sees this as his or her cause célèbre. Writer wants to help others in similar circumstances.

Nancy Mairs, in a *New York Times Book Review* commentary (1993), speaks of her contribution to this literature on victimization, survival, and healing:

Because my books have dealt candidly with my own multiple sclerosis, suicidal depression and agoraphobia, as well as my husband's melanoma, I am frequently asked to review or endorse works that belong to a distinct though largely unrecognized subgenre I've come to call, only half-facetiously, the Literature of Personal Disaster. . . .

> *The fact is that the true victim—the person set apart from ordinary human intercourse by temporary or permanent misfortune—has little enough time and even less energy for sniveling. . . . There are hands to be held and basins to be emptied and upper lips to be kept stiff. . . . Self-pity simply doesn't provide an adequate motive for going to the effort of writing a book about the ordeal. (pp. 1 and 25)*

Mair says that for many, the temptation to put their experience on paper is too great to resist. She also bemoans how the product too often is divorced and distant from the raw experience (mentioning William Styron's *Darkness Visible* about his severe bouts with depression as one such example). I do not think, however, that Mair's commentary considers adequately the value such works may have for the audience. Many readers may gain needed resolve and hope from such books. As for the benefit to the writer, if one has the drive to write—even if it is a half-legible personal diary that never will be made public—that drive probably signals the potential healing value of the activity. Certainly, the truest expression of pain may be the most valuable. But what is true or full expression to one person may be quite limited to another.

Whether or not people write about their lives and losses, I believe that telling one's story in some form is imperative to health. In the main, the following examples of stories of healing are just lines people have uttered to other people about events that jolted them and how they eventually dealt with the events. Sometimes, as noted at the beginning, these lines constitute the barest of stories in terms of number of words, paragraphs, or descriptive and interpretive material. While minute in content and form, however, they can be exceedingly revealing and affecting in meaning.

GRIEF SUPPORT GROUPS AND HOSPICES

> *A loving relationship is the therapy for all disorders of the human spirit.*
> —C.H. Patterson

Stories and storytelling are vital activities carried out in grief support groups and in hospices. In support groups, one hears countless stories and experiences a plethora of vicarious emotions as tellers share their struggles with the group. After an early period of grieving during which being alone may be quite essential to the survivor, it may help to join a support group. Most cities have many different kinds of support groups. Survivors need to do research before they join one. It probably will help to inquire of both leaders and regular members about the goals and activities of the relevant groups.

In *I'm Grieving as Fast as I Can* (1994), Linda Feinberg describes the value she found in a grief support group for young widowed persons after she lost her husband. She suggests that widowed people need to laugh and are good at it when given the chance. Sitting with a group for ten minutes can be an emotional roller coaster, as people tell their stories. People quickly learn that they are not the only ones sitting at home feeling miserable. She says that widowed young parents with children at home may feel a special sense of isolation. If left to their own devices, they will probably never even meet another young widowed person. That is where well-run grief groups are valuable. Survivors meet people like themselves. The group members can struggle together in dealing with the common feeling of being cheated out of a long and happy marriage.

As Gilda Radner endeavored to publicize before she died, there now are many excellent cancer wellness programs around the country. Central to these programs are support groups. Members may be dying of their cancer, but they also are trying to live as hopefully and fully as they can. And they are helping others in the process. Noting that friends and family may find stories of the cancer progression and treatment scary, members find that in these groups they can tell their stories without restraint. Humor bubbles up regularly during meetings. The humor may be black but it is appreciated.

Although many of us would like to die at home, we may need medical assistance in the form of nurses or medical technology. Hospices exist to provide a feeling of being at home coupled with appropriate medical assistance. In a hospice, which often is a regular home in a community, the emphasis is on the quality of life. The medical care is aimed primarily at controlling pain and restoring normal functioning. Hospice services are requested only after the person or physician believes that no treatment or cure is possible. Clients and their families are viewed as a unit. An attempt is made to keep clients free of pain. The role of the staff is on being with the client rather than doing something for the client, as in a hospital. The emphasis is on emotional and social support (Saunders, 1977).

STORIES OF HEALING FROM MAJOR LOSS

The *Chicago Tribune*, on June 2, 1994, ran an obituary for Wray McKenzie who died at age seventy-two. During World War II, McKenzie was a prisoner in Germany. It seems that he, as a bombardier on a B-17, was taken prisoner after his plane was shot down over Holland during a raid on Germany in July 1943. A Dutch girl who was riding by on a bicycle helped him from the wreckage, and in appreciation, he gave the girl the only thing he had in his pocket, a U.S. quarter. McKenzie later was captured and spent time in Stalag 17. In 1985, forty-two years after being shot down over Holland, he and his wife returned to Holland to visit the site where the plane crashed. They also located the widower of the girl who had rescued him. This man showed them a necklace she had worn all of her life. It was a chain holding a U.S. quarter with a hole drilled through it! In this little story, deep meaning is found in a quarter. It symbolized the bond of one human being's care for another—an act that spanned time, oceans, and other wars with other heroes and dramas of life and death.

Still another moving story is contained in Eva Fogelman's book, *Conscience and Courage* (1994), which tells the stories of rescuers of Jews during World War II. One of the people she highlighted was a small businessman in Warsaw, Poland, at the time of the Nazi takeover. When the Nazis created the Warsaw ghetto, from which Jews were shipped to concentration camps, this man said that he was curious about what was happening in the ghetto and found a way to visit it. He said that one transforming moment in that visit motivated him to spend the next four years risking his life and the lives of his family to help Jews hide from the Nazis. This moment was the sight of flies swarming over the bodies of dead and dying children.

The stories that follow also illustrate courage and exemplary actions in dealing with grievous personal loss. Quite apart from the ideas we as scholars use to try to explain these actions, they offer paradigms of hope for all people in dealing with their own losses. The quote on the title page of this book reflects only grace and strength in the face of death. In that one instant, the young man who, the former Vietnam nurse quotes, went to heroic lengths to express thanks—an act that not only stuck in the memories of his nurses but also will stick in the memories of all of us who hear about it.

Audrey Hepburn's Love for Children

Audrey Hepburn died of cancer at age sixty-three in early 1993. She had lived a life that involved surviving fear and hunger as a teenager in Holland during World War II and then going on to charm the world with her beauty, grace, and talent as she starred in twenty-five films and many television and Broadway productions, including the award-winning *Gigi* in 1952. But her greatest legacy, achieved over the last five years of her life, was her work on behalf of UNICEF, the United Nations International Children's Emergency Fund, in Ethiopia, Sudan, El Salvador, Guatemala, Honduras, Bangladesh, Vietnam, and Somalia. These five years of work gave her greater meaning than she had found in all of her film successes, and those she helped were blessed by her words and deeds. In commenting on the impact of her time in Nazi-held Holland, when the country was being punished by the Nazis for resistance, she said. "Your soul is nourished by all your experiences. It gives you ammunition for the future." She also said her mother's behavior was an inspiration for her desire to serve others:

It's that wonderful, old-fashioned idea that others come first, you come second. This was the whole ethic by which I was brought up. Others matter more than you do, so "Don't fuss, dear; get on with it." (People Extra, 1993, p. 65)

In reflecting on her experience with starving children in Somalia, she said:

No media report could have prepared me for the unspeakable agony I felt seeing countless little, fragile, emaciated children sitting under the trees, waiting to be fed, most of them ill. I'll never forget their huge eyes in tiny faces and the terrible silence. (People Extra, 1993, p. 66)

Hepburn's work on behalf of starving children became known and respected around the world. In the countries she visited, she held press conferences to tell the world of what she found in looking into the eyes of hungry, often dying children:

I do not want to see [Ethiopians, then in the middle of a civil war] digging graves for their children. As Gandhi said, "Wars cannot be won by bullets but only by bleeding hearts." (People Extra, 1993, p. 65)

Knowing that she had only a little time left, she made trips to Somalia to aid children there until near the end of her life. In an October 31, 1994, *People* article about Hepburn's legacy, her son Sean said that Hepburn did not feel dying was unjust but that it was part of nature. At the time of Hepburn's death, Shirley MacLaine said of her, "If there was a cross between the salt of the earth and a regal queen, then she was it" (*People Weekly*, 1993, p. 61). Film critic Rex Reed said, "She was living proof that God could still create perfection" (*People Weekly*, 1993, p. 64).

C.S. Lewis's Steps Toward Healing

I return now to C.S. Lewis's grief over the loss of his wife, Joy Davidman. As discussed in earlier chapters, Lewis intensely grieved Joy's death and wrote about his grief in a diary. After a couple of years of grieving, he began to find peace. Lewis records this period toward the end of his diary, which he later published as *A Grief Observed*.

Something quite unexpected has happened. For various reasons, not in themselves at all mysterious, my heart was lighter than it had been for many weeks. For one thing I suppose I am recovering from a good deal of mere exhaustion, and after ten days of low hung grey skies and motionless warm dampness, the sun was shining and there was a light breeze. And

suddenly, at the very moment when so far, I mourned [Joy] least, I remem-
bered her best. Indeed it was something almost better than memory: an in-
stantaneous unanswerable impression. To say it was like a meeting would
go too far. Yet there was that in it which tempts one to use those words. It
was as if the lifting of the sorrow removed a barrier. Why has no one told
me these things? How easily I have misjudged another man in the same
situation. I might have said, "He's got over it. He's forgotten his wife,"
when the truth was, "He remembers her better because he has partly got
over it." (1961, pp. 38–39)

Davidman and her courage near the time of her death opened Lewis up
to feelings that he never had experienced or expressed. In turn, his writing
about grief stands as a monument not only to this special relationship but
also to the eternal verities of the people's experience of loss and healing.

Ordinary Folk with Extraordinary Stories and Contributions

Beyond the well-known people with their stories of loss, recovery, and heroism are countless ordinary people who bear similar stories—many of which
never come to light. Stories of generative acts by survivors of great loss dot
the landscape. They may involve small acts such as the dying soldier's effort to thank his nurses, but they have enormous psychological value to
those involved and to those who hear about them. Symbolically they bring
care and compassion into a world that too often does not seem to have time
to care for its own. Suffering has ennobled the works of many common people who have experienced the depths of loss.

There are whole groups of people who have found a "survivor's mission," to use Judith Herman's (1992) term. Vietnam veterans constitute one
such group. Recently, women veterans have been at the forefront in enlarg-
ing the public's awareness of the losses and PTSD-type reactions still suffered by some nurses, Red Cross workers, and women serving in various
other positions twenty years after the end of that war. Over 11,000 women
served in Vietnam.

In November 1993, a bronze statue of three women—one of them
cradling a wounded soldier—was placed near the Vietnam Wall in Washington, D.C. Patricia Heyer, a theater instructor entertaining the troops in Vietnam, was working at Phuoc Binh with the 101st Airborne Division during the
deadly Tet offensive of 1968. She was in favor of the development of this
monument because another statue (showing three soldiers supporting one
another) recognizing U.S. male soldiers' roles in the war had been created and
placed near the Wall, but nothing had been specifically done to honor the
women's contribution. Here is what she said of her time in Vietnam:

You couldn't direct plays because you never knew who would be back that evening. Mostly we talked to the men and let them cry on our shoulders. We got the brunt of the Dear John letters from home [that were reported to them by soldiers receiving them from their now ex-girlfriends back home]. Because we were there for morale we had to be pleasant and walk around with a smile. We felt it was a major responsibility to be that way because we could be the last American women these guys would see. (Smith, 1993, p. C1)

At the time, the stress of it got to Heyer, who says that she would sit in her bathtub and cry. After she left Vietnam, however, for many years she didn't think about it until one day when she was washing her hair under a faucet she had a flashback to Phuoc Binh and the sounds of battle. Ms. Heyer then sought the help of a Vietnam veterans' support group and began to deal with her pain and unexpressed feelings of loss. This time it was the men who helped her. "Those men helped me, they took my hand" (Smith, 1993, p. C1).

Like many veterans of Normandy, women who served in Vietnam often reported that it was the central, most important time in their lives. For many the constant fight to save lives not only drained them but also gave their lives and work a meaning that they have not found since the war's end. For many in combat zones, the adrenalin high was of such magnitude that all that has occurred in their lives since then pales in comparison. Nurse Kathy Ormond said that her greatest fear occurred both right after she arrived and just before she left Vietnam. A memory that haunts her is of her last week in Vietnam, "I would go out to the fire bases, and I'd keep my sunglasses on as much as I could because I was crying so much. I felt like a traitor for leaving" (Smith, 1993, p. 8C).

Like many male combat veterans, quite a few of the women who served in Vietnam started to come out with reports of their trauma in the early 1980s. These women became galvanized behind the start-up of the Women's Vietnam Memorial campaign in the 1990s. This campaign became a step toward healing for many. One for whom it has meant greater meaning, hope, and healing is Carolyn Tanaka, a former Vietnam nurse. In November 1993, *People Weekly* profiled her and one of the men she helped during the war, Rory Bailey. He was an Army private who had had much of his face shot off. Tanaka's task in caring for him was to keep him from drowning in the blood gushing from his wounds. Over the years, they exchanged letters and calls, but Tanaka wondered if Bailey's disfigured face could ever be mended by plastic surgeons.

They finally had a date to meet again twenty-five years after she had suctioned blood from the hole that used to be his face. It was the unveiling of the Women's Memorial on Veteran's Day, 1993. They met at the monument. She hugged him and did not let go. He held her tight and did not say anything. Bailey has undergone two hundred surgeries to restore his face to more or less normal. There still is a long way to go to achieve that look and lessen the stares of strangers. Both Bailey and Tanaka have suffered. According to *People Weekly*, however, they both have constructive orientations toward what they are doing with their lives. Tanaka has been very active in the development of funds for the memorial. She indicated it was a "long-overdue thank-you to all the women who have served in every war, beginning with Florence Nightingale" (*People Weekly*, 1993, p. 52).

Following are the stories of some other regular people who have used loss and grief to spur them to unusual contributions.

- Students, parents, and teachers at Rolling Meadows High School outside of Chicago, in May 1994, created a memorial garden at the school dedicated to their twenty-eight friends, children, pupils, and teachers who have died in the twenty-three years since the school began. The garden was created also to remind students that they are mortal. Many of those remembered in the garden died in car accidents, often involving alcohol. This memorial eloquently suggests that we all need to be more vigilant in our recognition of how readily young people can die in "the flower of life."

- As described in Chapter 4, the Pan Am Flight 103 parents' organization has achieved many noble works to remember their children who died in the bombing of the plane over Scotland in 1988 and to capture the suspected terrorists who planted the bomb.

- Some of the most effective crusaders of the 1990s are the women's organizations that focus on dealing with the life-threatening problems women frequently experience. One such group is the Lynn Sage Cancer Research Foundation in Chicago. Sage died of breast cancer in 1984. Her very good friends Ellen Beda, Joan Epstein, and Diane Greengross—colleagues who had achieved unusual emotional intimacy as friends—led an effort to make her death more meaningful. They were scoffed at by a professional fundraiser who thought that their plans would never come to fruition. In nine years, they have raised $3 million and added a comprehensive breast cancer center to a woman's hospital in Chicago.

- In January 1994, Leslie and Dana Williams commemorated the first birthday since their sister Lea's death by running in a fundraiser to benefit the fight against cancer. Lea died of cancer after having been diagnosed in 1991. It was Leslie's first birthday without her twin sister, who would have been twenty-six. Dana is twenty-seven. Leslie and Dana had decided to run in honor of their sister who loved to run and who had been on track teams in high school and college. With knowledge of

Lea's possible death, the three sisters, who lived in different places, met in 1993 for one final reunion in Key West, Florida. They talked, dined, and danced to street music at a restaurant near the ocean. Lea fought for and lived life fully to the end. She was a graduate student in psychology at Duke University. She engaged in regular aerobic exercise and went rock climbing. After she was diagnosed, the sisters wrote and recorded a song, "Miracle of Life," about meeting cancer's challenge. Everyone in the family wears a gold angel necklace in memory of Lea. Leslie said, "I don't like people to feel sorry for us, because we were so blessed to have the time we did" (Swegle, 1994, p. 3A).

- Erica Mallard was thirteen in 1993 when she lost her grandfather. He had been one of the most important people in her life. When he died near the beginning of Erica's school year, she was confused and sank into despair. Soon after starting school, however, she met Emanuel Hughes, also thirteen, who had recently lost his father. They bonded in their grief and soon began a project that would transform their grief into courage to deal with their losses. They learned together how to heal through their project. They began a book about Erica's memories accompanied by pictures that Emanuel drew. As Erica told of how she cried and cried when she saw her grandfather lying in his casket and how she felt pain for her grandmother, Emanuel drew pictures that reflected her feelings. The book, *Remembrance*, was awarded one of the Young Authors Awards in the Chicago Public Schools in 1994.

- Former model and actress Shelley Smith gave up her work after her son Justin died three days after his birth in 1989 of a rare genetic condition. She said:

> It's a cliche to say that that changed my life, but it did. After he died, I felt like I was walking around under water. It was horribly traumatic, and I was suffering from post-traumatic stress disorder.
>
> After a while I realized that the only way I was going to be able to heal myself was to help other people who had suffered a similar loss. (Knaff, 1994, sec. 6, p. 3)

Smith went on to obtain training and begin a practice in marriage and family counseling. In 1991, she established the Surrogacy Program to offer a number of services to infertile couples.

- In 1980, a grieving mother named Candy Lightner started Mothers Against Drunk Driving after her daughter, age thirteen, was killed by a drunken driver. She quit her job as a California real estate agent to devote herself fully to the cause. Now the organization works in every state with hundreds of chapters nationwide. It is credited for changing both state and federal laws to increase the accountability of drunken drivers who kill someone. (Bartenders and bar owners are increasingly in the spotlight in litigation resulting from deaths occurring because of patrons' excessive drinking).

- Miya Rodolfo-Sioson's life was drastically changed on November 1, 1991, when she was shot by a recent Ph.D. in physics, Gang Lu, at the University of Iowa. Lu was upset that he was passed over for a university award for best dissertation that year in favor of another Ph.D. student in physics—his former friend who had become his rival. That day, Lu killed three of his former professors, a university administrator, his rival for the university award, and then himself. Ms. Rodolfo-Sioson, now paralyzed from the neck down, was the only survivor of Lu's shootings. Through over a year of slow rehabilitation and trying to begin a new life, she has maintained a positive attitude, and her life will stand as a model for others who suffer such losses. A gifted student, she has begun taking classes toward a second degree and wants to go to El Salvador to work as a volunteer as she had planned before Gang Lu's rampage. She is aided by a brother and sister who have come to live with her for the time being. They form a very close family. She indicates that she has no bitterness toward Gang Lu—such feelings would have no value now. She said that early after the shooting, she asked, " 'Why me?,' a lot. Then you figure out it's pretty much useless asking it. So, you don't do it anymore and just try to focus more on adapting to a new lifestyle and moving on" (DeWall, 1993, p. 5A).

DO SOME RECOVER WITHOUT GRIEVING?

Can people heal from great pain and suffering without grief, stories, and action designed to reconstruct their lives? Perhaps. Some people—emergency room medical personnel and police working in violent neighborhoods—may become inured to the sights and sounds of death and grieving. They put aside their feelings to keep going. The same is true of soldiers in combat. Becoming hardened to death, however, is not the same as healing. What has been argued throughout this book, and in much of the literature reviewed in this book, is that grieving major loss and putting one's life back together requires considerable work and good friends and confidants. The question remains, however: Do some people move on readily without much grief?

Researchers Camille Wortman and Roxane Silver (1992) have reported on the experience of parents who have lost children to sudden infant death syndrome. They interviewed the parents soon after their infant's death and again after one and one-half years. Wortman and Silver report that in the first interview parents showed some anxiety but also positive emotions and little major distress. Were these parents in denial? No, according to the researchers. Eighteen months later the parents continued to show strong signs of adaptation without major grief. Wortman and Silver have found that parents' religious devotion and participation in religious activities were positively related to coping. The mediating factor apparently was their feeling that they would see their children someday in heaven. However, it could be argued that even eighteen months may be too soon to see the effects of denial. It is possible that the parents who grieved little in this first year and a half will eventually need to come to grips with their grief. Otherwise, they may suffer in various ways physically and psychologically.

Wortman and Silver's work (1989, 1992) suggests the intricacies of the grieving experience and that we still know too little about its convolutions. In their 1992 study, the authors report that a sample of older persons who had lost spouses showed only a moderate degree of distress. Wortman and Silver speculate that these people may have grieved prior to their spouses' deaths and that the deaths in many cases may have been seen as positive events because of the spouses' extended period of suffering prior to death. Certainly, as we live long lives, we begin to experience regularly the deaths of kin and friends. It is in the nature of things that we have learned to expect and accept. Further, as our bodies age and become infirm in many ways, we may simply be tired of the living ourselves and recognize the blessing of death for our colleagues who also suffer.

Thus, for some of us as we become quite old, death is healing for ourselves and our loved ones. We do not necessarily articulate this reality, but we know it is true and accept it. Such a conclusion provides a fitting final irony to this book's message of the power of storytelling and confiding in dealing with loss and grief. For some near the end of long lives, there is no more story to develop, no more words to be spoken, no more tears to be wept. There is completion of the story in our acceptance of the life lived—there is meaning! Past sorrows no longer haunt and hurt.

A QUESTION TO THE READER

Just as I began with the proposition that grief is omnipresent in our lives, I end with a question about the overall value of life: In the big picture of things, what value do you wish to have ascribed to your life, or anything about you, 1,000 years from now? We so often talk about providing for our children and their children. But what about a time when the generations of our particular family have come to an end? What contribution would we hope to make that would last until then? I would suggest that we all face that ultimate type of loss—loss of our particular gene pool and bloodline. But should we necessarily despair? Our lives count for something in the ideas and values we put into practice that will continue to impact people indefinitely into the future. These ideas and beliefs are parts of the stories we form and tell about our lives. We, too, have received and benefited from past generations' contributions of stories. This continuity is generativity in its most cogent manifestation. Hence, in the end, the stories we form in our lives, particularly about those events that affect us most, are our unassailable contributions. They will continue and even flourish when our personal bloodline and genes have long ceased to exist.

> *Sorrow . . . turns out to be not a state but a process. It needs not a map but a history. . . . There is something new to be chronicled every day.*
> —C.S. Lewis

> *A human being is part of the whole called by us universe. . . . He experiences himself, his thoughts and feelings as something separated from the rest, a kind of optical delusion of his consciousness. This delusion is a kind of prison for us, restricting us to our personal desires and to affection for a few persons nearest to us. Our task must be to free ourselves from this prison by widening our circle of compassion to embrace all living creatures and the whole of nature in its beauty.*
> —Albert Einstein

Without the pain that comes from significant loss, there can be no story. Without the storytelling, there can be no meaning. Without meaning, there can be no healing.

NEW DIRECTIONS IN THE STORYTELLING APPROACH TO LOSS

Human beings are storytellers by nature. In many guises,
as folktale, legend, myth, epic, history, motion picture and
television program, the story appears in every known
human culture.

—Dan P. McAdams

In this book, I have sought to make a case for the merit of McAdams's statement. In this epilogue, I outline what I perceive to be the future directions
for this type of analysis of loss. In so doing, I again emphasize the argument
in Chapter 12 on the potential transcending value of loss—namely, that it
opens the survivor's eyes to the possibility that he or she can give back to
others who are suffering or will suffer similar types of losses.

The overall aim of this book on loss has been to empower all people,
whether or not they consider themselves victims or survivors, with greater
courage, the will to continue to try to live life fully, and a certain perspective
about the broad continuum of human suffering and loss. As emphasized in
Chapter 1, we are all interdependent and our brother's keepers. Every chapter and any piece of advice offered is based on the assumption that it is far
more empowering to live one's life, even in its final days, with as much
knowledge as possible of what is happening to the self and in the world at
large. Denial or avoidance have no place in this analysis.

I contend that it is decidedly more empowering to confront loss than it
is to run from loss, although both must have their limits. Certainly the per-

vasiveness of loss in human life does not need to be pushed down our throats all the time. Yet, at the same time, recognition of our mortality, the mortality of others, and the many ways we are diminished as humans can be both humanizing and enlightening.

TEACHING, RESEARCHING, AND WRITING STORIES OF LOSS

What stories can do, I guess, is make things present.
—Tim O'Brien

Novelists can disclose as much about the nature of people as psychologists and sociologists, not because writers occasionally behave "scientifically," or "systematically," but because psychologists and sociologists can only see the world in the same fundamental terms as novelists, no matter how much they envelop their research in esoteric techniques and abstruse jargon.
—Frank Smith

A major goal of this book is to enhance work on stories of loss, whether that work involves the development of college and high-school courses or more integrative research and writing. As I have espoused throughout this book, loss is a concept that brings together a host of diverse human experiences that may be better understood by viewing them as part of a life's constellation of losses. Focusing on stories of loss in different spheres can help to synthesize different experiences and aspects of loss. I believe that writing, teaching, and research on this topic will help people, including students, grow in their capacity to be empathic with others and give them greater strength in dealing with their own inevitable adversities.

Focusing on the stories and narratives of people who encounter loss facilitates learning. This theme is found in other writers' advocacy of greater study of people's use of narrative in dealing with life's dilemmas (e.g., Coles, 1989; Bruner, 1990). Narratives give us insight into people's thoughts, feelings, and words as they deal with issues of living, sometimes failing and sometimes succeeding. Stories both teach and heal as they construct versions of reality that endow experience with meaning. As Tim O'Brien suggests, stories make others' worlds come a bit more alive and palpable in our minds. O'Brien's tales, including his most recent novel *In the Lake of the Woods* (1994), tell of the faceless grief experienced by many Vietnam combat veterans and help us understand better what these individuals continue to experience and feel guilty about more than two decades after the fact. As the quotation from Frank Smith suggests, there is great power in the story to tap the heart of human affairs. For each of us, no matter what we do, some of the information we find most compelling about the nature of human life is derived from stories we have processed and reprocessed.

Since the beginning of the human species, storytelling has played an educational and inspirational role in people's lives. Certainly, gurus, shamans, witch doctors, diviners, priests, ministers, and religious folk of all stripes know and use the power of stories to tell people about loss and how to deal with it in their lives. An embrace of storytelling helps us to realize better the accessibility of cross-cultural perspectives and unites people in their nurturing of this activity, which Coles (1989) calls the bedrock capacity of the human being. Having recognized the value of storytelling, different types of therapists advocate greater use of stories in counseling people dealing with various stressors. For example, Joanne Bernstein (1976) has advocated bibliotherapy for grieving children. This approach would involve presenting the children with books that tell stories of other children encountering the death of a friend or loved one. Richard Gardner (1971) has proposed a mutual storytelling technique in which imaginative stories are elicited from children, and then the therapist retells the tale with a different resolution. In *Oriental Stories as Tools in Psychotherapy* (1982), Nossrat Peseschkian, an Iranian emigré living in Germany, includes many Islamic, Sufi, and Baha'i teaching tales along with accounts of the therapeutic situations in which he drew upon a particular story and reflections it provoked in his patient.

TYPES OF LOSSES NOT FULLY TREATED IN THIS BOOK

Loss in all of its manifestations is the touchstone of depression—in the progress of the disease and, most likely, in its origin . . . devastating loss in childhood figured in my own disorder.

—William Styron

In no way does this book represent a complete discussion of the various types of losses people experience. As Styron has suggested, the millions of sufferers of depression probably have their own closets full of losses that are associated with their condition. I touched on this disease only in the chapter on lifespan losses. There are many other types of losses, also. In our rapidly paced, ever-changing world, there may be a loss of self. Dancer and choreographer Bill T. Jones addressed the issue of subtle yet potent losses in our lives in his 1994 dance piece, "Still/Here." This work began as an attempt to consider the process of accepting illness and the potential for imminent death. Jones has been diagnosed as HIV positive and has lost many friends and close others to AIDS in the past decade. In developing the piece, Jones and a friend who was recovering from a double mastectomy began to discover that survivors have many things in common, not the least of which is the will to live. In describing his work, Jones said:

But there's another kind of loss, perhaps epidemic of this technological age more than any other: the loss of self. What does it mean to be told that your breast being cut off wasn't enough, the cancer has spread, you're going to die? What does it mean to know that a virus that causes AIDS is in your blood? I know. I know how one can be terrified of what might happen and at the same time fascinated and amused. I know how it feels to be driven at times to the point of madness because of the fear of not finishing one's work, while being at the same time utterly resigned to disappointment. To be profoundly sad, and at the same time absurdly happy. Many people know what this loss is, what this dichotomy means. We're still here, and we struggle with survival every day! (Jones, 1994)

Thus, loss of self is yet another construction of the nature of loss that is consistent with Gergen's (1991) concept of the "saturated self." Gergen suggests that our mobility, technology, and pace of living undercut contemplative activity and communion among people and, therefore, have negative implications for self-identity and self-growth. Fax machines, e-mail, phone machines, and other such means of communication all hinder people's face-to-face interaction with others. They also lessen our faltering ability and inclination to share parts of our lives with close others by letters. Losses of self or of important parts of self-identity represent subtle losses that are becoming common as we approach the twenty-first century.

Other types of losses not fully treated in this book include the loss of close interactive friendships when people move apart, the loss of inspiration or talent a writer feels when she or he has encountered an insuperable block or when an athlete cannot attain a cherished goal or defeat a rival; and the loss of freedom when people are incarcerated or put into mental institutions.

In an article for the *Chicago Tribune*, Eric Zorn (1994) discusses the "secret casuality of Alzheimer's: sex." In his article, Zorn discusses how a great dilemma sometimes occurs in the lives of people who care for individuals with advanced cases of Alzheimer's disease. Those with the disease often are both needy and self-centered. They may become insistent on having sexual relations with their spouses. Indeed they may become much more demanding than before they became so ill. Conversely, the individuals caring for them may totally lose interest in sex and physical contact. The well partner may end up feeling quite guilty if the ill partner demands sex but the well partner does not want to comply. On the other hand, the well partner may feel degraded if he or she does comply and feels that the sex is just mechanical. Zorn mentions the possibility that for many Alzheimer's patients, sexual relations with their spouses may be an oasis of familiarity and comfort in their increasingly confused worlds.

The situation surrounding the intimacy encountered by spouses and caretakers of persons in advanced stages of Alzheimer's disease is similar to that confronting the loved ones of persons who have suffered serious brain injuries. In Chapter 7, I alluded to the deep, unrelenting loss to survivors of their partner's "companionship of the mind." In these situations, a survivor must somehow come to grips with the fact that, in effect, there is a new person inhabiting the body of their partner. It literally becomes a world of the surreal—your partner is dead, but not really! We as scholars and caring people do not begin to understand the pathos of these lives.

There no doubt are many more types of losses that could be pinpointed. That is another reason why this broad field deserves efforts at integrating types of losses and their consequences with connections in writing and teaching.

LOSS AS GROWTH: MAKING LOSS PART OF WHO WE ARE

There is always hope. It shouldn't be a selfish hope. . . . While a cure may not be found in time for me, we can look forward to the time it will be found for other survivors of AIDS.

—Arthur Ashe

Bill T. Jones's use of his HIV-positive condition to challenge people to confront death and achieve their life contributions suggests that loss can lead to great personal growth. How do we make loss, however harsh and traumatic, into something to grow with—even if we have very little time left to live? How do we make loss a part of who we are, a part that makes us stronger and wiser and more sensitive to others' struggles?

Albert Ellis's lecturing and his book, *A Guide to Rational Living* (1975), make good points about the imperative of work in overcoming adversity. In a lecture at Governor's State University in Chicago, Illinois, on October 14, 1994, Ellis put it in his typically colorful way, "You have to push your ass." He went on to say that when loss or adversity strikes us, we have the choice of falling into depression and despair, and essentially not moving out of those states or choosing grief, sadness, regret, and similar "movement-oriented" emotions. They are movement oriented because most of us learn the pathway through them to adaptation and recovery, whereas depression and despair lead nowhere. Of course, it is easy to say as much but difficult to do when you have just learned that your loving, longtime spouse has suddenly died of a heart attack. Still, Ellis's rational-emotional-behavioral therapy makes a lot of sense, because it emphasizes that we do have choices—some of which would be drastically bad for our future health—and that we can act on our grief. He argues that we have the choice, for example, of ripping up the "shoulds" others impose on us, our tendencies to "awfulize" our fate, and our feeling that there are some crises we simply cannot bear. Recall from Chapter 4 that Elizabeth Neeld (1990) also wrote about choices in her moving account of her husband's sudden death at midlife in *Seven Choices*.

In December 1994, the actress Marlo Thomas played a mother in a television movie entitled *Reunion*. Her role was that of a grieving mother who had to struggle to move beyond the death of her young son. Her grief was so great that she often went to the cemetery to talk to her deceased son. These conversations were not depicted as pathological in the movie, though she did need to get to a point at which they could be terminated. In an interview with Michael Ryan in the December 4, 1994, *Parade Magazine*, Thomas said that playing this role appealed to her because it echoed and verified a lesson she had learned in her own life:

> *The real reunion is to reunite with the rest of your family, to take your loss and fold it into your life and make it part of who you are. . . . It's just not enough to be a survivor—you have to thrive. And my character [in the movie] will go on to thrive. (Ryan, 1994, p. 5)*

In the interview, Thomas linked her character's loss and conversations with her dead son to the real personal loss she had experienced when her father, comedian Danny Thomas, died unexpectedly at age seventy-nine in 1991 and to her continued communion with Danny's spirit: "There's something that my father left behind. It's human. There's a spiritual conversation that still goes on with him. He's still there. If that weren't true, it would be unbearable" (Ryan, 1994, p. 5).

LOSS AS A STIMULANT TO CONTRIBUTE TO OTHERS

The capacity to wear glory with grace.
—The Reverend Jesse Jackson

I hope that a strong message of this book is that everyone can be a hero when it comes to showing courage and care about our fellow human beings in times of suffering and pain. As I noted in Chapter 12, there are countless examples of extraordinary courage and action on the part of ordinary people. I want to reinforce that message in this epilogue.

In September 1994, as his family's month-long vacation to Italy was coming to an end, Nicholas Green, age seven, was killed by robbers as his father drove along a desolate highway. Nicholas, sleeping in the backseat, was struck by bullets that penetrated the back door of the car. In an act that Italians found tremendously moving and compassionate, Nicholas's parents, Reg and Maggie Green, decided to donate his organs to seven Italians who needed organ transplants. Maggie said, "I know we have a long time of grief ahead of us" (*People Weekly*, 1994, p. 62). His parents went on to say that Nicholas was an intelligent little guy who read widely and had a great future ahead of him. They said that they knew Nicholas would want his life to reach as far as possible in its contribution to others.

In September 1994, Barbara Fassbinder died of AIDS. She had been a pioneer in the prevention of AIDS among health-care workers. She was infected with the AIDS virus in 1986 when she assisted in the care of an infected man in an emergency room. Fassbinder decided to go public with her situation in the late 1980s to help institute new medical practices (including wearing protective gloves and masks) to make medical personnel less vulnerable to the AIDS virus. In a 1991 interview, she said:

> *If this can happen to me, it can happen to anybody. I just couldn't live with myself not warning people. . . .*
>
> *Think of it this way. You're traveling down a mountain road. You see a guardrail. How many people had to go over the edge before they put a guardrail up? We were a few of those people who had to go over the rail. (Associated Press, 1994)*

LOSS AS AN INTEGRATING CONCEPT FOR DIVERSE PHENOMENA

In this book, I have shown that many otherwise discrete phenomena can be brought together and viewed as instances of personal or interpersonal loss. I believe that the concept of loss represents one large area for future work among laypersons and scholars, representing both the social and behavioral sciences, humanities, and medicine. The value of such a synthesis, I believe, lies in the breadth we gain in our understanding of the very nature of being human and of human life—how loss is a universal human experience and pervasive throughout the life of each human. At the same time, we learn that loss is a human construction. We can view these many phenomena— from aging to divorce to stigmatization to death—as opportunities for the renewal of survivors and the impetus for constructive accomplishment that otherwise would not occur. We construe our lives almost every instant (Kelly, 1955; Heider, 1958). It is possible, therefore, to construe the very process of dying as natural and conducive to further progress of the species and its achievements, if not the individual. Is that not simply rationalization or denial that "It's over. Finished. Why not just admit it and that life amounts to nothing more than that"? Perhaps. But that, too, is merely another construction, and I prefer the former!

For both the scholar and the layperson, there are specific benefits in viewing loss in this broad, integrative way. For example, it gives us perspective both on the similarities and differences among types of losses. There are many differences even within a particular category, such as the loss of a close other through death. Losing a spouse and losing a child are quite different experiences with different implications for the survivor. As important, the age of the deceased person and the circumstances of his or her death will also have considerable impact on the experience of loss and grief of the survivor. Similarly, for some people, the personal loss associated with aging is more dramatic and demoralizing than it is for others. Simply recognizing these differences suggests some of the countless questions about the relativity of loss that can be raised for theoretical, research, and application purposes. The fact that loss is such a relative concept is, in itself, a powerful message for the survivor: No one other than you has the right to construe your loss as diminished; no one but you has the right to say, "Now you should be getting on with your life."

There are also many commonalities across types of major losses. Each diminishes our resources, whether it is the closeness and interaction of a deceased loved one, the agency afforded by a lost physical ability, or our general selfhood. While our grief may vary greatly in nature and intensity, the sense of loss remains daunting and often dismayingly disempowering. For most of us, there is a consolidation of losses and grieving over time. As noted at different points in this book, how else could it be? Major loss often comes in multiples. When we think hard about our lives, multiple instances of loss always are present. At midlife, when we experience a divorce, a death in the family, unemployment, or an illness, or a combination of these, which staggers us and changes the course of our lives, we may still be grieving the loss through dissolution of an early relationship in our lives. A famous quote from Dante notes: "In the middle of the journey of our life I came to myself within a dark wood where the straight way was lost."

It is human to lose our path and a lot more, not just bad luck! Given the indefinite nature of human memory, it is entirely possible that each new instance of major loss triggers our memories of other major losses. As implied in Chapter 5, the very instant at which we begin a new close relationship is both cause for celebration and cause for grief: grief, because ultimately that relationship will end. The start is a point along the progression to the end, the stage of parting that happens in all human relationships.

This line of reasoning on the unity of the concept of loss, thus, brings into focus both the frailty of being human and the amazing resiliency of a species that is able to contemplate, grieve, remember so well its losses, and yet keep going and construe positive aspects associated with those losses. Even as we have so much left to do to understand the differences among different types of losses and grief, we also have a long way to go to recognize and realize the value of examining different types of losses under the unitary category of major loss. Such a direction may be most helpful to survivors as well as scholars in this field.

REDUX ON WE GRIEVE

Heart vainly seeks the links that will connect it again.
—Albert Camus

Forty years after the kidnapping and killing of her child, Anne Morrow Lindbergh published *Hour of Gold, Hour of Lead* (1973). As quoted in *Time* magazine (1973), she noted:

I do not believe that sheer suffering teaches. If suffering alone taught, all the world would be wise, since everyone suffers. To suffering must be added mourning, understanding, patience, love, openness and the willingness to remain vulnerable. (p. 35)

Lindbergh's message remains true today. What this integrative view of loss suggests is that to grow and contribute, we must be willing to suffer to the end of our life. We must continue to reach out to others, even in our grief and anguish, realizing that we have something to offer.

John Brantner (1977) presented an important paper to a conference on death on dying, entitled "Positive Approaches to Dying." His paper focused on the centrality of close relationships to happiness. He noted that all relationships end in separation and that one never fully gets over grief but hopes to enter a new state of having one's energy charged and directed by personal loss of relationships and consequent suffering. He suggested that some people grow and become enriched from suffering and loss. They have learned in dealing with the deaths of close others that grieving and mourning can transform a person. This is where positive use of death is to be focused. This is the great opportunity that most of us flee, even in these times when death preoccupies us. We avoid the open griever; we hope (and we often say this aloud) that others will not grieve at our death. Brantner offered a strategy for empowering us in our understanding of loss. He suggested that we make a list of our own dead, then study our relationships with these individuals and how they have changed over time:

Reopen these relationships; examine them. . . . What is the significance of these relationships? They are not over. They are not finished. They do not end. They are fresh. The emotions are there and stir us still. In some sense, the person is still there, still meaningful, still influential in our lives. These are the people we know, as we know no living person. They are a part of us, unchanged, for the rest of our lives. . . .

These, the dead, teach us the meaning of relationships; they teach us the importance of intensity, passion, and vulnerability. They teach us that duration, the number of hours or days or years in a relationship is not the significant dimension. (p. 301)

> *The best way that I understand to live life is to live the reality of death simultaneously. These folks help me live that out. Because of that, I think I live a better life.*
>
> *—Mary Kay Mattiace*

BIBLIOGRAPHY

Abzug, B. (1990, July/August). Martin, what should I do now? *Ms.*, pp. 95–96.

Ackner, L.F. (1993). *How to survive the loss of a parent*. New York: Morrow.

Adams, H. (1994, August 21). *Chicago Tribune*, section 5, p. 4.

Adler, J. (1994, January 10). *Newsweek*, p. 43.

Allport, G.W. (1968). The historical background of modern social psychology. In G. Lindzey & E. Aronson (Eds.), *Handbook of social psychology* (2d ed.) (Vol. 1, pp. 9–33). Reading, MA: Addison-Wesley.

Altman, I., & Taylor, D. (1973). *Social penetration*. New York: Holt, Rinehart & Winston.

Arias, R. (1993, August 23). [Interview with the family of Tammy Zywicki]. *People Weekly*, p. 39.

Auden, W. H. (1976). *Collected poems*. New York: Random House.

Bass, E., & Davis, L. (1988). *The courage to heal*. New York: Harper & Row.

Baum, A.S., & Burnes, D. W. (1993). *A nation in denial*. Boulder, CO: Westview Press.

Baumeister, R.F. (1991). *Meanings of life*. New York: Guilford Press.

Beatty, J. (1994, September 25). *Chicago Tribune*, p. A1.

Becker, E. (1973). *The denial of death*. New York: Free Press.

Belsky, J. (1994). Aging in later life. In J. L. Ronch, W. V. Ornum, & N. C. Stillwell (Eds.), *Counseling approaches throughout the lifespan* (pp. 484–485). New York: Crossroads.

Berger, J. (1994, September 1). [Interview with Rabbi Gordon Tucker]. *New York Times*, p. B8.

Bernstein, J.E. (1975). Helping young children to cope with acute grief. In V. R. Pine (Ed.), *Acute grief and the funeral* (pp. 274–280). Springfield, IL: Charles Thomas.

Berscheid, E. (1994). Interpersonal relationships. *Annual Review of Psychology, 45,* 79–129.

Boswell, J. (1791/1992). *Life of Johnson*. New York: Knopf.

Bowlby, J. (1960). Separation anxiety. *International Journal of Psychoanalysis, 41,* 89–113.

Bowlby, J. (1979). *The making and breaking of affectional bonds*. London: Tavistock.

216

Bowlby, J. (1980). *Attachment and loss: Vol. 3. Loss: Sadness and depression.* London: Hogarth.

Brando, M. (1994). *Brando: Songs my mother taught me.* New York: Random House.

Brantner, J. (1977). Positive approaches to dying. *Death Education, 1,* 293–304.

Brende, J.O., & Parson, E. R. (1985). *Vietnam veterans: The road to recovery.* New York: Plenum.

Brotman, B. (1994, July 17). *Chicago Tribune,* section 6, pp. 1, 9.

Brown, R.M. (1991). *The quotable woman.* Philadelphia: The Running Press.

Bruner, J. (1990). *Acts of meaning.* Cambridge: Harvard University Press.

Buchwald, A. (1994). *Leaving home.* New York: G. P. Putnam.

Carver, R. (1986). *Ultramarine.* New York: Vintage.

Clark, K. (1994, May 29). [Interview with Charles Durning]. *Chicago Tribune,* TV Week, p. 3.

Cleland, M. (1982). *Strong at the broken places.* New York: Chosen Books.

Cochran, L., & Claspell, E. (1987). *The meaning of grief.* Westport, CT: Greenwood Press.

Cohen, R. (1994, September 29). *Cedar Rapids Gazette.*

Cohn, V. (1990, May 24). *Washington Post,* p. 6B.

Coles, R. (1989). *The call of stories.* Boston: Houghton Mifflin.

Corr, C.A., Nabe, C. M., & Corr, D. M. (1994). *Death and dying: Life and living.* Pacific Grove, CA: Brooks/Cole.

Cousins, N. (1989). *Head First.* New York: Penguin.

Crompton, V. (1994). *Teen dating violence.* Unpublished manuscript, University of Iowa, Department of Psychology, Iowa City.

Davis, D.L. (1991). *Empty cradle, broken heart.* Golden, CO: Fulcrum.

Davis, R. (1993, November 26). *USA Today,* p. 8A.

de Botton, A. (1993). *On love.* New York: Atlantic Monthly Press.

Dee, E. (1990). *Souls on board.* Sioux City, IA: Loess Hills Press.

Delaney, S., & Delaney, B. (1994). *The Delaney sisters book of everyday wisdom.* New York: Farrar, Straus, & Giroux.

Delbo, C. (1990). *Days and memory.* Marlboro, VT: Marlboro.

DeSpelder, L. A., & Strickland, A. L. (1992). *The last dance* (3rd ed.). Mountain View, CA: Mayfield.

DeWall, T. (1993, November 1). *Daily Iowan,* p. 5A.

Dickens, C. (1859/1960). *A tale of two cities.* New York: New American Library.

Dickinson, E. (1960). *Complete poems.* Boston: Little, Brown.

Didinger, R. (1990, December 16). Packer strength coach a perfect example. *Chicago Tribune,* p. 6C.

Doka, K.J. (1989). Disenfranchised grief. In K. J. Doka (Ed.), *Disenfranchised grief: Recognizing hidden sorrow* (pp. 1–11). Lexington, MA: Lexington Books.

Donne, J. (1952). *Complete poetry and selected prose.* New York: Modern Library.

Downs, H. (1994, August 21). *Parade Magazine.*

Duck, S. (1994). *Meaningful relationships: Talking, sense, and relating.* Newbury Park, CA: Sage.

Dunn, J. (1988). *The beginnings of social understanding.* Cambridge, MA: Harvard University Press.

[Article on Virginia Eddy]. (1994, September 4). *Cedar Rapids Gazette,* p. 8F.

Ellis, A. (1975). *A guide to rational living*. Englewood Cliffs, NJ: Prentice Hall.

Erhlichman, J. (1993, August 29). *Parade Magazine*, p. 4.

Erickson, E. (1963). *Childhood and society* (2d ed.). New York: Norton.

Erickson, E. (1969). *Gandhi's truth*. New York: Norton.

Ewart, G. (1945). War dead. In Oscar Williams (Comp.), *War poets: An anthology of war poetry of the twentieth century*. New York: John Day.

Faulkner, W. (1962). Complete works. New York: Modern Library.

Feinberg, L. (1994). *I'm grieving as fast as I can*. Far Hills, NJ: New Horizon Press.

Fine, B. (1994, August 28). *Cedar Rapids Gazette*.

Fogelman, E. (1994). *Conscience and courage*. New York: Doubleday / Anchor Books.

Frazier, S.H. (1994). *Psychotrends*. New York: Simon & Schuster.

Freedy, J.R., Saladin, M. E., Kilpatrick, D. G., Resnick, H. S., & Saunders, B. E. (1994). *Journal of Traumatic Stress, 7*, 257–273.

Fulton, R. (1979). Anticipatory grief, stress, and the surrogate griever. In J. Taché, H. Selye, & S. Day (Eds.), *Cancer, stress, and death*. New York: Plenum.

Furstenberg, F.F., Jr., & Cherlin, A. (1991). *Divided families*. Newbury Park, CA: Sage.

Gardner, R. (1971). *Therapeutic communication with children*. New York: Jason Aronson.

Gergen, K. (1991). *The saturated self: Dilemmas of identity in contemporary life*. New York: Basic Books.

Gergen, K., & Gergen, M. (1987). Narratives as relationship. In R. Burnett, P. McGhee, & D.C. Clarke (Eds.), *Accounting for relationships* (pp. 269–315). London: Meuthen.

Gergen, K., & Gergen, M. (1988). Narrative and self as relationship. *Advances in Experimental Social Psychology, 21*, 17–56.

Gillis, E. (1986). A single parent confronting the loss of an only child. In T. A. Rando (Ed.), *Parental loss of a child* (pp. 315–319). Champaign, IL: Research Press.

Glaser, E., & Palmer, L. (1991). *Absence of Angels*. New York: G. P. Putnam's Sons.

Gleser, G.C., Green, B.L., & Winget, C. (1981). *Prolonged psychosocial effects of disaster: A study of Buffalo Creek*. New York: Academic Press.

Glick, I.O., Weiss, R.S., & Parkes, C.M. (1974). *The first year of bereavement*. New York: Wiley.

Goffman, E. (1959). *The presentation of self in everyday life*. New York: Doubleday / Anchor Books.

Goffman, E. (1963). *Stigma*. Englewood Cliffs, NJ: Prentice Hall.

Green, B.L., Grace, M.C., Lindy, J.D., Gleser, G.C., Leonard, A. C., & Kramer, T. L. (1990). Buffalo Creek survivors in the second decade. *Journal of Applied Social Psychology, 20*, 1033–1050.

[Article on Nicholas Green]. (1994, October 24). *People Weekly*, p. 62.

Greenberger, D. (1993). *Duplex planet*. New York: Faber and Faber.

Greene, B. (1994, May 4). *Chicago Tribune*.

Greenspan, H. (1992). Lives as text: Symptoms as modes of recounting in the life histories of holocaust survivors. In G.C. Rosenwald & R.L. Ochberg (Eds.), *Storied Lives* (pp. 145–164). New Haven: Yale University Press.

Griessman, E. (19   ).

Gubrium, J.F. (1993). *Speaking of life: Horizons of meaning for nursing home residents*. New York: Aldine De Gruyter.

Gunn, T. (1992). The gas-poker. *The Three Penny Review*. Berkeley, CA.

Hall, M. (1993, December 9). *USA Today*, p. 8A.

Harrison, B. (1994, April 27). *Atlanta Journal*, p. C1.

Harvey, J.H. (1987). Attributions in close relationships: Research and theoretical developments. *Journal of Social and Clinical Psychology, 4*, 420–434.

Harvey, J.H., Agostinelli, G., & Weber, A.L. (1989). Account-making and the formation of expectations about close relationships. *Review of Personality and Social Psychology, 10*, 39–62.

Harvey, J.H., Barnes, M.K., Carlson, H.R., & Haig, J. (1995). Held captive by their memories. In S. Duck & J. Wood (Eds.), *Relationship challenges* (pp. 210–233). Newbury Park, CA: Sage.

Harvey, J.H., & Davidson, C. (1994). [Interviews with D day veterans and family survivors]. Unpublished raw data.

Harvey, J.H., Flanary, R., & Morgan, M. (1986). Vivid memories of vivid loves gone by. *Journal of Social and Personal Relationships, 3*, 359–373.

Harvey, J.H., & Martin, R. (in press). Celebrating the story in social perception, communication, and behavior. *Advances in social cognition* (Vol. 7). Hillsdale, NJ: Erlbaum.

Harvey, J.H., Orbuch, T.L., Chwalisz, F., & Garwood, G. (1991). Coping with sexual assault: The roles of account-making and confiding. *Journal of Traumatic Stress, 4*, 515–531.

Harvey, J.H., Orbuch, T.L., & Weber, A.L. (1990). A social psychological model of account-making in response to severe stress. *Journal of Language and Social Psychology, 9*, 191–207.

Harvey, J.H., Orbuch, T.L., & Weber, A.L. (1992). (Eds.). *Attributions, accounts, and close relationships.* New York: Springer-Verlag.

Harvey, J.H., Orbuch, T.L., Weber, A.L., Merbach, N., & Alt, R. (1992). House of pain and hope: Accounts of loss. *Death Studies, 16*, 99–124.

Harvey, J.H., Weber, A.L., & Orbuch, T.L. (1990). *Interpersonal accounts: A social psychological perspective.* Oxford: Blackwell.

Harvey, J.H., Wells, G.H., & Alvarez, M.D. (1978). Attribution in the context of conflict and separation in close relationships. In J. H. Harvey, W. Ickes, & R. F. Kidd (Eds.), *New directions in attribution research* (Vol. 2, pp. 235–259). Hillsdale, NJ: Erlbaum.

Hazan, C., & Shaver, P. (1987). Romantic love conceptualized as an attachment process. *Journal of Personality and Social Psychology, 52*, 511–524.

Heider, F. (1958). *The psychology of interpersonal relations.* New York: Wiley.

Helmreich, W. (1992). *Against all odds.* New York: Simon & Schuster.

Hemispheres. (1994). [summary of J. Rosemund's views on telling children about divorce]. United Airlines.

Hemingway, E. (1952). *The old man and the sea.* New York: Scribner's.

Herman, J. (1992). *Trauma and recovery.* New York: Basic Books.

Hill, C.T., Rubin, Z., & Peplau, L.A. (1976). Breakups before marriage: The end of 103 affairs. *Journal of Social Issues, 32*, 147–168.

Hill, R. (Ed.). (1971). *Tennyson's poetry: Authoritative texts, juvenilia, and early response to criticism.* New York: Norton.

Holden, S. (1994, September 21). How's love in the '90s? Depressing. *New York Times*, p. 3.

Holtzworth-Munroe, A., & Jacobson, N.J. (1985). Causal attributions of married couples. *Journal of Personality and Social Psychology, 48,* 1399–1412.

Horowitz, M.J. (1976). *Stress response syndromes.* (2d ed.). Northvale, NJ: Jason Aronson.

Howard, G.S. (1991). Cultural tales: A narrative approach to thinking, cross-cultural psychology, and psychotherapy. *American Psychologist, 46,* 187–197.

Hoyt, E.P. (1993). *One hundred and ninety-nine days: The battle of Stalingrad.* New York: Tor Publishing Company.

Hunt, M. (1966). *The world of the formerly married.* New York: McGraw-Hill.

Interview with President William J. Clinton. (1994, May 8). *USA Weekend.*

Interview with Linda Corwin. (1988, July 17). *Chicago Tribune,* section 5, p. 5.

Interview with B. Fassbinder. (1994, September 22). Associated Press.

Interview with Robert Redford. (1994, May 15). *Chicago Tribune,* p. 4.

Jacobs, S. (1993). *Pathologic grief.* Washington: American Psychiatric Press.

Janoff-Bulman, R. (1992). *Shattered assumptions.* New York: Free Press.

Johnson, R. (1993, June 1). Only scars are shared in a friendly divorce. *Dallas Morning News,* p. 3C.

Jones, B. T. (1994). [Promotional material for "Still/Here"].

Jones, E. E., Farina, A., Hastorf, A. H., Markus, H., Miller, D. T., & Scott, R. A. (1984). *Social stigma.* New York: Freeman.

Kahn, E.J. (1994, September 12). [Interview with Grace Corrigan]. *Boston Globe,* p. 13A.

Kaplan, D. (1993, October 24). *Chicago Tribune,* section 6, p. 1.

Kelly, G. (1955). *The psychology of personal constructs.* New York: Norton.

Kessler, S. (1975). *The American way of divorce.* Chicago: Nelson Hall.

Kierkegaard, S. K. (1843/1954). *Fear and trembling and the sickness unto death.* New York: Doubleday.

Kleber, R.J., & Brom, D. (1992). *Coping with trauma: Theory, prevention, and treatment.* Amsterdam: Swets & Zeitlinger.

Kleinke, C. (1991). *Coping with life's challenges.* New York: Freeman.

Knaff, D. (1994, July 10). Inner beauty. *Chicago Tribune,* section 6, p. 3.

Kovaleski, S. (1994, March 20). *Washington Post,* p. B1.

Kramer, H., & Kramer, K. (1993). *Conversations at Midnight.* New York: Morrow.

Kübler-Ross, E. (1969). *On death and dying.* New York: Collier.

Kuenning, D.E. (1990). *Life after Vietnam.* New York: Paragon House.

Landman, J. (1993). *Regret.* New York: Oxford University Press.

Langer, L.L. (1991). *Holocaust testimonies: The ruins of memory.* New Haven: Yale University Press.

Larson, D. (1993). *The helper's journey.* Champaign, IL: Research Press.

Laughlin, J. (1993). The departure. *Iowa Review, 29,* 3, 63.

Lavin, C. (1993, August 1). Being dumped for the first time is no easier for an adult. *Chicago Tribune,* p. 3C.

Leash, R.M. (1994). *Death notification.* Hinesburg, VT: Upper Access.

Lesser, W. (1994, August 14). Thom Gunn's sense of movement. *Los Angeles Times Magazine,* p. 39.

Levi, P. (1988). *The drowned and the saved.* New York: Summit.

Levinger, G. (1992). Close relationship loss as a set of inkblots. In T. L. Orbuch (Ed.), *Close relationship loss* (pp. 213–221). New York: Springer-Verlag.

Levinson, D.J., Darrow, C.N., Klein, E.B., Levinson, M.H., & McKee, B. (1978). *The seasons of a man's life*. New York: Knopf.

Lewis, C.S. (1961). *A grief observed*. New York: Farrar, Straus & Giroux.

Lifton, R.J., & Olson, E. (1976). The human meaning of total disaster: The Buffalo Creek experience. *Psychiatry, 39*, 301–318.

Lin, M.Y. (1987). Introduction. In *The Wall*. New York: Collins.

Lincicome, B. (1993, August 16). *Chicago Tribune*, section 3, p. 1.

Review of Anne Morrow Lindbergh, *Hour of gold, hour of lead*. (1973, February 5). *Time*, p. 35.

Lindeman, B. (1994, July 31). [Interview with Paul Reese]. *Chicago Tribune*, p. 6F.

Loew, A. (1993, May 2). *Parade Magazine*, p. 18.

Loewald, H.W. (1960). On the therapeutic action of psychoanalysis. *International Journal of Psychoanalysis, 41*, 16–33.

Macdonald, B. (1983). *Look me in the eye: Old women, aging, and ageism*. San Francisco: Spinsters Ink.

Mairs, N. (1993, February 21). *New York Times Book Review*, pp. 1, 25.

Marshall, S. (1994, April 26). *USA Today*, p. 1A.

McAdams, D. (1993). *The stories we live by*. New York: Morrow.

McCarren, J. (1994, September 25). *Chicago Tribune*, section 7, p. 2.

McDonald, W. (1976). *Caliban in blue and other poems*. Lubbock: Texas Tech University Press.

McIntosh, D.N., Silver, R. C., & Wortman, C. B. (1993). Religion's role in adjustment to a negative life event: Coping with the loss of a child. *Journal of Personality and Social Psychology, 65*, 812–821.

McLemore, D. (1993, December 26). *Dallas Morning News*, p. 50A.

McMurran, K. (1991, February 4). [Interview with Elizabeth Glaser]. *People Weekly*, p. 96.

Meeks, E.M. and Marks, J. (1994, March). Making peace with the past: one woman's story. *McCall's*, pp. 50–59.

Meichenbaum, D. (1985). *Stress inoculation training*. New York: Pergamon Press.

Meichenbaum, D., & Fitzpatrick, D. (1992). A constructivist narrative perspective on stress and coping. In L. Goldberger & S. Breznitz (Eds.), *Handbook of stress* (pp. 28–43). New York: Free Press.

Miller, A. (1958). *Death of a salesman*. New York: Viking Press.

Monette, P. (1994). *Last watch of the night*. New York: Harcourt Brace.

Morrell, D. (1988). *Fireflies*. New York: Dutton.

Morris, W. (1990, June). Here lies my heart. *Esquire*, pp. 00–175.

Mueller, L. (1986). Face lift. *Second language poems*. Baton Rouge: Louisiana State University Press.

Myers, D.G. (1992). *The pursuit of happiness*. New York: Morrow.

Neeld, E. (1990). *Seven choices: Taking the steps to a new life after losing someone you love*. New York: Delta.

Nichols, J. (1987). *American blood*. New York: Henry Holt.

Nigro, G., & Neisser, U. (1983). Point of views in personal memories. *Cognitive Psychology, 15*, 467–482.

Staff. 900-year-old letter casts light on spurned love. (1993, November 26). *Washington Post*.

Nolen-Hoeksema, S., & Morrow, J. (1991). A prospective study of depression and posttraumatic stress symptoms after a natural disaster. *Journal of Personality and Social Psychology, 61,* 115–121.

Nuland, S.B. (1994). *How we die.* New York: Knopf.

Obituary for Elizabeth Glaser. (1994, December 4). *Des Moines Register,* p. 2A.

Obituary for Audrey Hepburn. (1993, February 1). *People Weekly.*

Obituary for Theresia M. Lawrence. (1993, June 20). *Cedar Rapids Gazette,* p. 14A.

Obituary for Wray McKenzie. (1994, June 2). *Chicago Tribune.*

Obituary for Lewis Puller, Jr.. (1994, May 30). *People Weekly,* p. 68.

O'Brien, T. (1994). *In the lake of the woods.* Boston: Houghton Mifflin.

O'Brien, T. (1990). *The things they carried.* Boston: Houghton Mifflin.

Oliner, S., & Oliner, P. (1988). *The altruistic personality.* New York: Free Press.

Orbuch, T.L. (1988). *Responses to and coping with nonmarital relationship terminations.* Unpublished Ph.D. dissertation, University of Wisconsin, Madison.

Orbuch, T.L., Harvey, J. H., Davis, S.H., & Merbach, N. (1994). Account-making and confiding as acts of meaning in response to sexual assault. *Journal of Family Violence, 9,* 249–264.

Orvis, B.R., Kelley, H.H., Butler, D. (1976). Attributional conflict in young couples. In J.H. Harvey, W.J. Ickes, & R.F. Kidd (Eds.), *New directions in attribution research* (Vol. 1, pp. 353–386). Hillsdale, NJ: Erlbaum.

Painter, K. (1994, May 6). *USA Today,* p. 6A.

Palmer, L. (1987). *Shrapnel in the heart.* New York: Random House.

Parkes, C.M. (1972). *Bereavement: Studies of grief in adult life.* London: Tavistock.

Parkes, C.M. (1988). Bereavement as psychosocial transition: Processes of adaptation to change. *Journal of Social Issues, 44,* 53–65.

Parkes, C.M., & Weiss, R. S. (1983). *Recovery from bereavement.* New York: Basic Books.

Patty, M. (1994, May 26). *Rocky Mountain News,* p. 36A.

Paulson, D.S. (1991). Myth, male initiation and the Vietnam veteran. In E. Tick (Ed.), *Healing a generation* (pp. 156–165). New York: Guilford.

Pennebaker, J. (1990). *Opening up.* New York: Morrow.

Peseschkian, N. (1982). *Oriental stories as tools in psychotherapy.* New York: Springer-Verlag.

Peskin, H. (1993). Neither broken hearts nor broken bonds. *American Psychologist, 48,* 990–991.

Petry, S., & Avent, H. (1992). Stepping stone: A haven for displaced youths. In M. J. Robertson & M. Greenblatt (Eds.), *Homelessness: A national perspective* (pp. 299–305). New York: Plenum.

Phillips, D.H. (1982). *Living with Huntington's disease.* Madison: University of Wisconsin Press.

Pop, V. (1994, January 30). A life after death. *Chicago Tribune,* section 6, p. 3.

Powell, J. (1994). *Things I should have said to my father.* New York: Avon.

Price, R. (1994, March 20). Cancer activist's legacy: "Never give up." *USA Today,* p. 2A.

Pusey, A. (1994, September 8). [Article on the sinking of the Titanic]. *Dallas Morning News.*

Radner, G. (1989). *It's always something.* New York: Simon & Schuster.

Rando, T.A. (1993). *Treatment of complicated mourning*. Champaign, IL: Research Press.

Raphael, B. (1983). *The anatomy of bereavement*. New York: Basic Books.

Rasdal, D. (1992, January 30). 2 lives forever changed. *Cedar Rapids Gazette*, pp. 1B, 2B.

Rawlings, M. (1938). *The yearling*. New York: Scribner.

Ray, D. (1968). *Sam's Book*. Middletown, CT: Wesleyan University Press.

Richards, M.G. (1994). *When someone you know is hurting*. New York: Harper & Row.

Robertson, B.A., & Rutherford, M. (1988). *The living years*. London: Hit and Run Music.

Robertson, M.J., & Greenblatt, M.D. (Eds.). (1992). *Homelessness: A national perspective*. New York: Plenum.

Rosenblatt, P. (1983). *Bitter, bitter tears*. Minneapolis: University of Minnesota Press.

Ryan, D.R. (1992). Raymond: Underestimated grief. In K.J. Doka (Ed.), *Disenfranchised grief: Recognizing hidden sorrow* (pp. 127–133). Lexington, MA: Lexington Books.

Ryan, M. (1994, December 4). *Parade Magazine*, p. 5.

Sacks, O. (1970). *The man who mistook his wife for a hat*. New York: Harper & Row.

Salaman, E. (1970). *A collection of moments: A study of involuntary memories*. New York: St. Martin's Press.

Sales, R. (1994, June 6). *The Stars and Stripes*, p. 8.

Sanders, C.M. (1980). A comparison of adult bereavement in the death of a spouse, child and parent. *Omega, 10*, 303–322.

Sanders, C.M. (1982). Effects of sudden vs. chronic illness death on bereavement outcome. *Omega, 13*, 227–241.

Saunders, C. (1977). Dying they live: St. Christopher's Hospice. In H. Fiefel (Ed.), *New meanings of death* (pp. 45–55). New York: McGraw-Hill.

Savage, J.A. (1989). *Mourning unlived lives: A psychological study of childbearing loss*. Wilmette, IL: Chiron Publications.

Schank, R., & Abelson, R. (1977). *Scripts, plans, goals, and understanding*. Hillsdale, NJ: Erlbaum.

Scherer, J. (1991). *Introductory medical-surgical nursing*. Philadelphia: Lippincott.

Schleifer, S.J., Keller, S.E., & Stein, M. (1979). *The influence of stress and other psychosocial factors on human immunity*. Paper presented at the thirty-sixth annual meeting of the American Psychosomatic Society.

Schoenberg, B., Carr, A., Peretz, D., & Kutscher, A. (1970). *Loss and grief*. New York: Columbia University Press.

Schwartz, L. (1987). *So you're going to have a new body*. New York: Harper & Row.

Scott, M.B., & Lyman, S. (1968). Accounts. *American Sociological Review, 33*, 46–62.

Shakespeare, W. (1952/1971). *Complete Works of William Shakespeare*. New York: Spring Books.

Shaw, C. (1982). *Come out, come out, wherever you are*. New York: American R. R. Publishing Company.

Shirer, W. (1960). *The rise and fall of the third reich*. New York: Simon & Schuster.

Schucter, S. R. (1986). *Dimensions of grief*. San Francisco: Jossey-Bass.

Siegel, B. (1994). *How to live between office visits*. New York: Harper & Row.

Simpkins, D. (1993, January 24). Timeless love. *Chicago Tribune*, p. 8.

Smith, F. (1990). *To think*. New York: Teachers College, Columbia University Press.

Smith, J. (1994, September 4). Help wanted: Metro Detroit jobs unfilled. *Detroit News*, p. 6C.

Smith, S. (1994, March 20). Getting through the night. *Chicago Tribune*.

Smith, S.D. (1993, November 7). [Interview with Patricia Heyer and Kathy Ormand]. *Cedar Rapids Gazette*, pp. C1, C8.

Stearns, D.P. (1994, March 15). Making the dying light the brightest. *USA Today*, p. 2D.

Steinbergh, J. (1988). *A living any time*. Boston: Talking Stone Press.

Stone, A. (1994, April 28). For a tiny town, innocence lost. *USA Today*, p. 5A.

Stroebe, M., Gergen, M., Gergen, K., & Stroebe, W. (1992). Broken hearts or broken bonds: Love and death in historical perspective. *American Psychologist, 47*, 1205–1212.

Stroebe, W., & Stroebe, M. (1987). *Bereavement and health: The psychological and physical consequences of partner loss*. New York: Cambridge University Press.

Styron, W. (1990). *Darkness visible: A memoir of madness*. New York: Random House.

Sullivan, H. (1953). *Conceptions of modern psychiatry*. New York: Norton.

Sutker, P.B., Uddo, M., Brailey, D., Vasterling, and Errera, P. (1994). Psychopathology in war-zone deployed Operation Desert Storm troops assigned graves registration duties. *Journal of Abnormal Psychology, 103*, 383–390.

Swegle, L. (1994, January 24). *Iowa City Press-Citizen*, p. 3A.

Article on Carolyn Tanaka. (1993, November). *People Weekly*, p. 52.

Tavris, C. (1993, January 3). *New York Times Book Review*.

Tender words on paper possible legacy of crash. (1977, April 7). [Nashville] *Tennessean*.

Terman, J.L. (1992). *Trauma and recovery*. New York: Basic Books.

Tick, E. (Ed.). (1991). *Voices: Healing a generation*. New York: Guilford. (p. 30).

Titchner, J.L., & Kapp, F.T. (1976). Family and character change at Buffalo Creek. *American Journal of Psychiatry, 133*, 295–299.

A tribute to Audrey Hepburn. (1993, Winter). *People Extra, Collector's Edition*.

Tulsa World. (1994, June 20). P. 5A.

Tyler, A. (1985). *The accidental tourist*. New York: Knopf.

Uleman, J.S., & Bargh, J.A. (Eds.). (1989). *Unintended thought*. New York: Guilford Press.

Vaughn, D. (1986). *Uncoupling*. New York: Oxford University Press.

Viorst, J. (1986). *Necessary losses*. New York: Fawcett.

Volkan, V.D., & Zintl, E. (1993). *Life after loss*. New York: Scribner's.

Wallerstein, J.S., & Kelly, J.B. (1980). *Surviving the break-up*. New York: Harper & Row.

Watts, B. (1991). Missing. In E. Tick (Ed.), *Voices: Healing a generation* (p. 127). New York: Guilford.

Wear, D., & Nixon, L. (1994). *Literary anatomies: Women's bodies and health in literature*. Albany: State University of New York Press.

Weenolsen, P. (1988). *Transcendence of loss over the life span*. New York: Hemisphere.

Wegner, D.M. (1989). *White bears and other unwanted thoughts: Suppression, obsession, and the psychology of mental control*. New York: Penguin.

Wegner, D.M. (1991). *Fanning old flames*. Paper presented at the annual meeting of the American Psychological Association. San Francisco, CA.

Weisel, E. (1960). *Night* (S. Rodway, Trans). New York: Farrar, Strauss & Giroux.

Weisel, E. (1978). A plea for survivors. In *A Jew today* (M. Weisel, Trans.). New York: Random House.

Weisman, A.D. (1975). *Coping capacity*. New York: Human Sciences Press.

Weiss, R.S. (1975). *Marital separation*. New York: Basic Books.

Weiss, R.S. (1988). Loss and recovery. *Journal of Social Issues, 44*, 37–52.

Welwood, J. (1990). *Journey of the heart*. New York: Collins.

Wild, L. (1994). *I remember you: A grief journal*. New York: Harper & Row.

Winer, R. (1994). *Close encounters*. New York: Jason Aronson.

Wolff, T. (1989, September). Raymond Carver had his cake and ate it too. *Esquire*, pp. 240–248.

Woodson, M. (1994). *The toughest days of grief*. Grand Rapids, MI: Zondervan Publishing House.

Worden, J.W. (1982). *Grief counseling and grief therapy: A handbook for the mental health practitioner*. New York: Springer Verlag.

Wortman, C.B., & Silver, R.C. (1989). The myths of coping with loss. *Journal of Consulting and Clinical Psychology, 57*, 349–357.

Wortman, C.B., & Silver, R.C. (1992). Reconsidering assumptions about coping with loss: An overview of current research. In L. Montada, S. Filipp, & M. J. Lerner (Eds.), *Life crises and experiences of loss in adulthood* (pp. 341–365). Hillsdale, NJ: Erlbaum.

Wuthnow, R. (1994). *Sharing the journey: Support groups and America's new quest for community*. New York: Free Press.

Yalom, I.D. (1985). *The theory and practice of group psychotherapy* (3rd ed.). New York: Basic Books.

Yarborough, T.E. (1988). Finding peace in crisis. In O. S. Margolis, A. Kutscher, E. Marcus, H. Raether, & V. Pine (Eds.). *Grief and the loss of an adult child*. New York: Praeger.

INDEX